WIZARDS WITH CRIMSON EYES

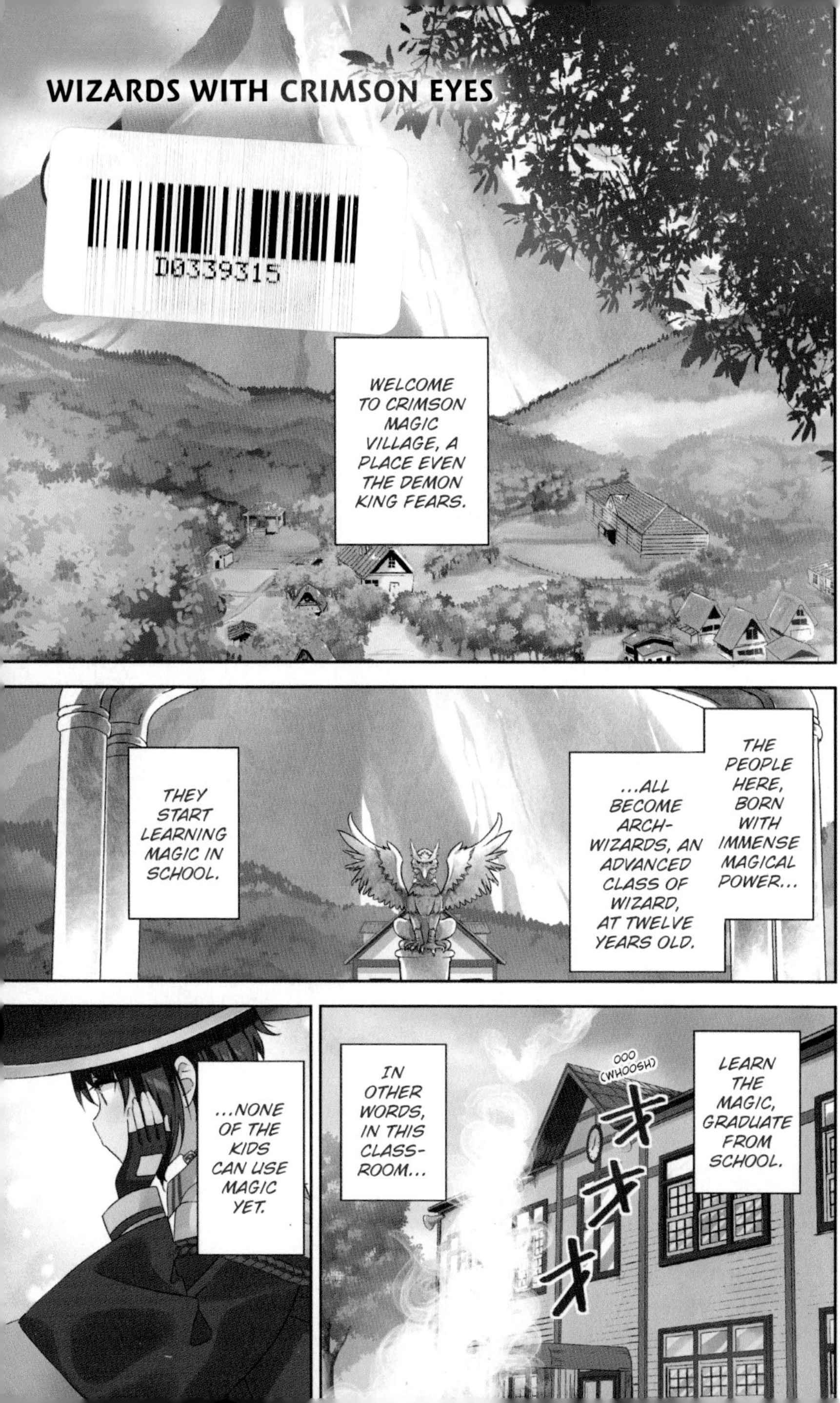
WELCOME TO CRIMSON MAGIC VILLAGE, A PLACE EVEN THE DEMON KING FEARS.
THE PEOPLE HERE, BORN WITH IMMENSE MAGICAL POWER...
...ALL BECOME ARCH-WIZARDS, AN ADVANCED CLASS OF WIZARD, AT TWELVE YEARS OLD.
THEY START LEARNING MAGIC IN SCHOOL.
LEARN THE MAGIC, GRADUATE FROM SCHOOL.
OOO (WHOOSH)
IN OTHER WORDS, IN THIS CLASS-ROOM...
...NONE OF THE KIDS CAN USE MAGIC YET.

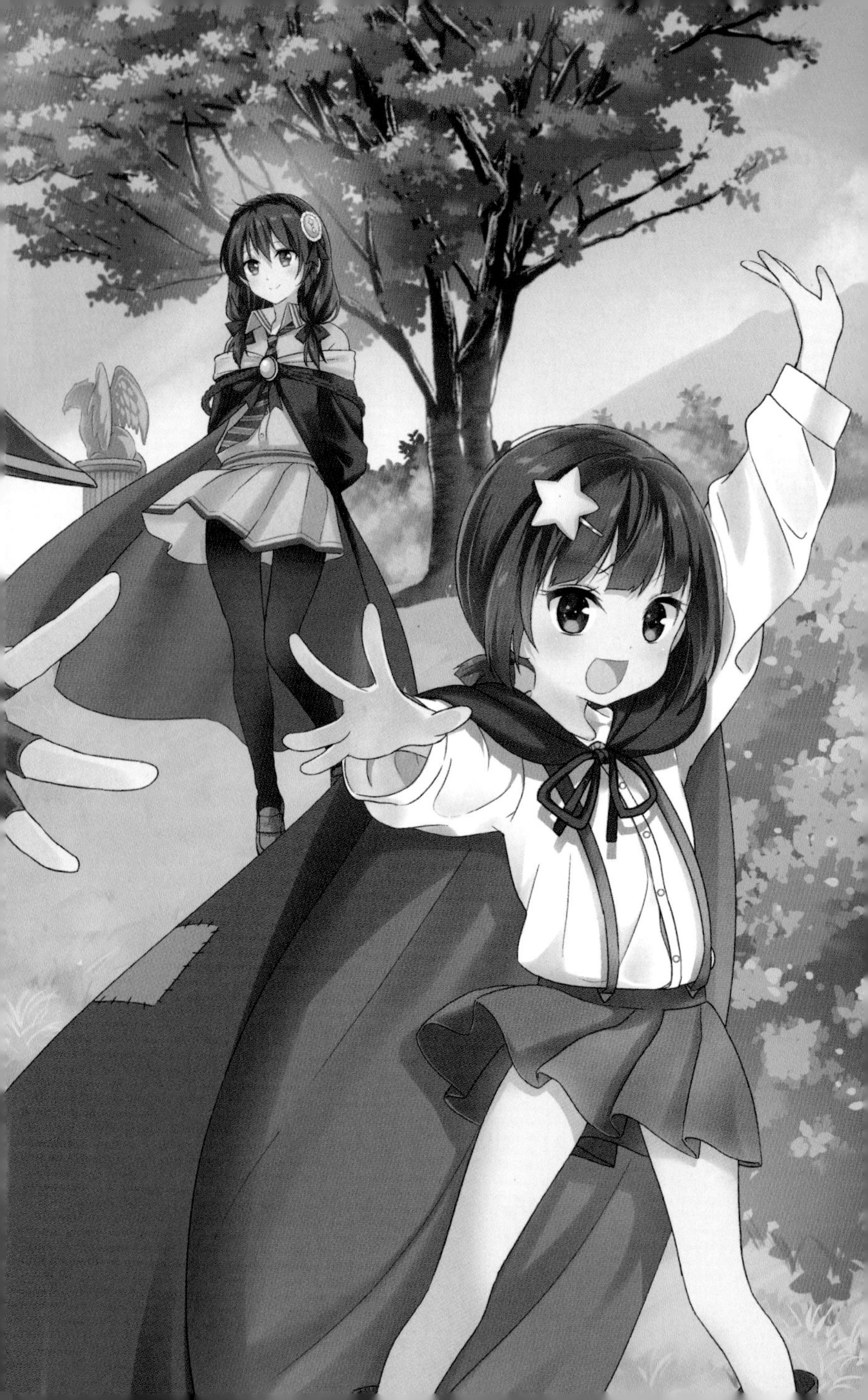

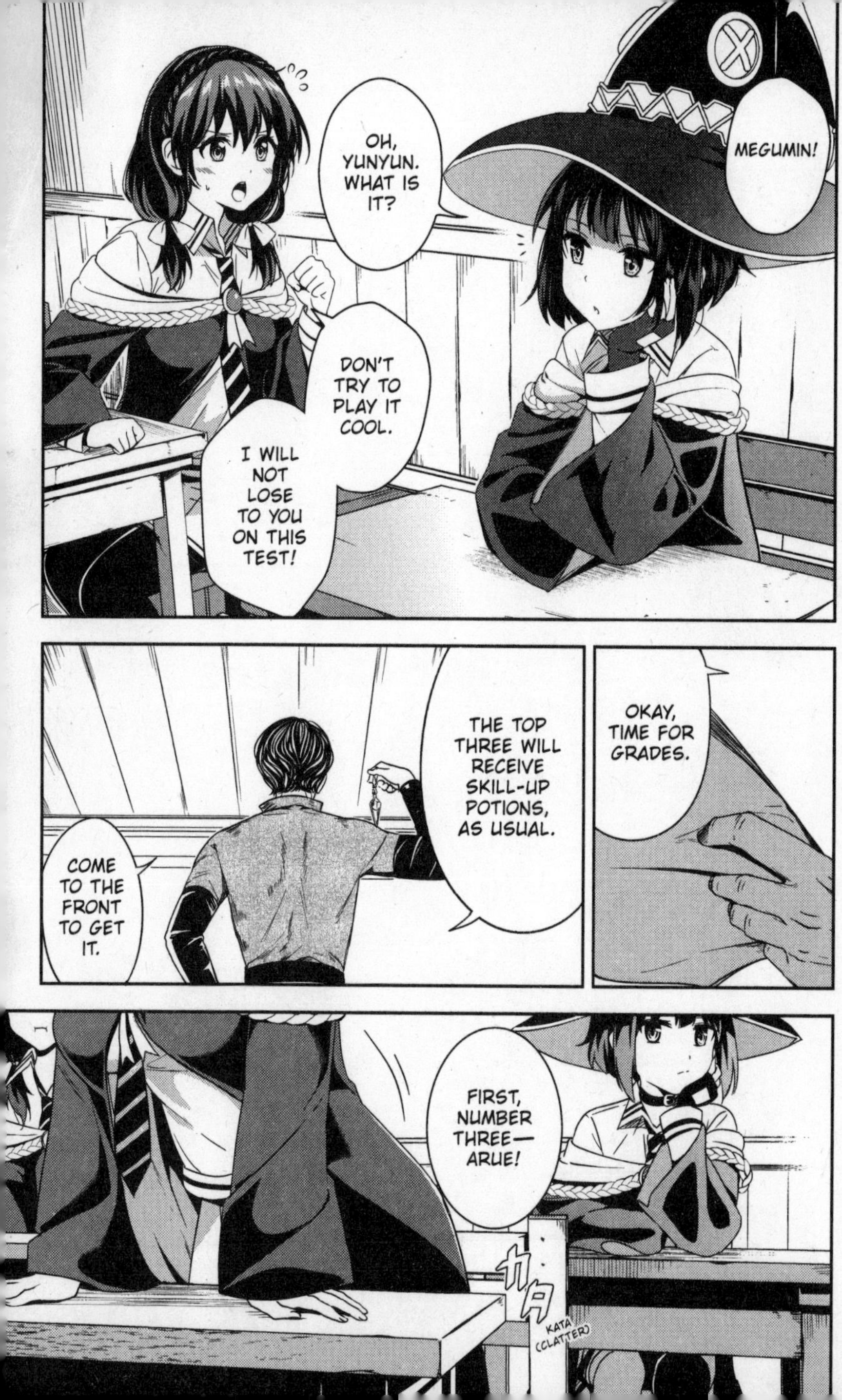
MEGUMIN!
OH, YUNYUN. WHAT IS IT?
DON'T TRY TO PLAY IT COOL.
I WILL NOT LOSE TO YOU ON THIS TEST!
OKAY, TIME FOR GRADES.
THE TOP THREE WILL RECEIVE SKILL-UP POTIONS, AS USUAL.
COME TO THE FRONT TO GET IT.
FIRST, NUMBER THREE—ARUE!
KATA (CLATTER)

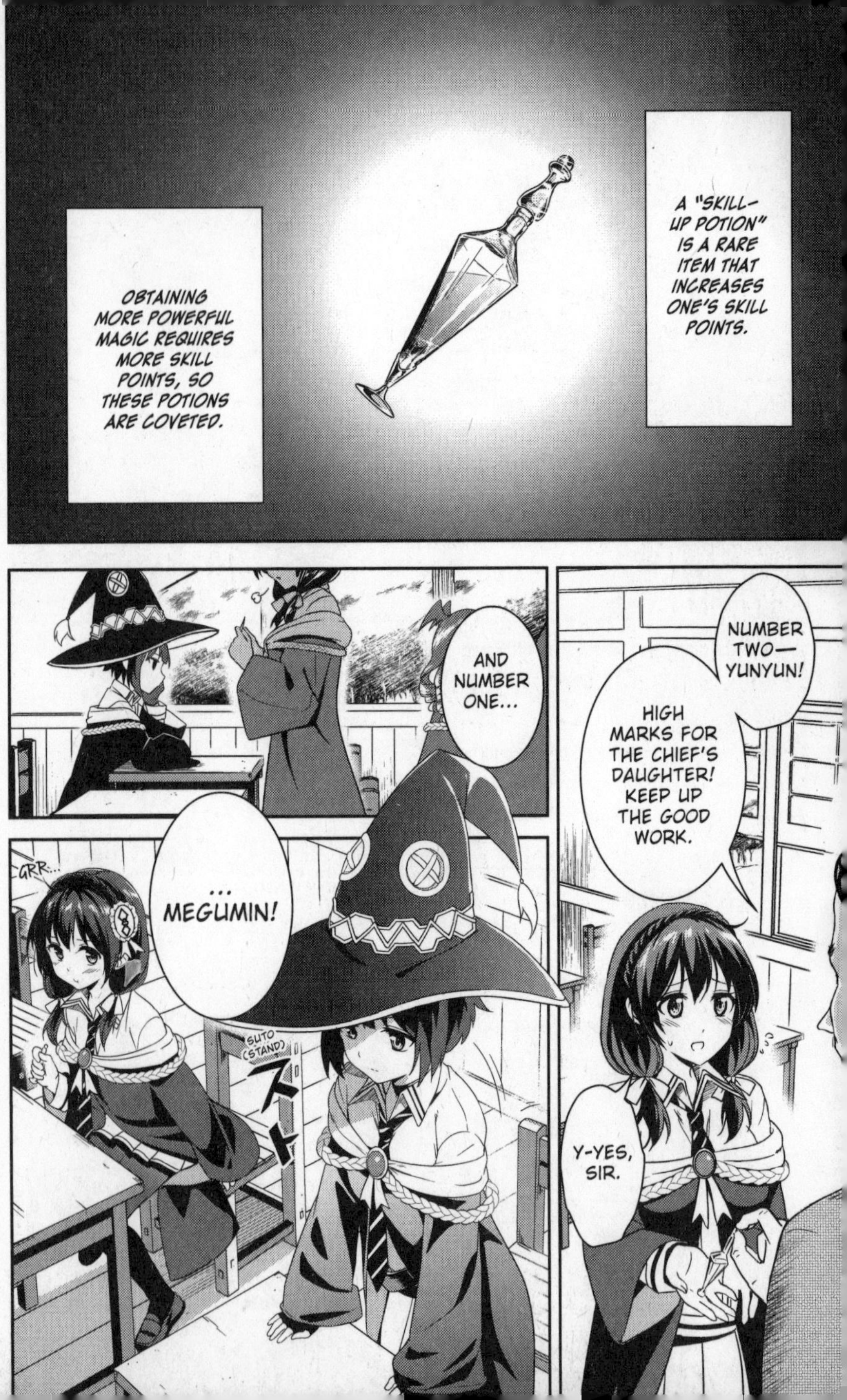
A "SKILL-UP POTION" IS A RARE ITEM THAT INCREASES ONE'S SKILL POINTS.
OBTAINING MORE POWERFUL MAGIC REQUIRES MORE SKILL POINTS, SO THESE POTIONS ARE COVETED.
NUMBER TWO—YUNYUN!
HIGH MARKS FOR THE CHIEF'S DAUGHTER! KEEP UP THE GOOD WORK.
Y-YES, SIR.
AND NUMBER ONE...
...MEGUMIN!
SUTO (STAND)
GRR...

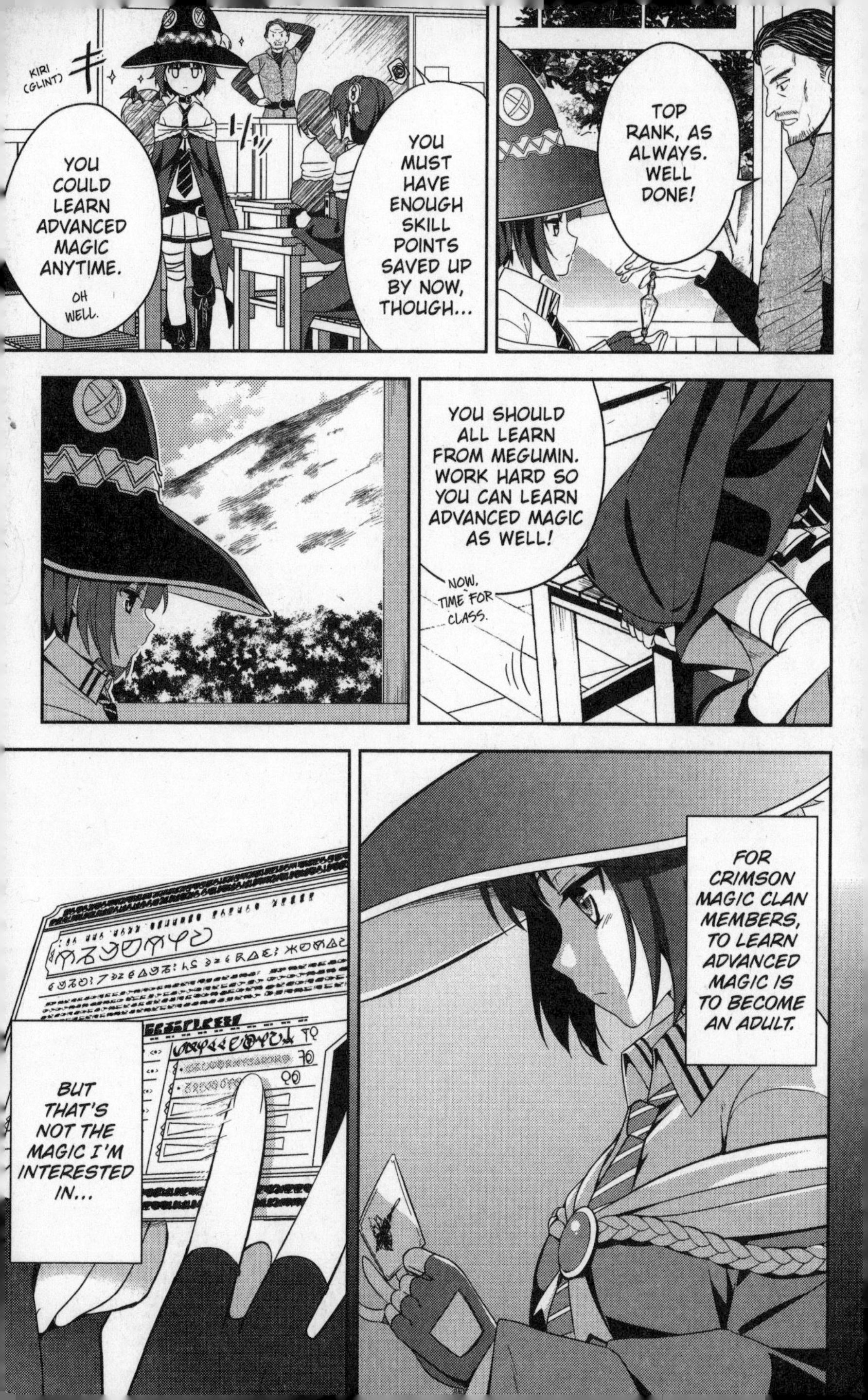
TOP RANK, AS ALWAYS. WELL DONE!
YOU MUST HAVE ENOUGH SKILL POINTS SAVED UP BY NOW, THOUGH...
KIRI (GLINT)
YOU COULD LEARN ADVANCED MAGIC ANYTIME.
OH WELL.
YOU SHOULD ALL LEARN FROM MEGUMIN. WORK HARD SO YOU CAN LEARN ADVANCED MAGIC AS WELL!
NOW, TIME FOR CLASS.
FOR CRIMSON MAGIC CLAN MEMBERS, TO LEARN ADVANCED MAGIC IS TO BECOME AN ADULT.
BUT THAT'S NOT THE MAGIC I'M INTERESTED IN...

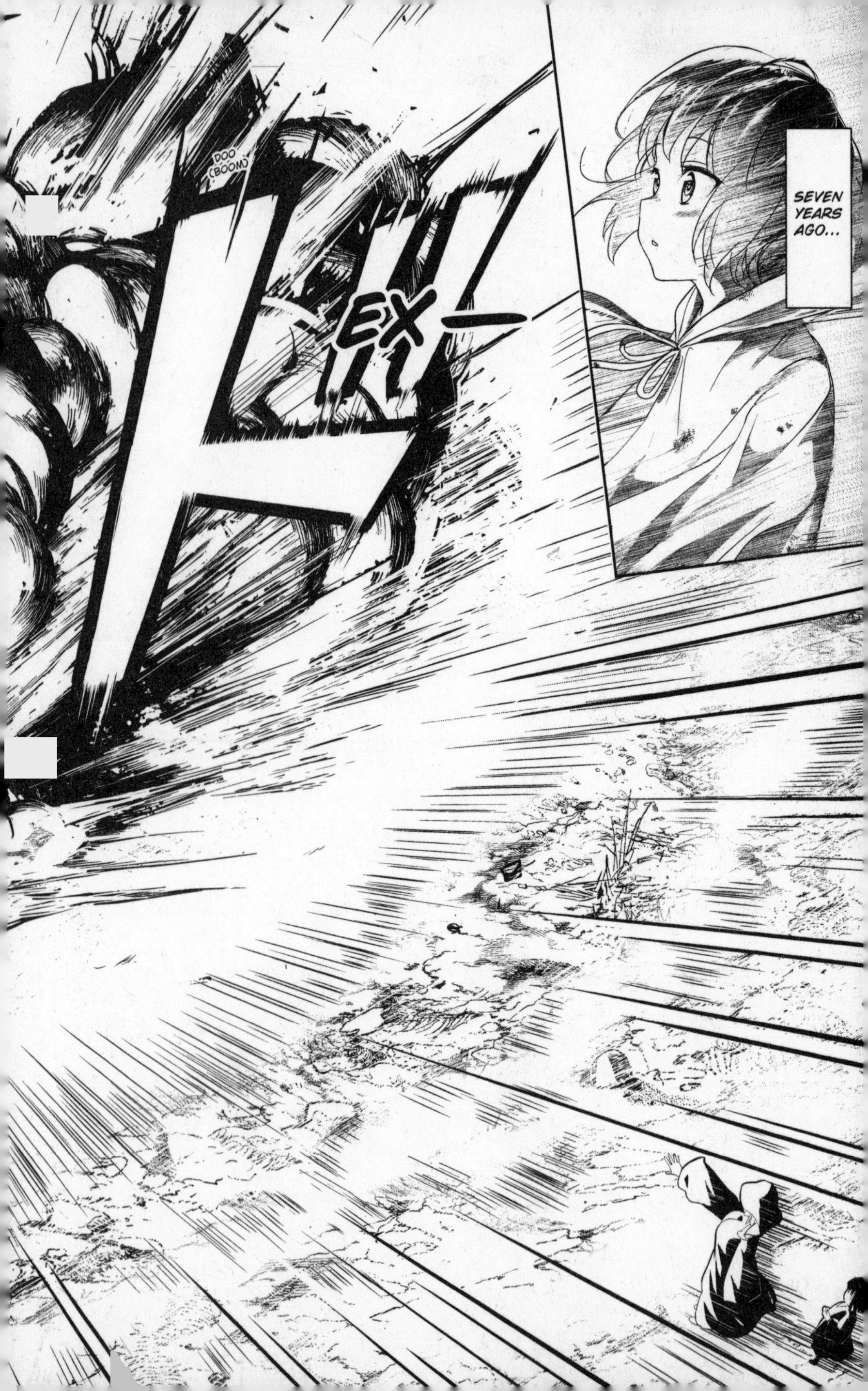
SEVEN YEARS AGO...
DOO (BOOM)
EX—

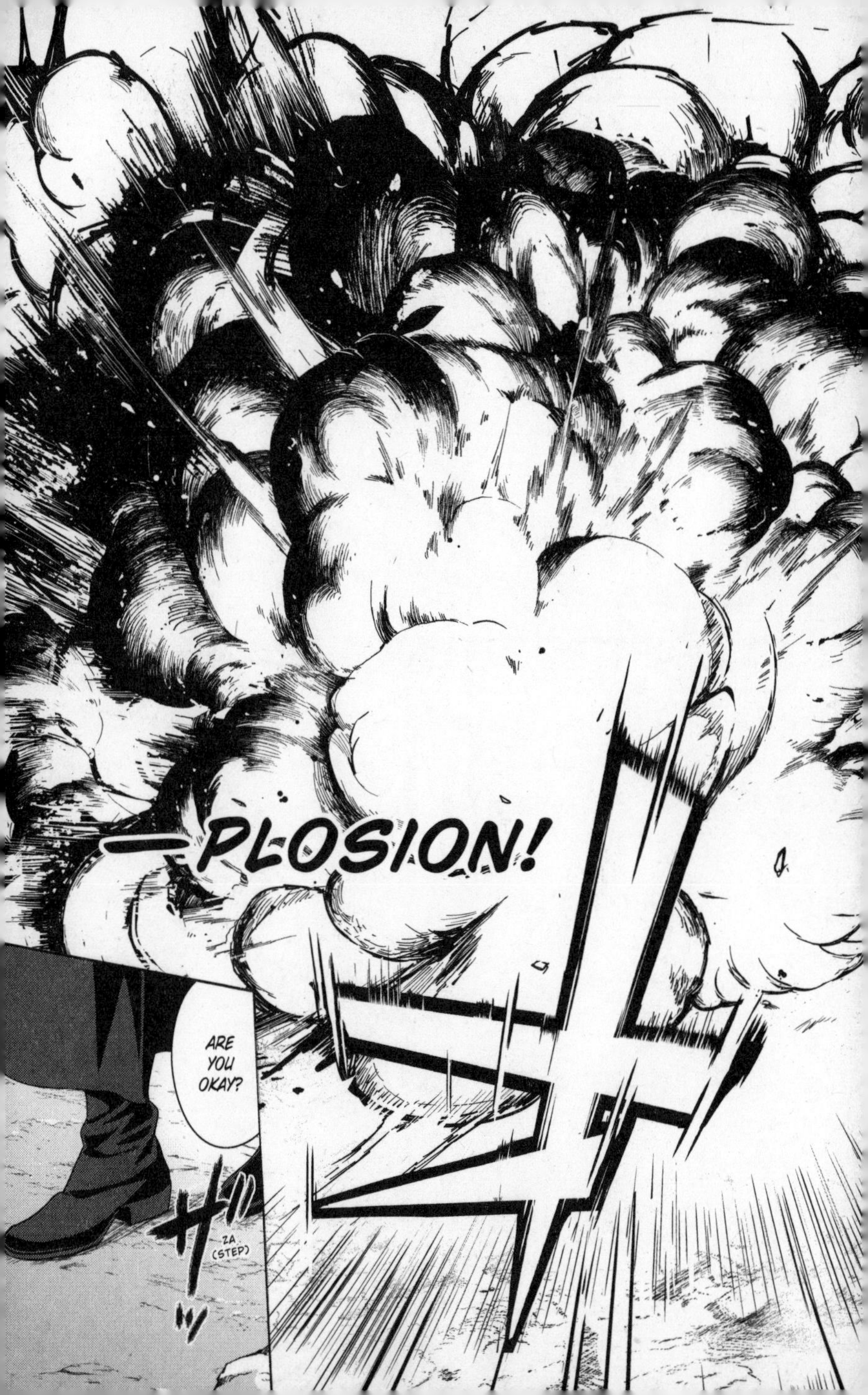
—PLOSION!
ZA (STEP)
ARE YOU OKAY?

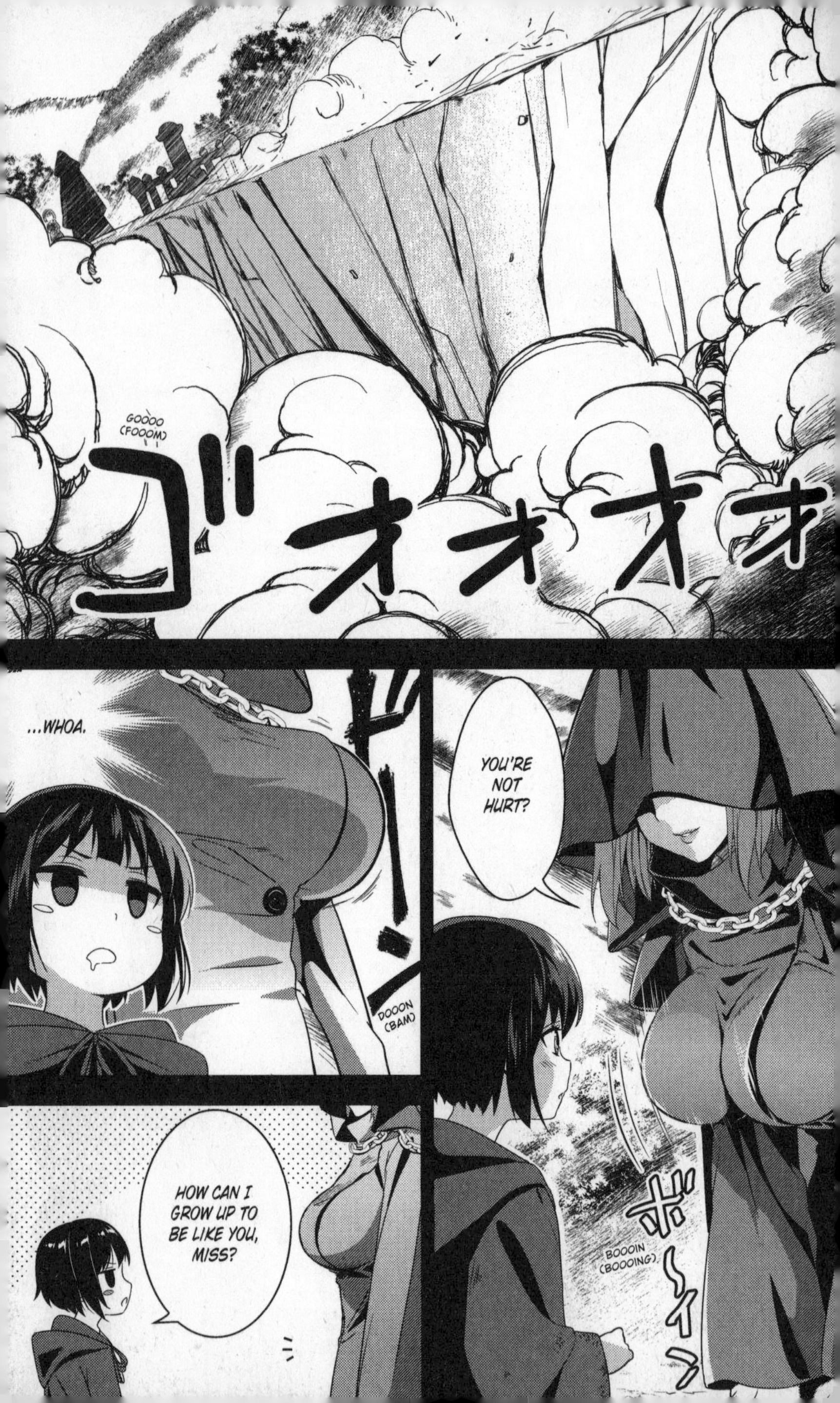

GOOOO
(FOOOM)
ゴオォオォ
YOU'RE NOT HURT?
BOOOIN
(BOOOING)
...WHOA.
DOOON
(BAM)
HOW CAN I GROW UP TO BE LIKE YOU, MISS?

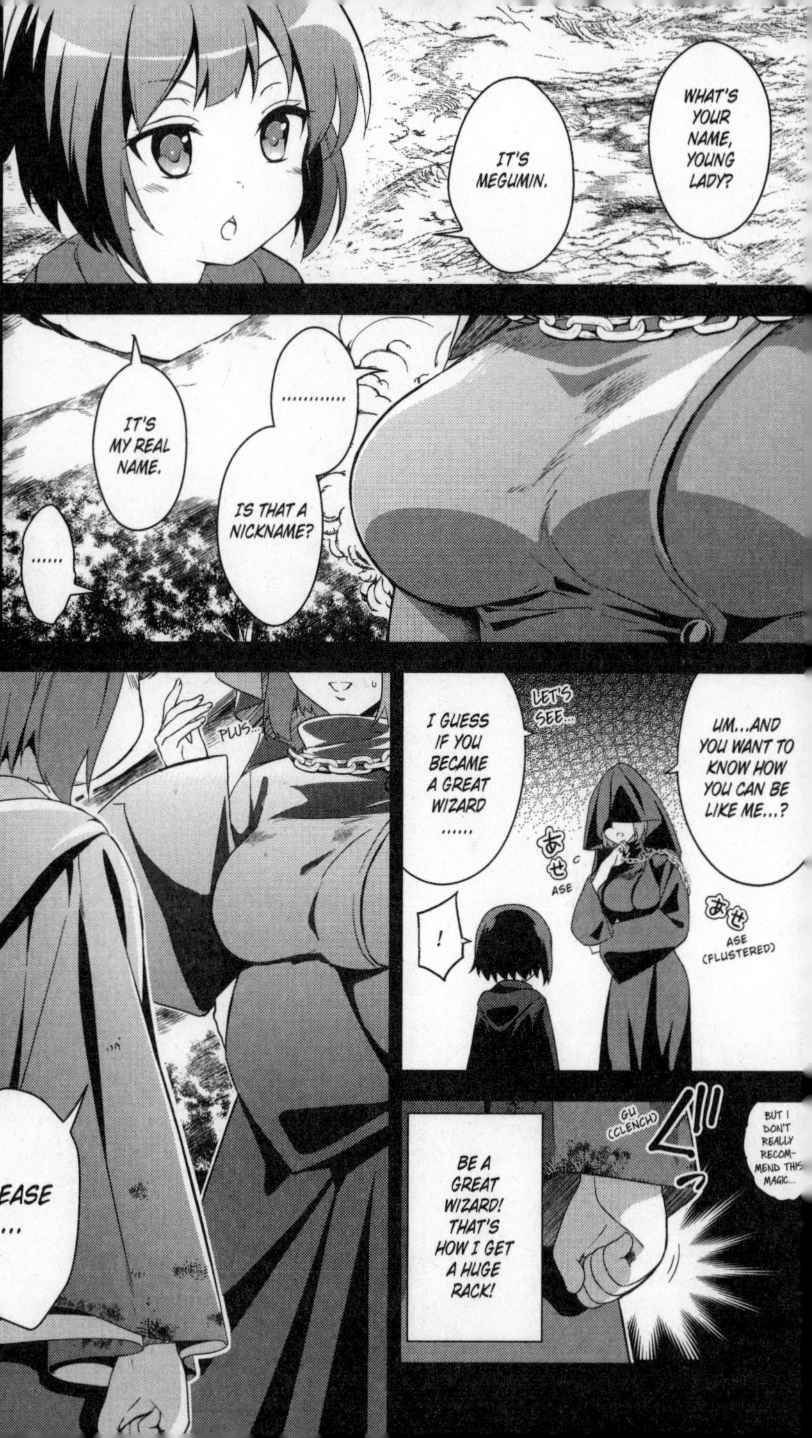
WHAT'S YOUR NAME, YOUNG LADY?
IT'S MEGUMIN.
....
IS THAT A NICKNAME?
IT'S MY REAL NAME.
......
UM...AND YOU WANT TO KNOW HOW YOU CAN BE LIKE ME...?
LET'S SEE...
I GUESS IF YOU BECAME A GREAT WIZARD ......
あせ ASE (FLUSTERED)
あせ ASE
!
BUT I DON'T REALLY RECOM-MEND THIS MAGIC...
GU (CLENCH)
BE A GREAT WIZARD! THAT'S HOW I GET A HUGE RACK!
PLUS...
PLEASE ...

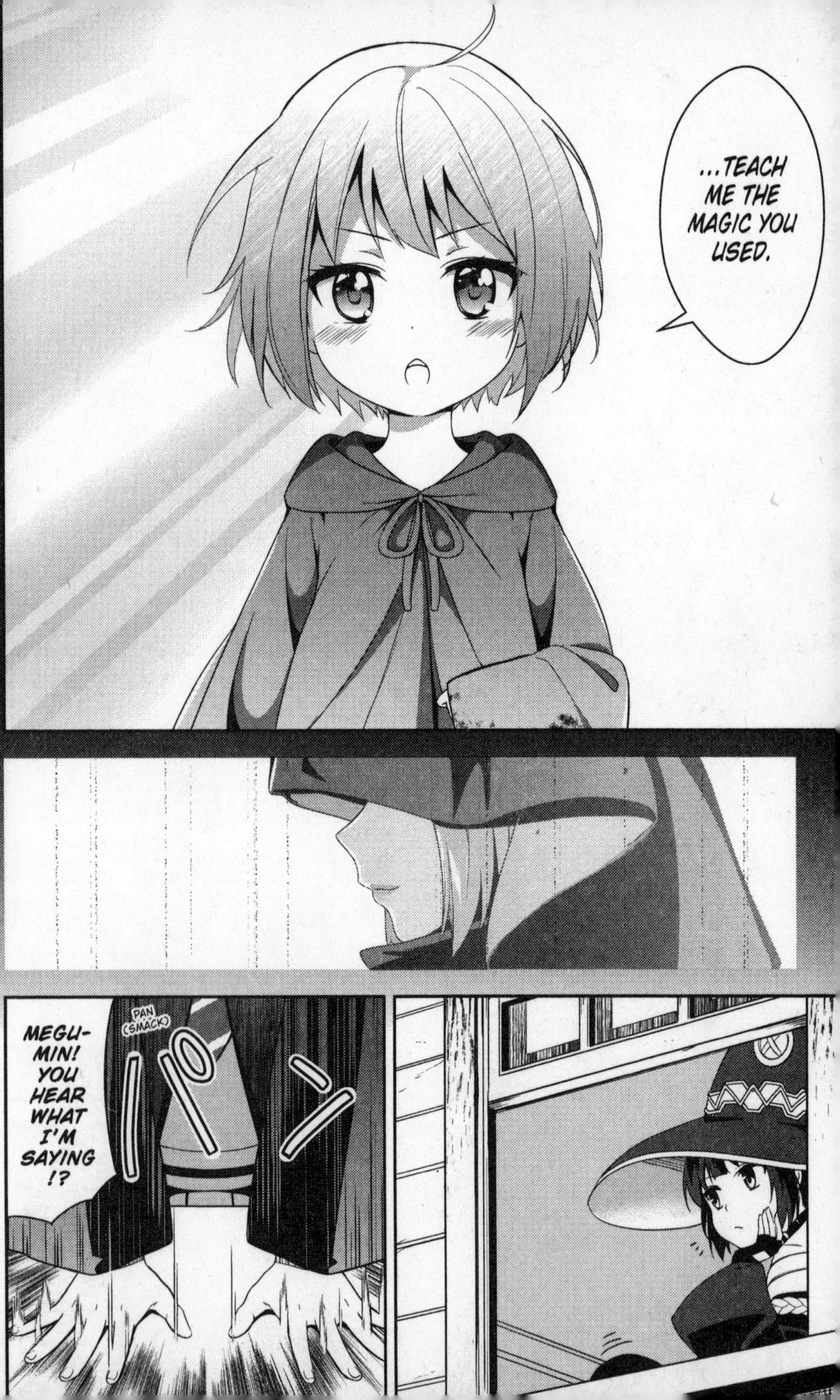
...TEACH ME THE MAGIC YOU USED.
PAN (SMACK)
MEGU-MIN! YOU HEAR WHAT I'M SAYING!?

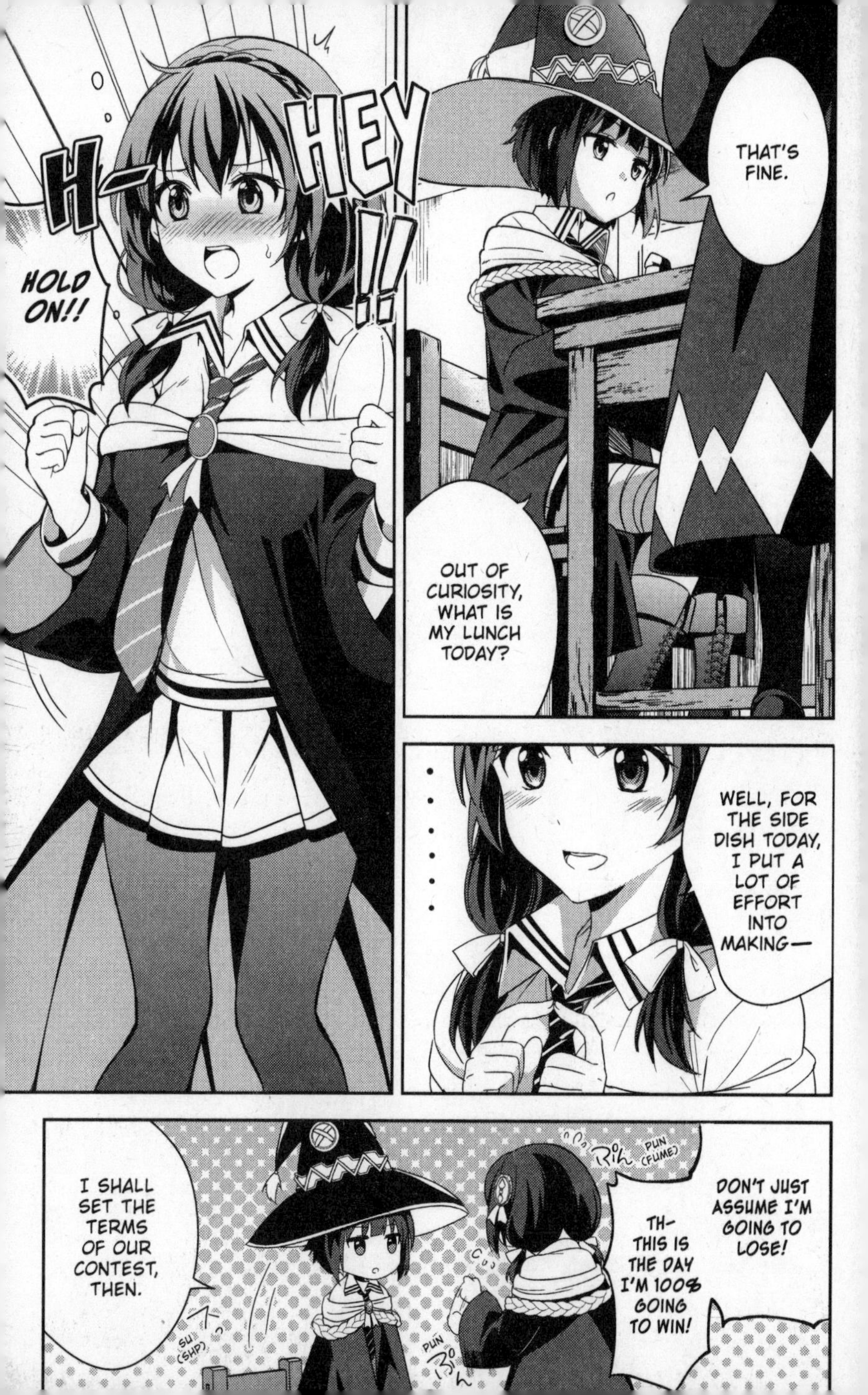
THAT'S FINE.
OUT OF CURIOSITY, WHAT IS MY LUNCH TODAY?
......
WELL, FOR THE SIDE DISH TODAY, I PUT A LOT OF EFFORT INTO MAKING—
H-HEY!!
HOLD ON!!
PUN (FUME)
DON'T JUST ASSUME I'M GOING TO LOSE!
TH- THIS IS THE DAY I'M 100% GOING TO WIN!
I SHALL SET THE TERMS OF OUR CONTEST, THEN.
SU (SHP)
PUN

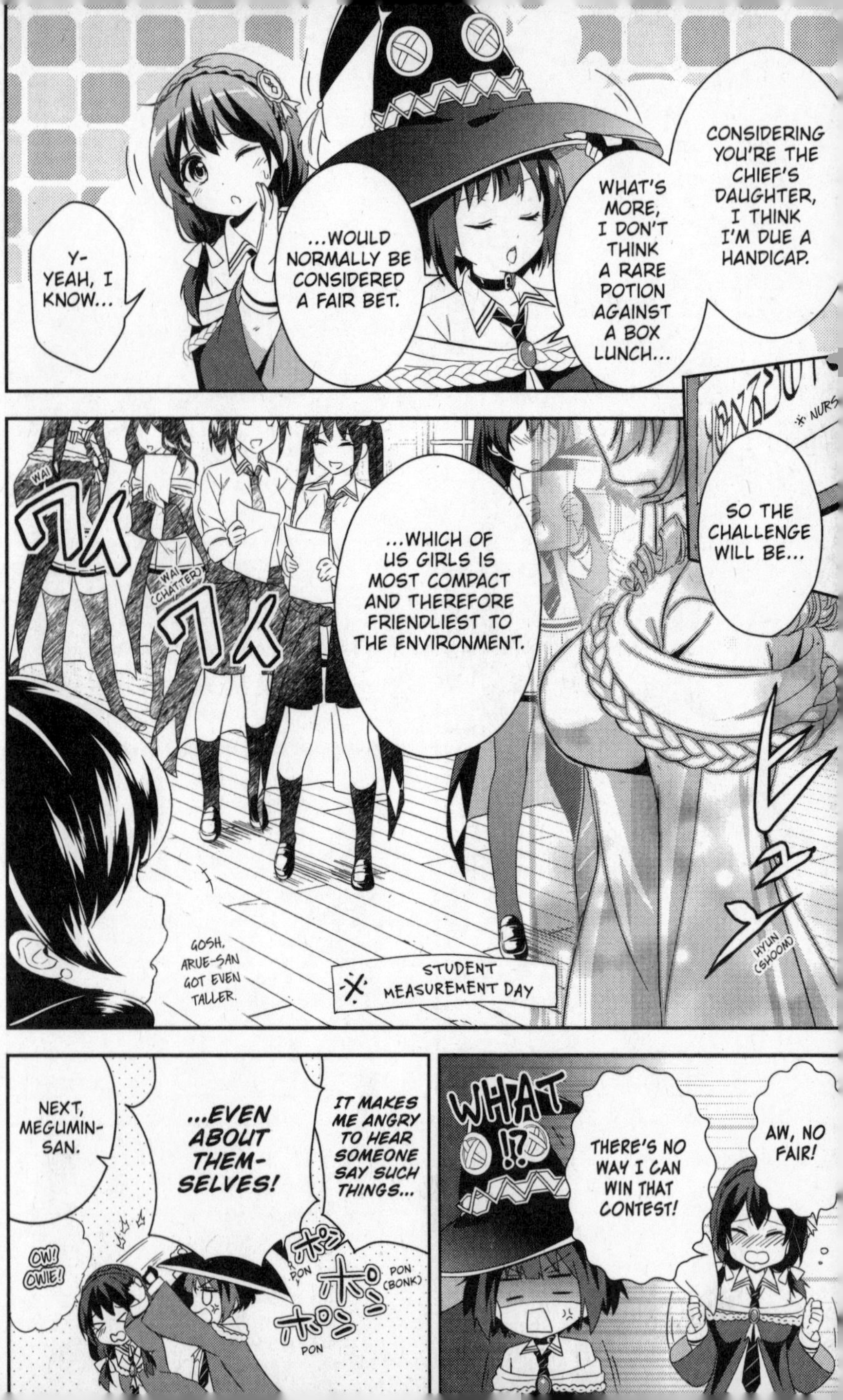

CONSIDERING YOU'RE THE CHIEF'S DAUGHTER, I THINK I'M DUE A HANDICAP.
WHAT'S MORE, I DON'T THINK A RARE POTION AGAINST A BOX LUNCH...
...WOULD NORMALLY BE CONSIDERED A FAIR BET.
Y-YEAH, I KNOW...
SO THE CHALLENGE WILL BE...
HYUN (SHOOM)
...WHICH OF US GIRLS IS MOST COMPACT AND THEREFORE FRIENDLIEST TO THE ENVIRONMENT.
WAI (CHATTER)
WAI
STUDENT MEASUREMENT DAY
GOSH, ARUE-SAN GOT EVEN TALLER.
AW, NO FAIR!
THERE'S NO WAY I CAN WIN THAT CONTEST!
WHAT!?
IT MAKES ME ANGRY TO HEAR SOMEONE SAY SUCH THINGS...
...EVEN ABOUT THEMSELVES!
NEXT, MEGUMIN-SAN.
PON (BONK)
PON
PON
OW! OWIE!

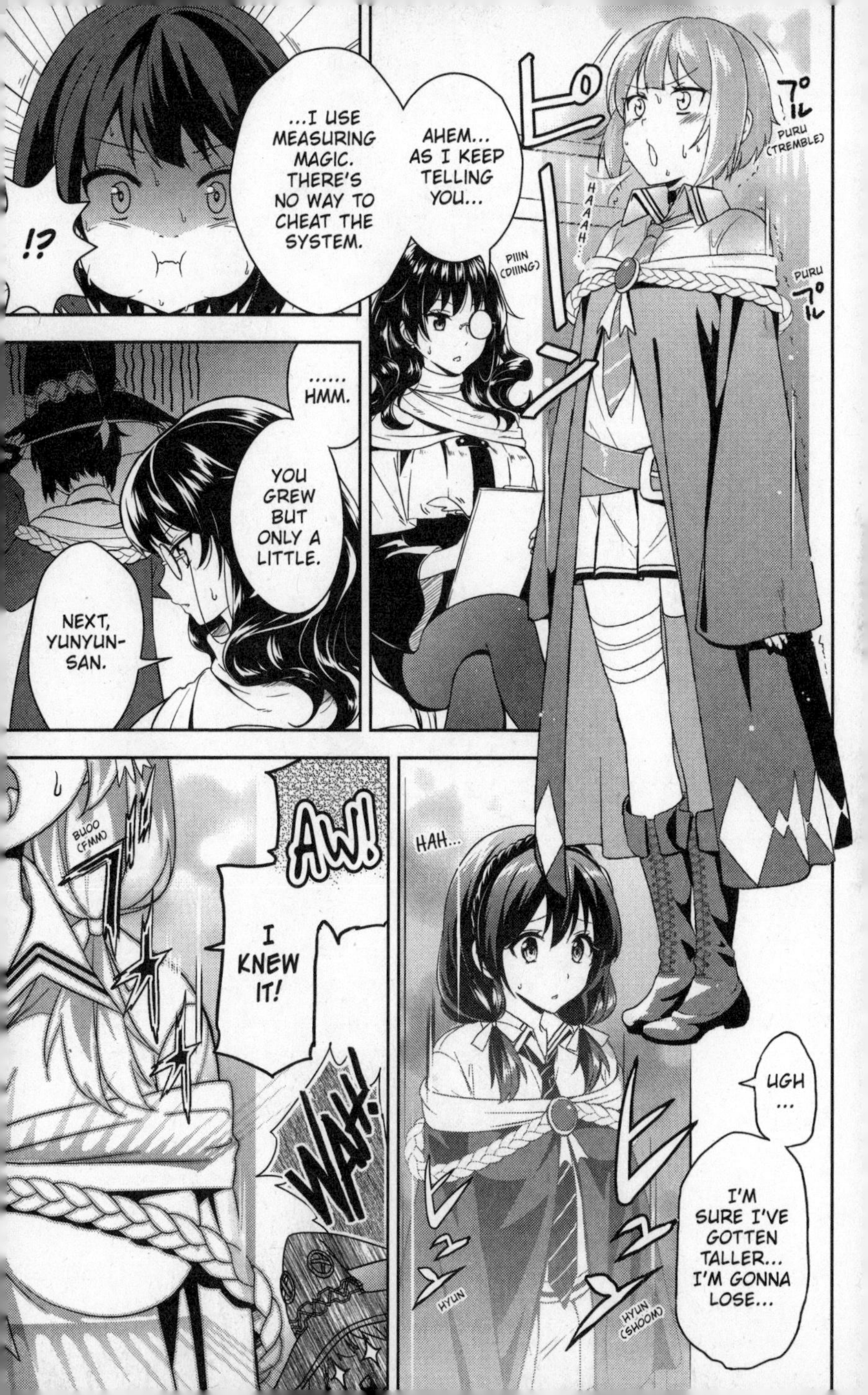
PURU (TREMBLE)
PURU
HAAAAH...
PIIIN (DIIING)
AHEM... AS I KEEP TELLING YOU...
...I USE MEASURING MAGIC. THERE'S NO WAY TO CHEAT THE SYSTEM.
!?
...... HMM.
YOU GREW BUT ONLY A LITTLE.
NEXT, YUNYUN-SAN.
HAH...
UGH ...
I'M SURE I'VE GOTTEN TALLER... I'M GONNA LOSE...
HYUN (SHOOM)
HYUN
AW!
I KNEW IT!
WAH!
BUOO (FMM)

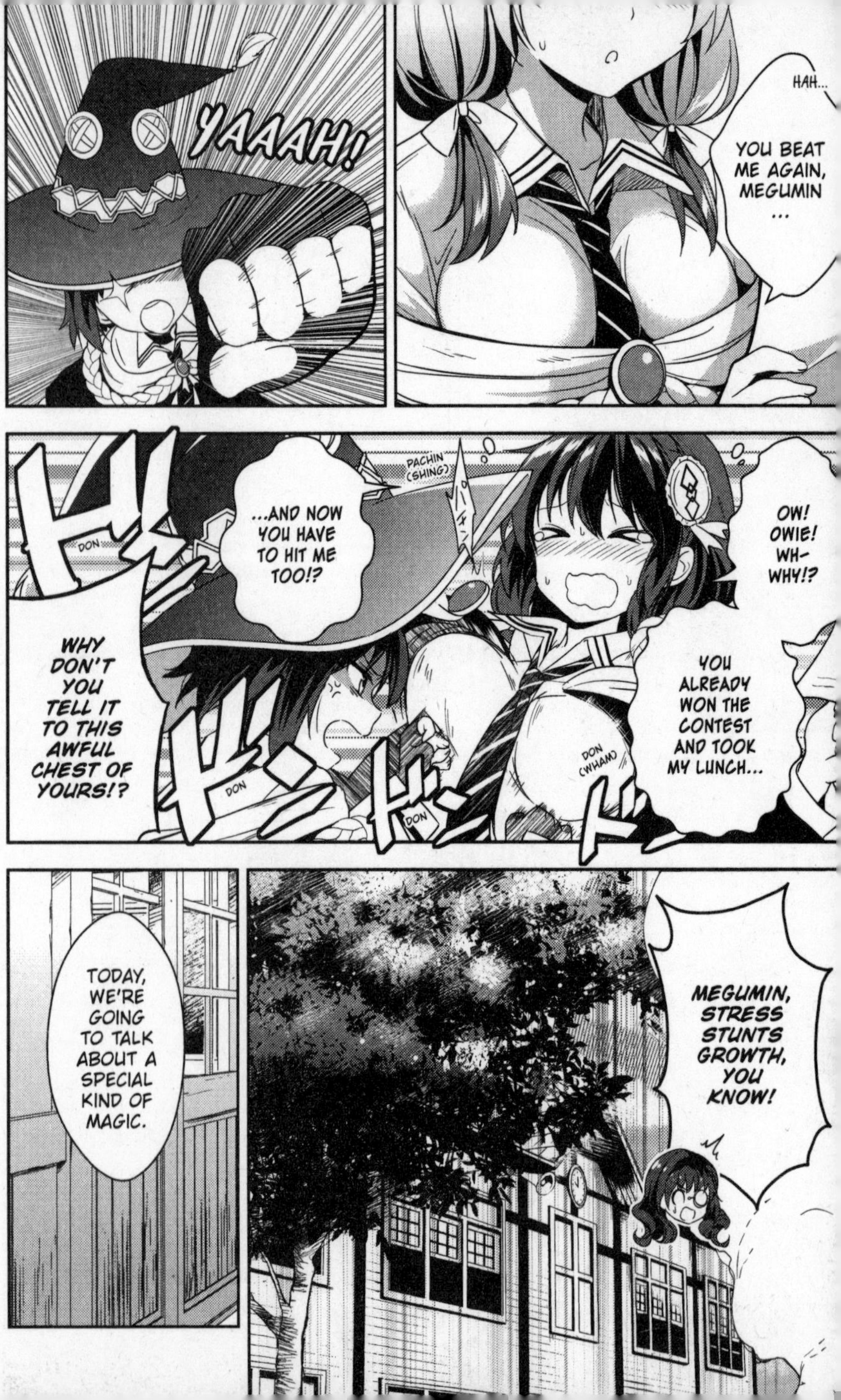
HAH...
YOU BEAT ME AGAIN, MEGUMIN...
YAAAH!
OW! OWIE! WH-WHY!?
PACHIN (SHING)
...AND NOW YOU HAVE TO HIT ME TOO!?
YOU ALREADY WON THE CONTEST AND TOOK MY LUNCH...
DON (WHAM)
DON
WHY DON'T YOU TELL IT TO THIS AWFUL CHEST OF YOURS!?
DON
DON
MEGUMIN, STRESS STUNTS GROWTH, YOU KNOW!
TODAY, WE'RE GOING TO TALK ABOUT A SPECIAL KIND OF MAGIC.

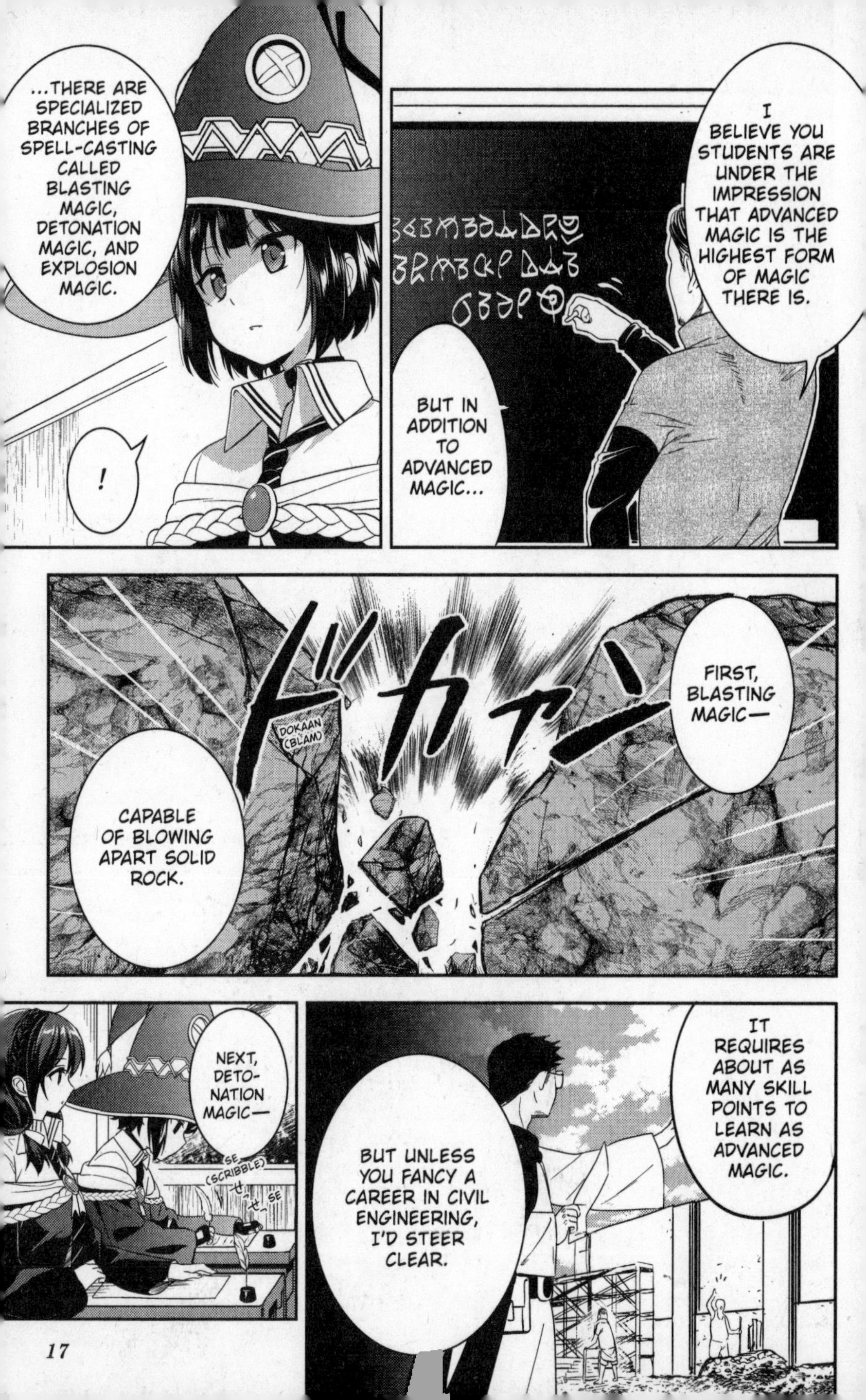
I BELIEVE YOU STUDENTS ARE UNDER THE IMPRESSION THAT ADVANCED MAGIC IS THE HIGHEST FORM OF MAGIC THERE IS.
BUT IN ADDITION TO ADVANCED MAGIC...
...THERE ARE SPECIALIZED BRANCHES OF SPELL-CASTING CALLED BLASTING MAGIC, DETONATION MAGIC, AND EXPLOSION MAGIC.
!
FIRST, BLASTING MAGIC—
DOKAAN (BLAM)
CAPABLE OF BLOWING APART SOLID ROCK.
IT REQUIRES ABOUT AS MANY SKILL POINTS TO LEARN AS ADVANCED MAGIC.
BUT UNLESS YOU FANCY A CAREER IN CIVIL ENGINEERING, I'D STEER CLEAR.
NEXT, DETONATION MAGIC—
SE (SCRIBBLE) SE

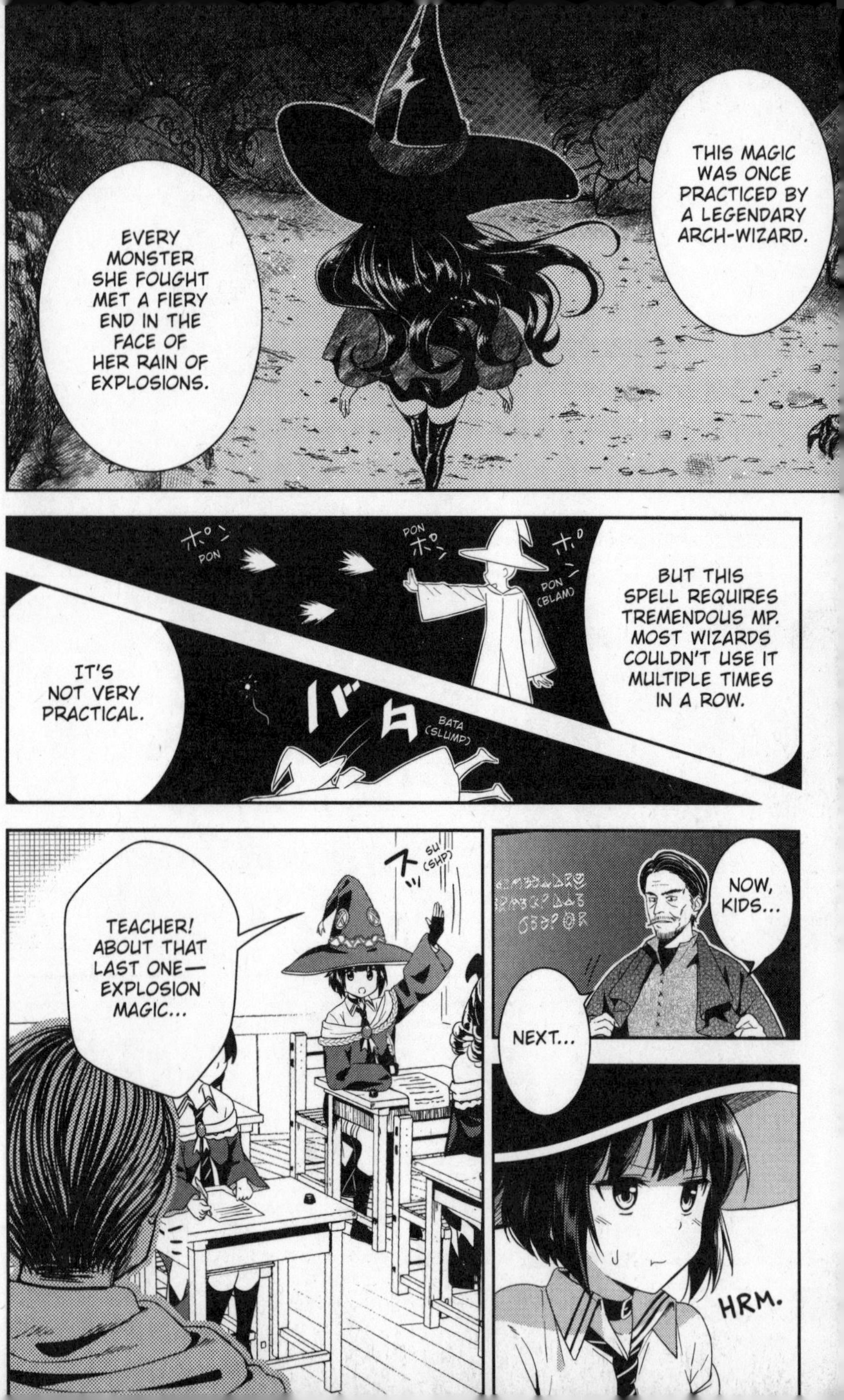
THIS MAGIC WAS ONCE PRACTICED BY A LEGENDARY ARCH-WIZARD.
EVERY MONSTER SHE FOUGHT MET A FIERY END IN THE FACE OF HER RAIN OF EXPLOSIONS.
BUT THIS SPELL REQUIRES TREMENDOUS MP. MOST WIZARDS COULDN'T USE IT MULTIPLE TIMES IN A ROW.
ポン
PON (BLAM)
ポン
PON
ポン
PON
IT'S NOT VERY PRACTICAL.
バタ
BATA (SLUMP)
NOW, KIDS...
NEXT...
HRM.
ス
SU (SHP)
TEACHER! ABOUT THAT LAST ONE—EXPLOSION MAGIC...

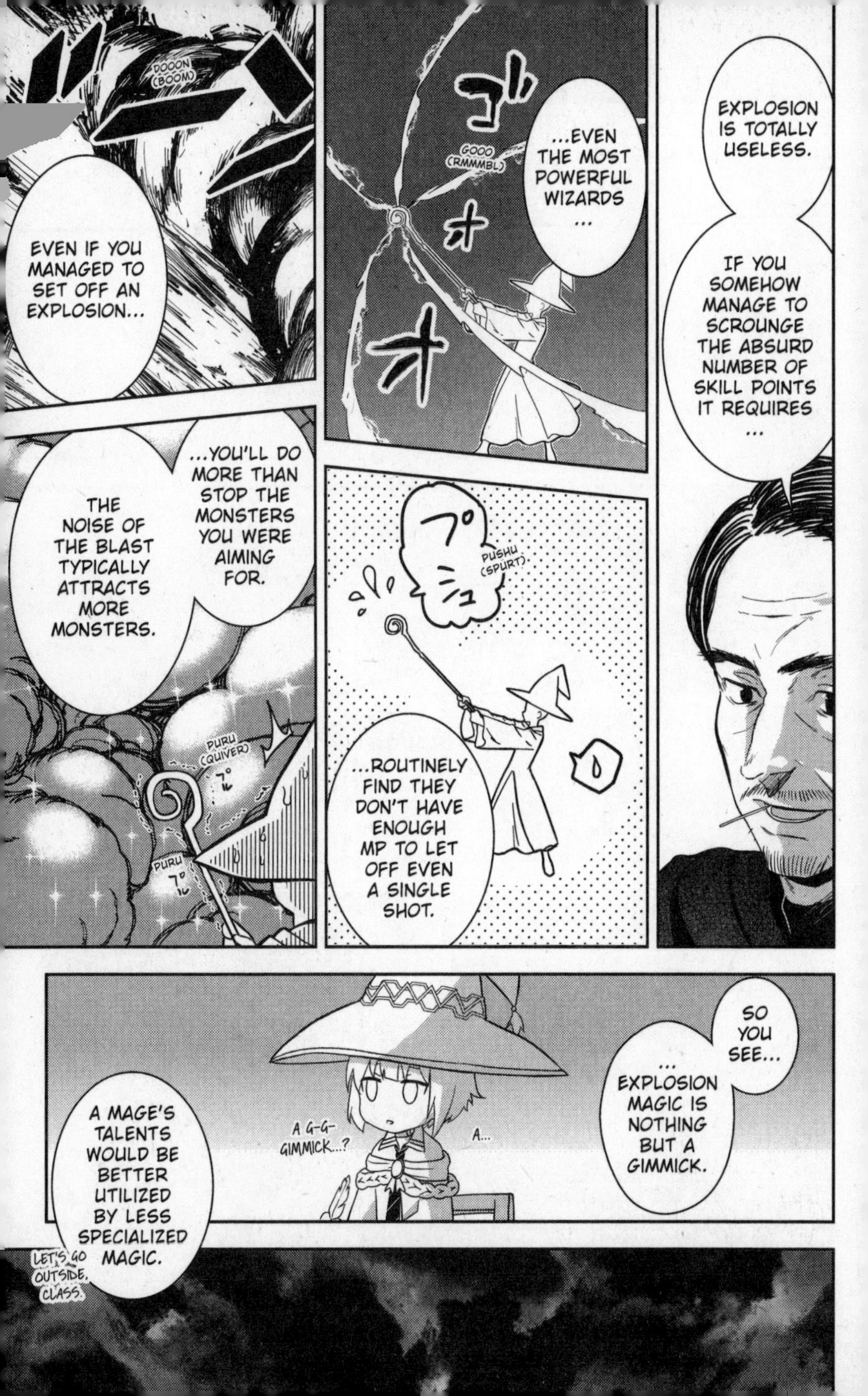
EXPLOSION IS TOTALLY USELESS.
IF YOU SOMEHOW MANAGE TO SCROUNGE THE ABSURD NUMBER OF SKILL POINTS IT REQUIRES ...
GOOO (RMMMBL)
...EVEN THE MOST POWERFUL WIZARDS ...
PUSHU (SPURT)
...ROUTINELY FIND THEY DON'T HAVE ENOUGH MP TO LET OFF EVEN A SINGLE SHOT.
DOOON (BOOM)
EVEN IF YOU MANAGED TO SET OFF AN EXPLOSION...
...YOU'LL DO MORE THAN STOP THE MONSTERS YOU WERE AIMING FOR.
THE NOISE OF THE BLAST TYPICALLY ATTRACTS MORE MONSTERS.
PURU (QUIVER)
PURU
SO YOU SEE...
... EXPLOSION MAGIC IS NOTHING BUT A GIMMICK.
A...
A G-G-GIMMICK...?
A MAGE'S TALENTS WOULD BE BETTER UTILIZED BY LESS SPECIALIZED MAGIC.
LET'S GO OUTSIDE, CLASS.

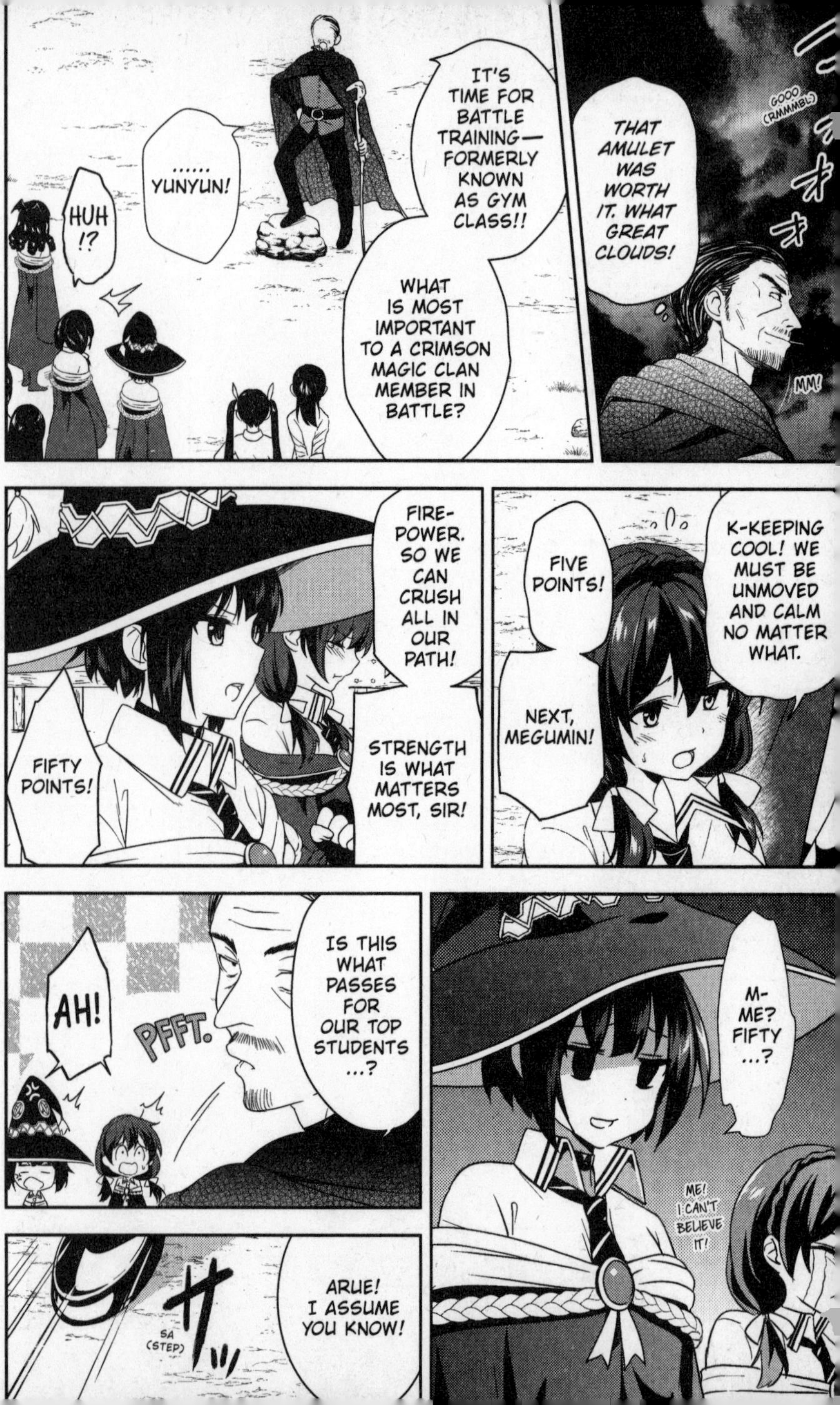
GOOO (RMMMBL)
THAT AMULET WAS WORTH IT. WHAT GREAT CLOUDS!
MM!
IT'S TIME FOR BATTLE TRAINING—FORMERLY KNOWN AS GYM CLASS!!
WHAT IS MOST IMPORTANT TO A CRIMSON MAGIC CLAN MEMBER IN BATTLE?
......YUNYUN!
HUH!?
K-KEEPING COOL! WE MUST BE UNMOVED AND CALM NO MATTER WHAT.
FIVE POINTS!
NEXT, MEGUMIN!
FIRE-POWER. SO WE CAN CRUSH ALL IN OUR PATH!
STRENGTH IS WHAT MATTERS MOST, SIR!
FIFTY POINTS!
M-ME? FIFTY...?
ME! I CAN'T BELIEVE IT!
IS THIS WHAT PASSES FOR OUR TOP STUDENTS...?
PFFT.
AH!
ARUE! I ASSUME YOU KNOW!
SA (STEP)

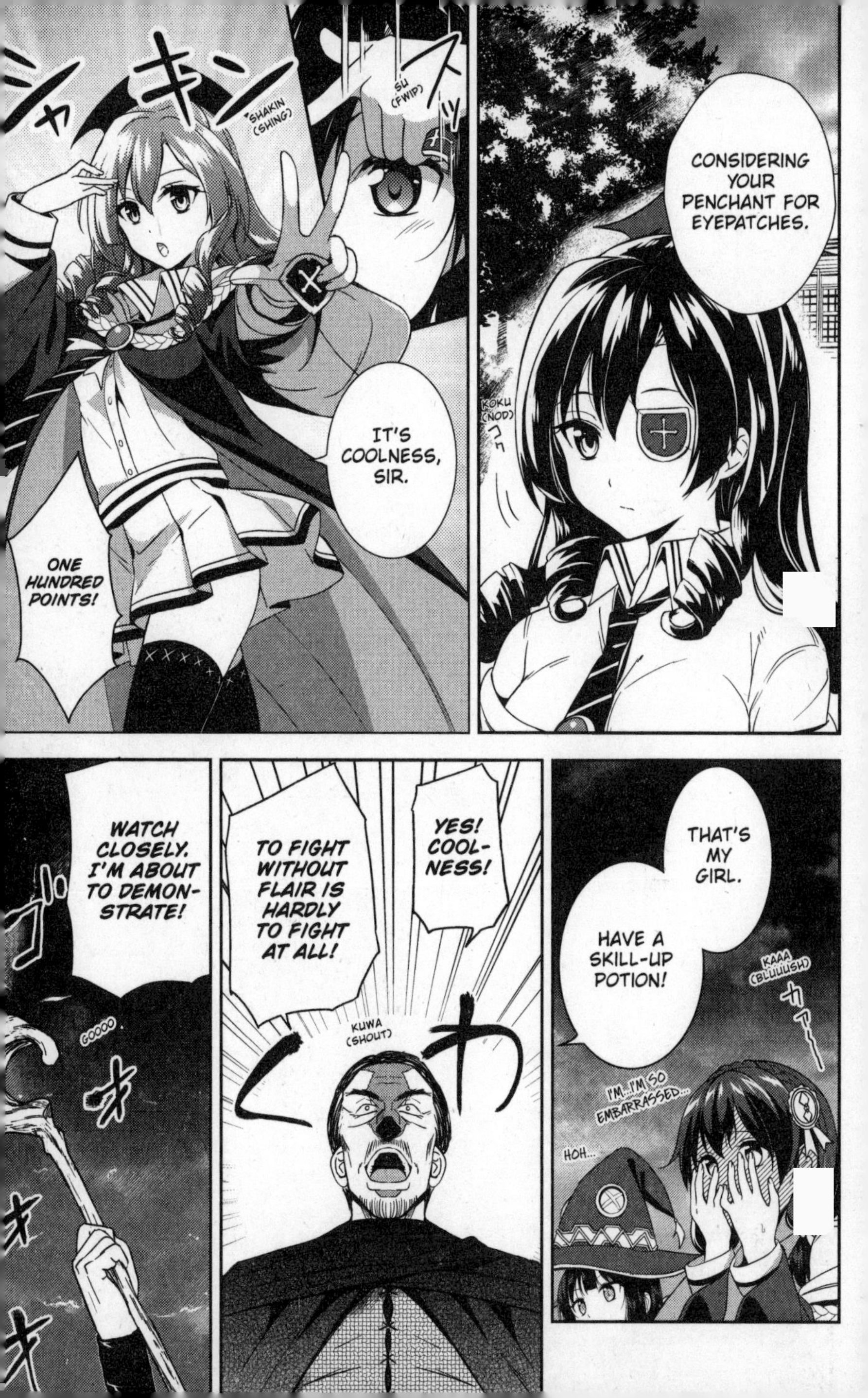
CONSIDERING YOUR PENCHANT FOR EYEPATCHES.
KOKU (NOD)
SU (FWIP)
SHAKIN (SHING)
IT'S COOLNESS, SIR.
ONE HUNDRED POINTS!
THAT'S MY GIRL.
KAAA (BLUUUSH)
HAVE A SKILL-UP POTION!
I'M...I'M SO EMBARRASSED...
HOH...
YES! COOL-NESS!
TO FIGHT WITHOUT FLAIR IS HARDLY TO FIGHT AT ALL!
KUWA (SHOUT)
WATCH CLOSELY. I'M ABOUT TO DEMON-STRATE!
GOOOO

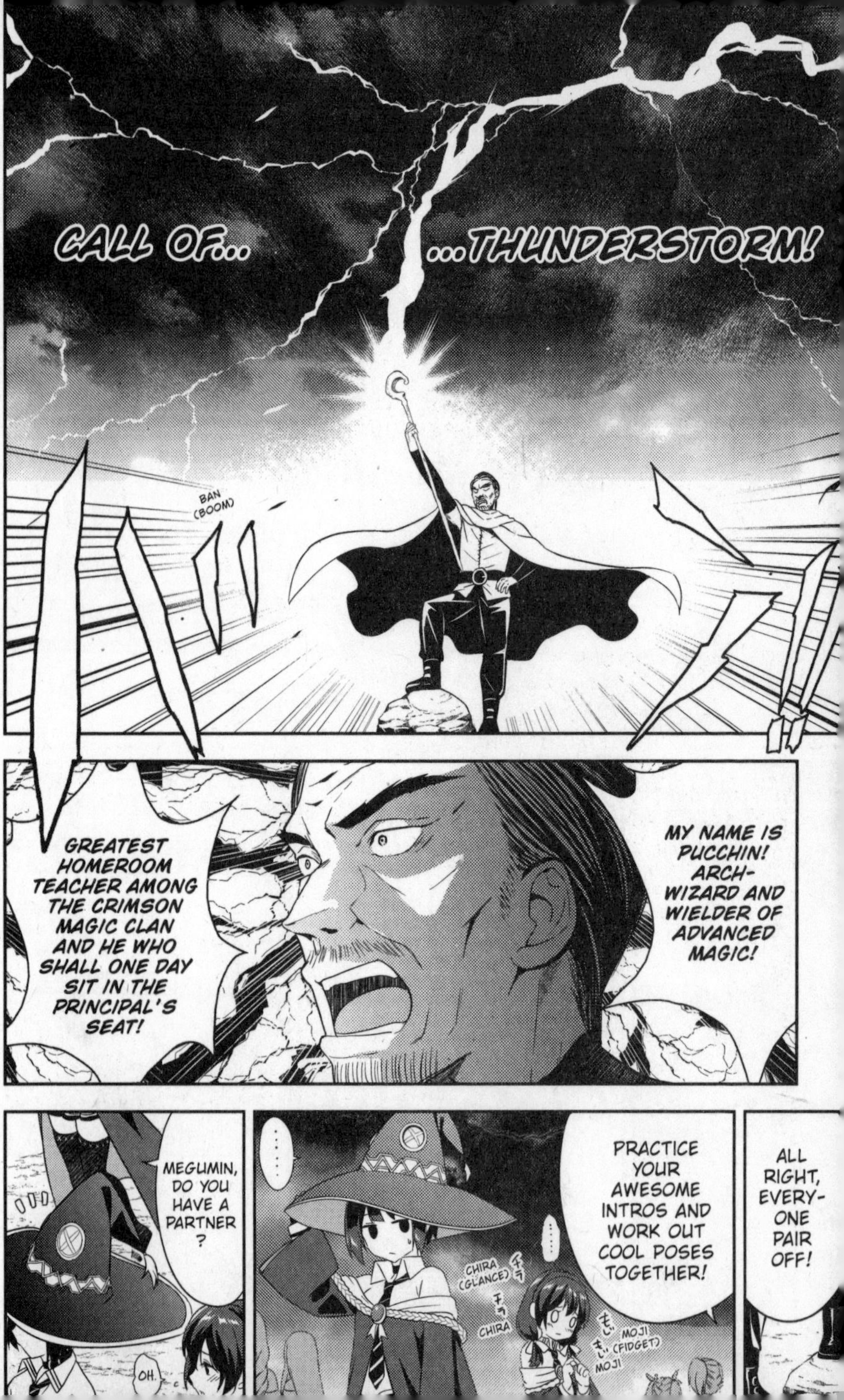
CALL OF...
...THUNDERSTORM!
BAN (BOOM)
MY NAME IS PUCCHIN! ARCH-WIZARD AND WIELDER OF ADVANCED MAGIC!
GREATEST HOMEROOM TEACHER AMONG THE CRIMSON MAGIC CLAN AND HE WHO SHALL ONE DAY SIT IN THE PRINCIPAL'S SEAT!
ALL RIGHT, EVERYONE PAIR OFF!
PRACTICE YOUR AWESOME INTROS AND WORK OUT COOL POSES TOGETHER!
......
......
CHIRA (GLANCE)
CHIRA
MOJI (FIDGET) MOJI
MEGUMIN, DO YOU HAVE A PARTNER?
OH.

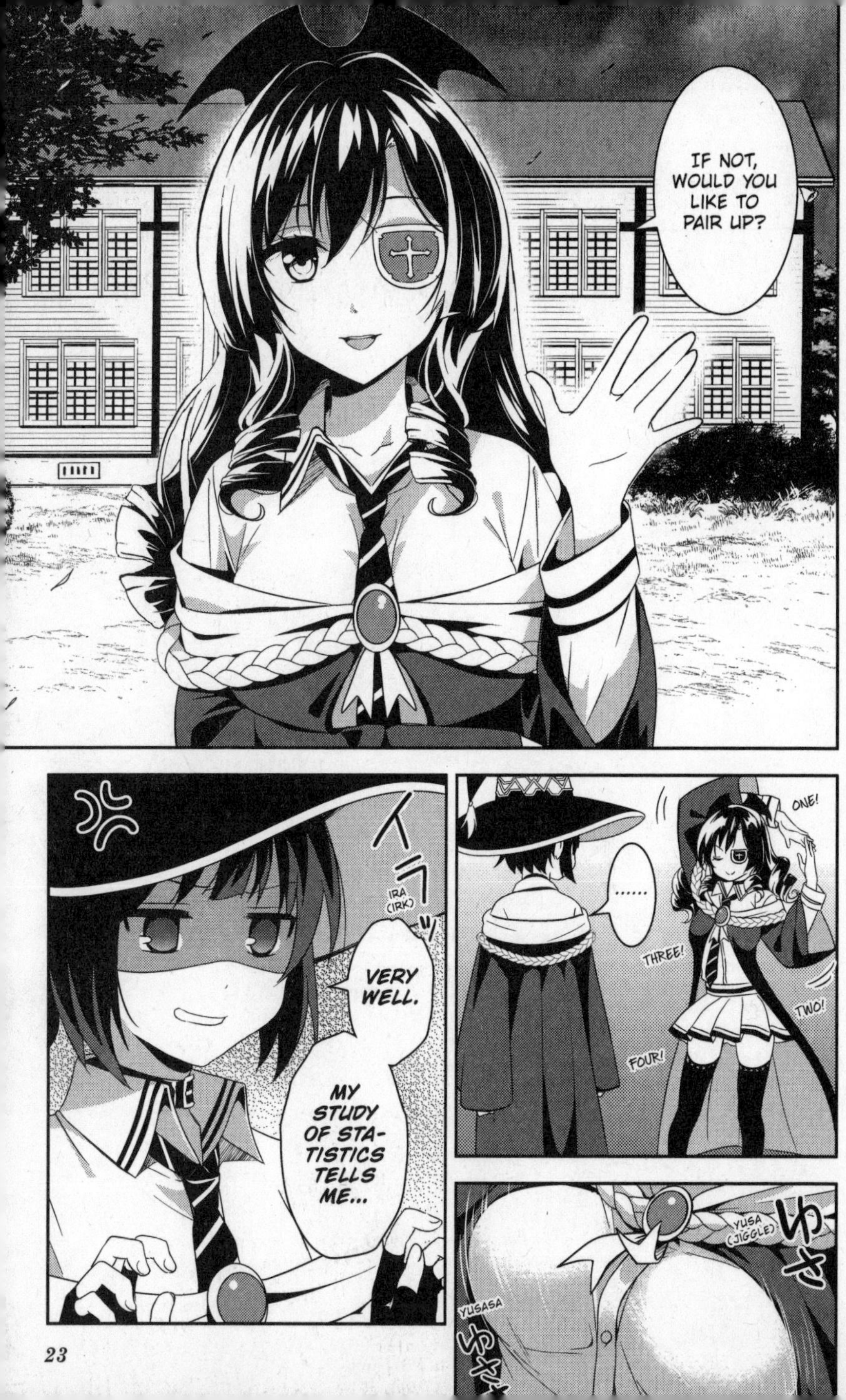
IF NOT, WOULD YOU LIKE TO PAIR UP?
ONE!
......
THREE!
TWO!
FOUR!
YUSA (JIGGLE)
YUSASA
IRA (IRK)
VERY WELL.
MY STUDY OF STA-TISTICS TELLS ME...

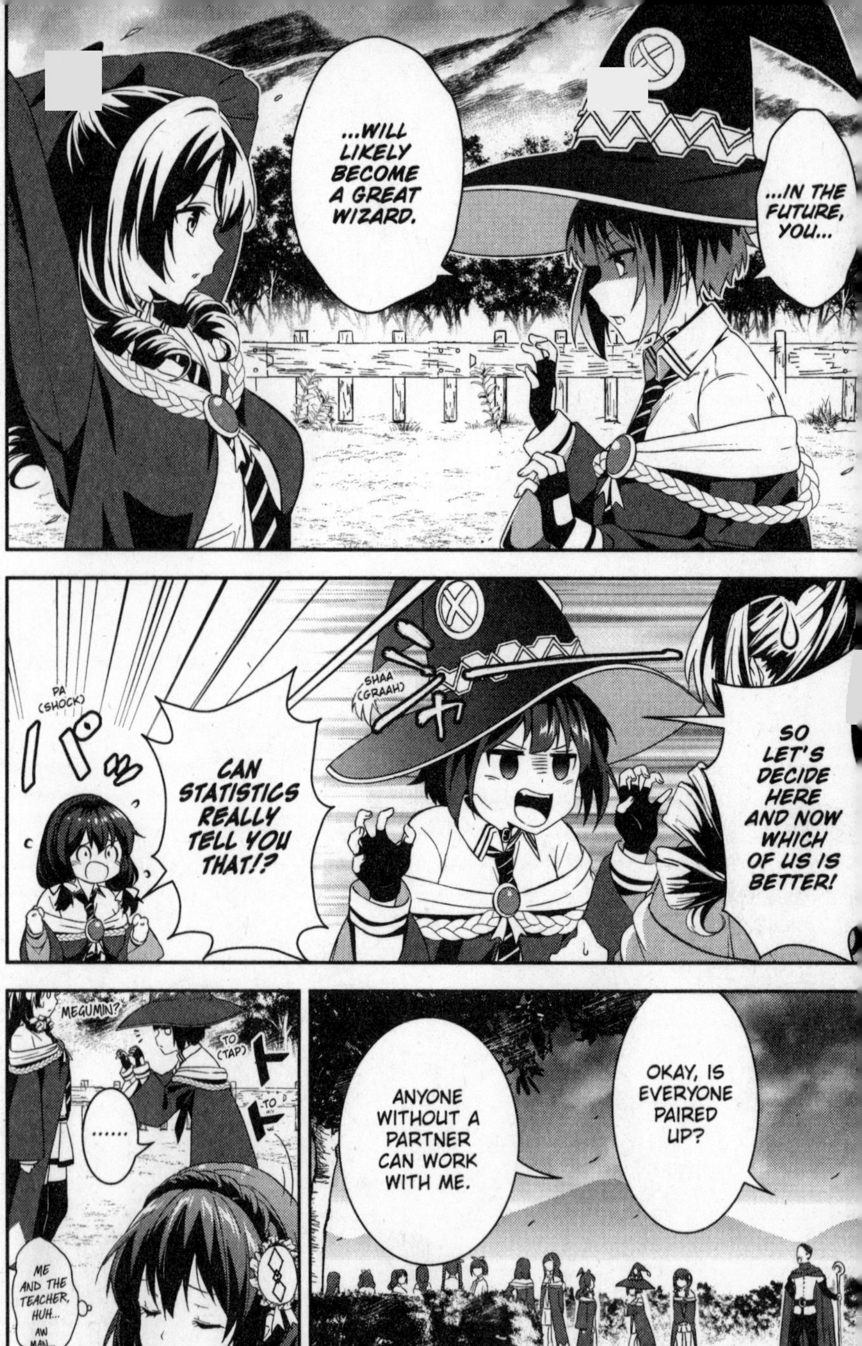
...IN THE FUTURE, YOU...
...WILL LIKELY BECOME A GREAT WIZARD.
SO LET'S DECIDE HERE AND NOW WHICH OF US IS BETTER!
SHAA (GRAAH)
CAN STATISTICS REALLY TELL YOU THAT!?
PA (SHOCK)
OKAY, IS EVERYONE PAIRED UP?
ANYONE WITHOUT A PARTNER CAN WORK WITH ME.
MEGUMIN?
TO (TAP)
TO
......
ME AND THE TEACHER, HUH...
AW MAN...
HAH...

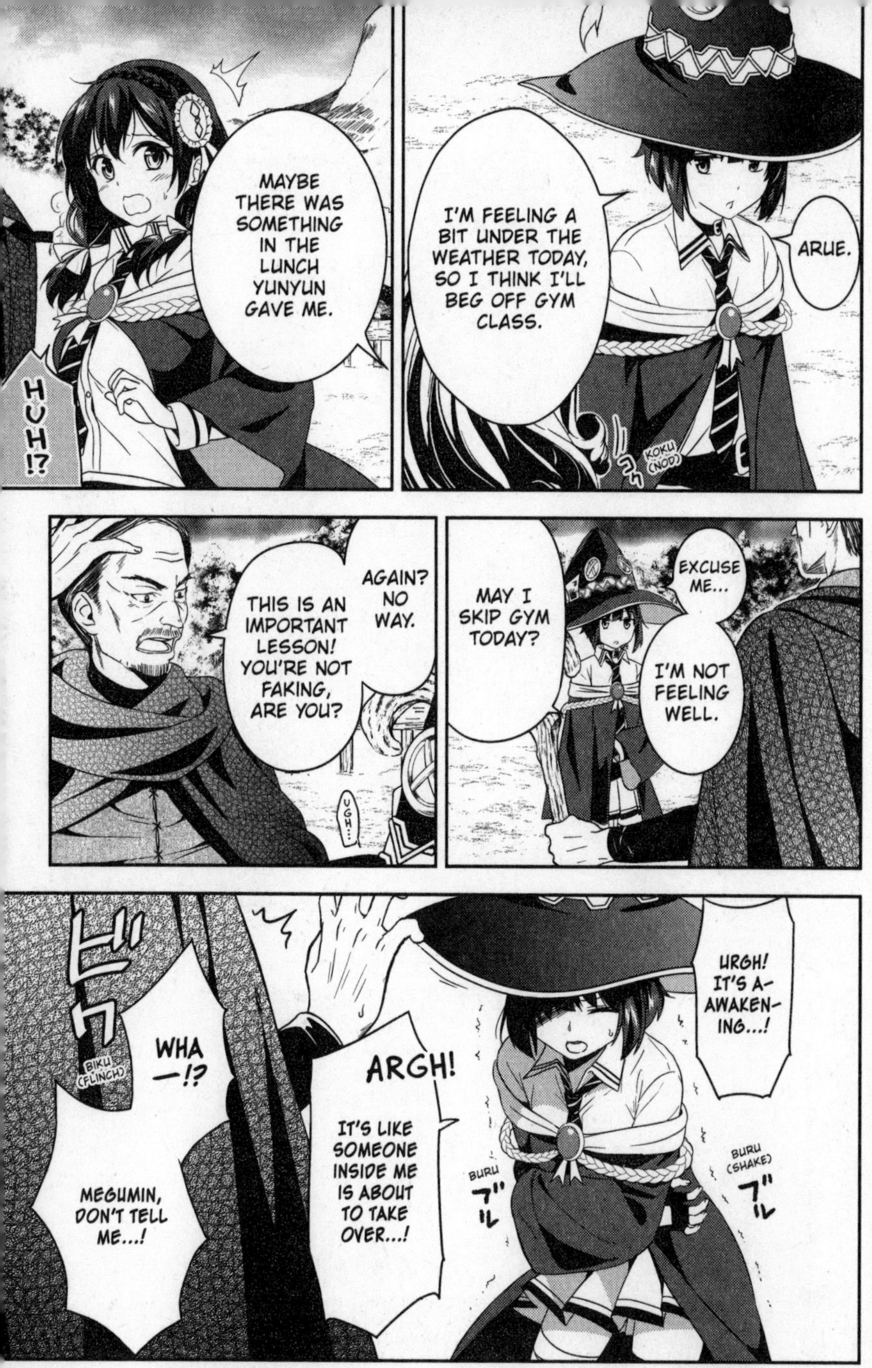
ARUE.
I'M FEELING A BIT UNDER THE WEATHER TODAY, SO I THINK I'LL BEG OFF GYM CLASS.
KOKU (NOD)
MAYBE THERE WAS SOMETHING IN THE LUNCH YUNYUN GAVE ME.
HUH!?
EXCUSE ME...
I'M NOT FEELING WELL.
MAY I SKIP GYM TODAY?
AGAIN? NO WAY.
THIS IS AN IMPORTANT LESSON! YOU'RE NOT FAKING, ARE YOU?
UGH...
URGH! IT'S A-AWAKENING...!
BURU (SHAKE)
ARGH!
IT'S LIKE SOMEONE INSIDE ME IS ABOUT TO TAKE OVER...!
BURU
WHA—!?
BIKU (FLINCH)
MEGUMIN, DON'T TELL ME...!

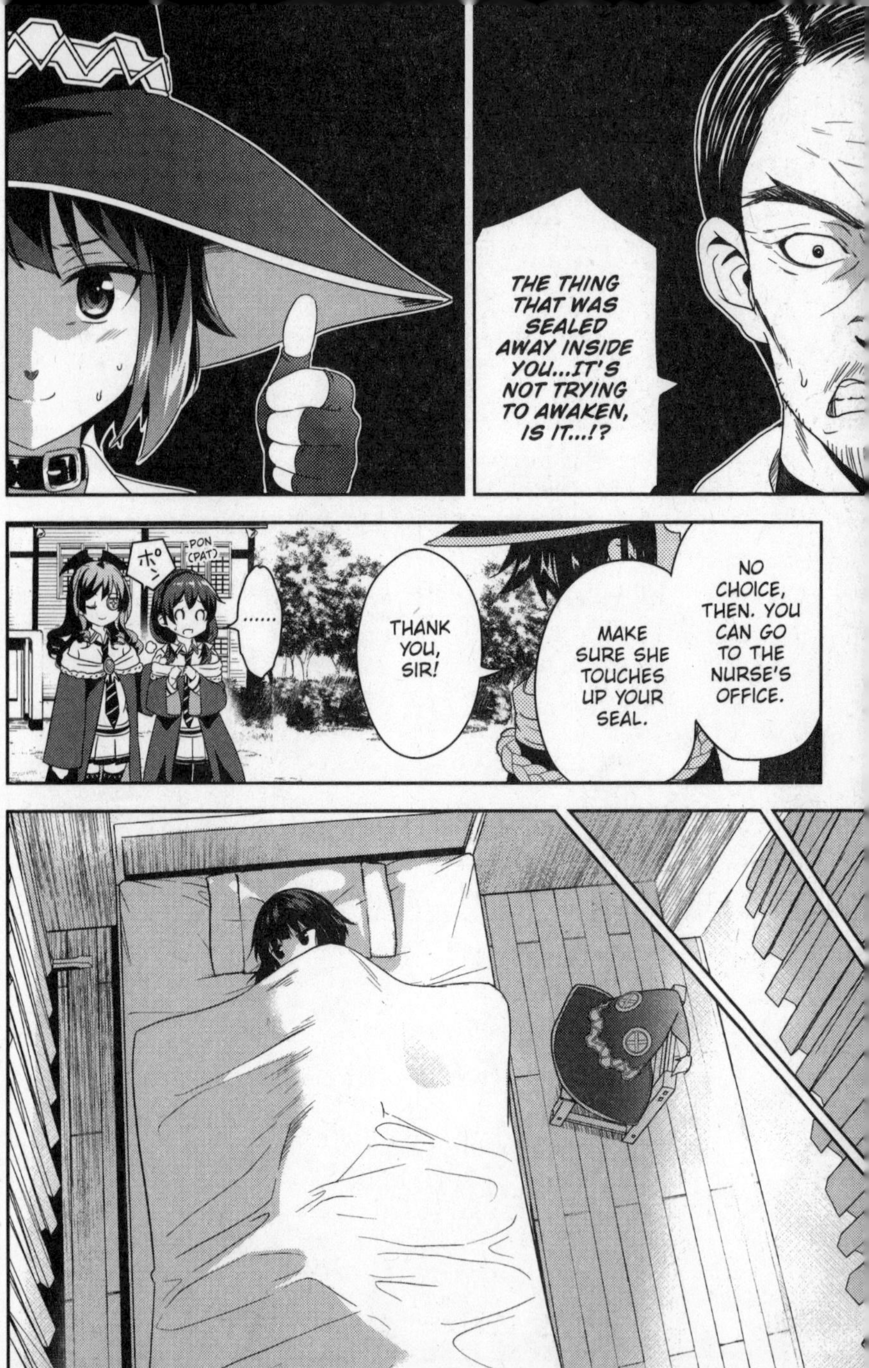
THE THING THAT WAS SEALED AWAY INSIDE YOU...IT'S NOT TRYING TO AWAKEN, IS IT...!?
NO CHOICE, THEN. YOU CAN GO TO THE NURSE'S OFFICE.
MAKE SURE SHE TOUCHES UP YOUR SEAL.
THANK YOU, SIR!
......
ポン
PON (PAT)

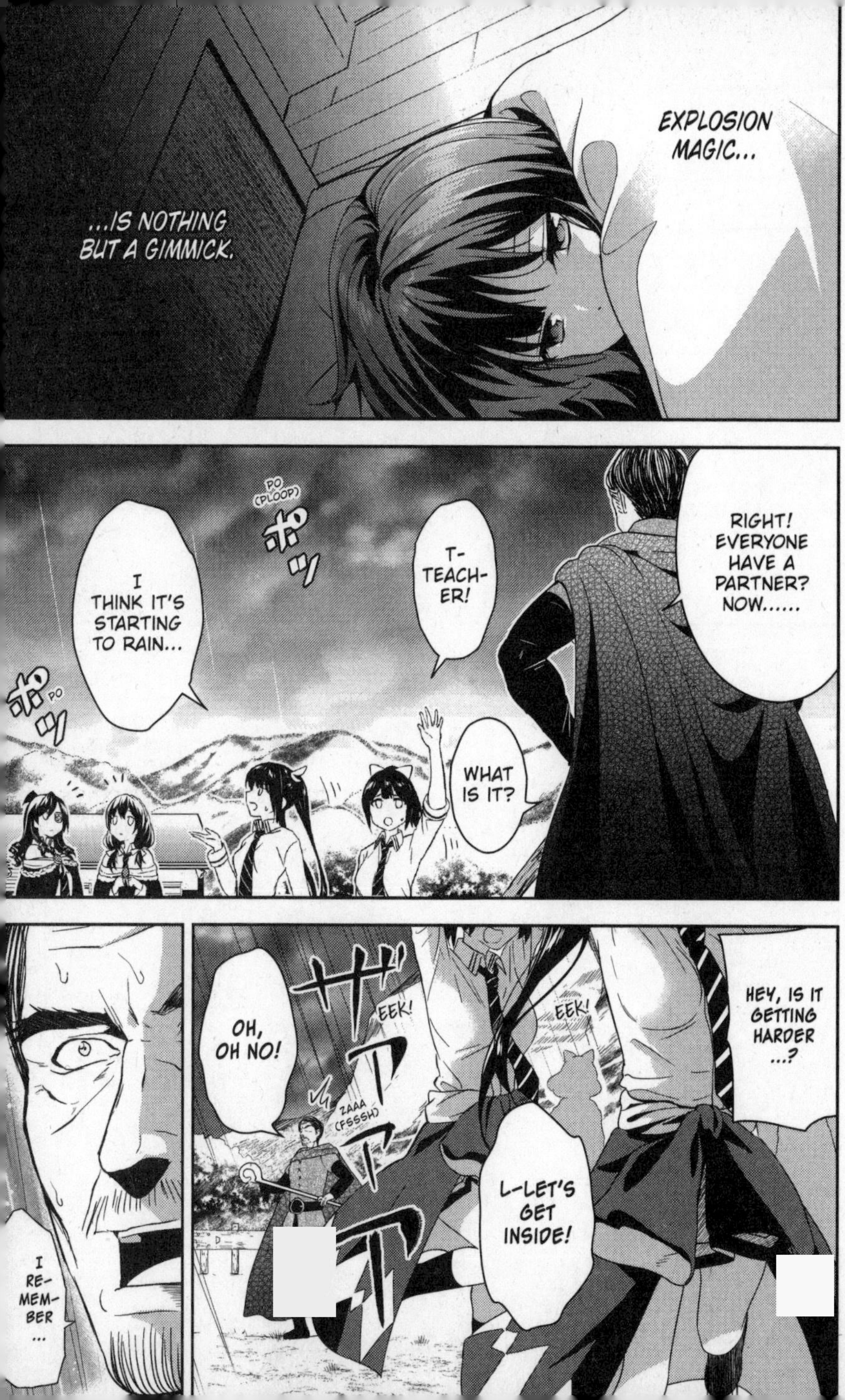
EXPLOSION MAGIC...
...IS NOTHING BUT A GIMMICK.
RIGHT! EVERYONE HAVE A PARTNER? NOW......
T-TEACHER!
PO (PLOOP)
I THINK IT'S STARTING TO RAIN...
WHAT IS IT?
PO
HEY, IS IT GETTING HARDER ...?
EEK!
EEK!
OH, OH NO!
ZAAA (FSSSH)
L-LET'S GET INSIDE!
I RE-MEM-BER ...

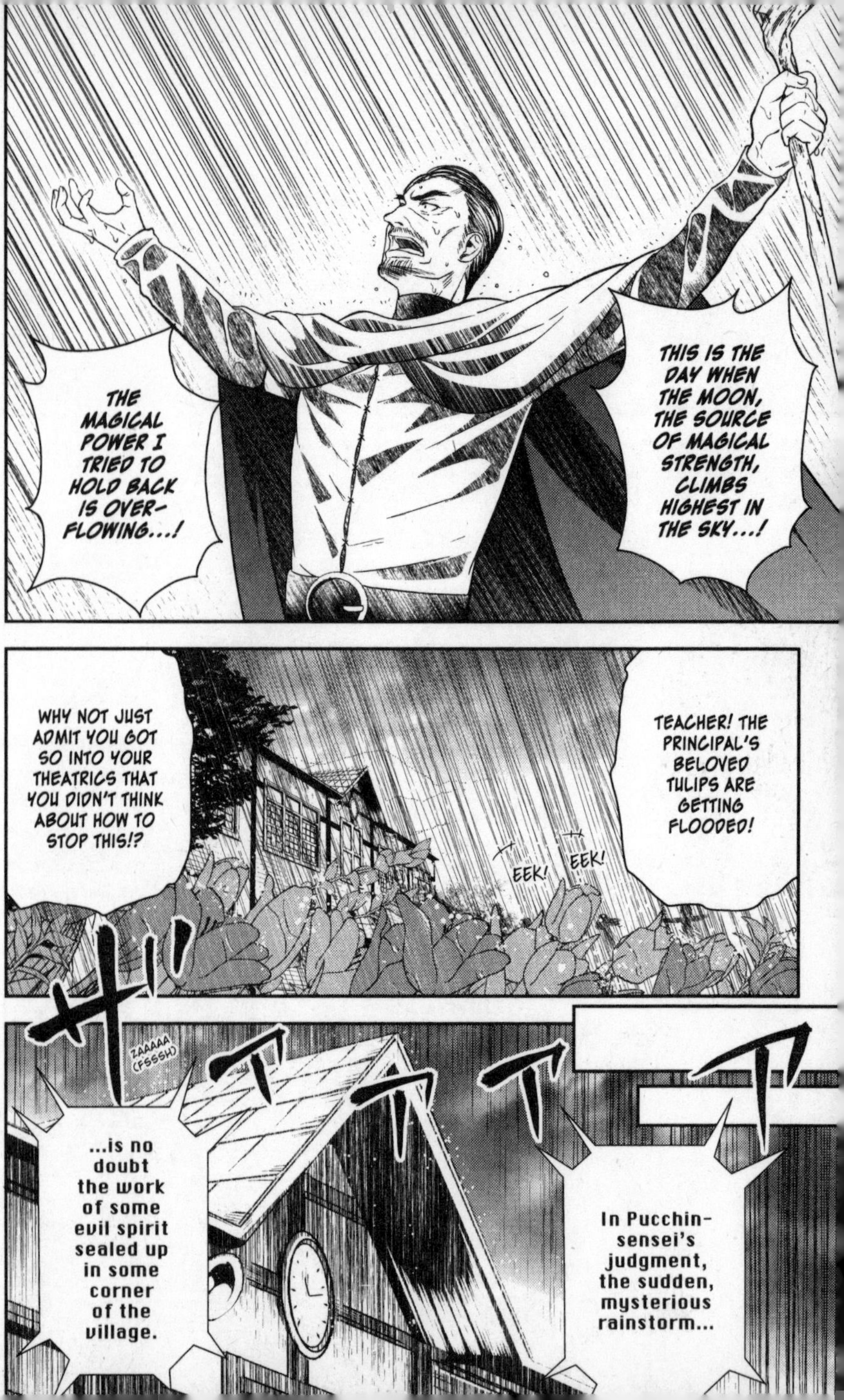

THIS IS THE DAY WHEN THE MOON, THE SOURCE OF MAGICAL STRENGTH, CLIMBS HIGHEST IN THE SKY...!
THE MAGICAL POWER I TRIED TO HOLD BACK IS OVER-FLOWING...!
TEACHER! THE PRINCIPAL'S BELOVED TULIPS ARE GETTING FLOODED!
EEK!
EEK!
WHY NOT JUST ADMIT YOU GOT SO INTO YOUR THEATRICS THAT YOU DIDN'T THINK ABOUT HOW TO STOP THIS!?
ZAAAAA (FSSSH)
In Pucchin-sensei's judgment, the sudden, mysterious rainstorm...
...is no doubt the work of some evil spirit sealed up in some corner of the village.

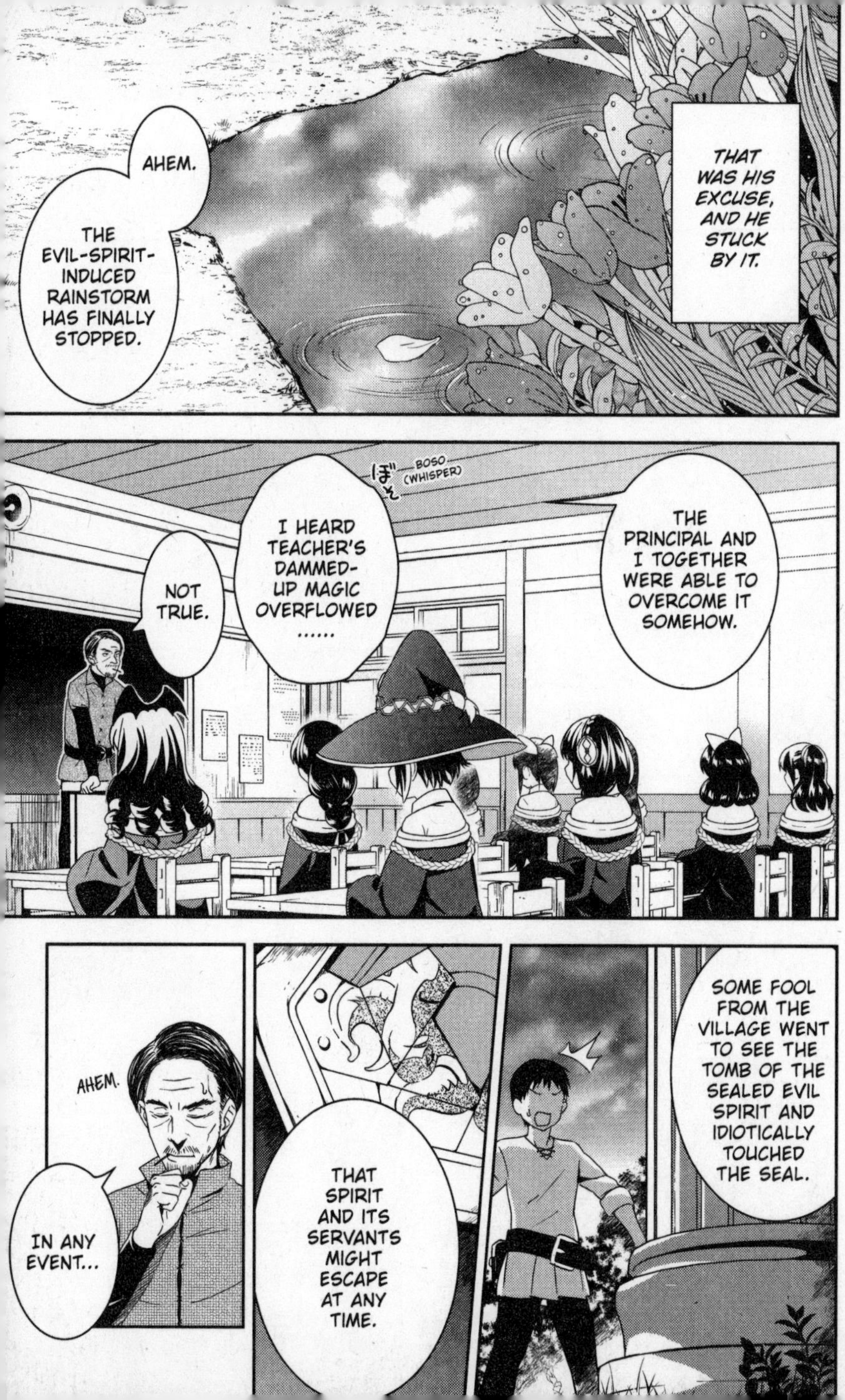
THAT WAS HIS EXCUSE, AND HE STUCK BY IT.
AHEM.
THE EVIL-SPIRIT-INDUCED RAINSTORM HAS FINALLY STOPPED.
THE PRINCIPAL AND I TOGETHER WERE ABLE TO OVERCOME IT SOMEHOW.
ぼそ BOSO (WHISPER)
I HEARD TEACHER'S DAMMED-UP MAGIC OVERFLOWED ......
NOT TRUE.
SOME FOOL FROM THE VILLAGE WENT TO SEE THE TOMB OF THE SEALED EVIL SPIRIT AND IDIOTICALLY TOUCHED THE SEAL.
THAT SPIRIT AND ITS SERVANTS MIGHT ESCAPE AT ANY TIME.
AHEM.
IN ANY EVENT...

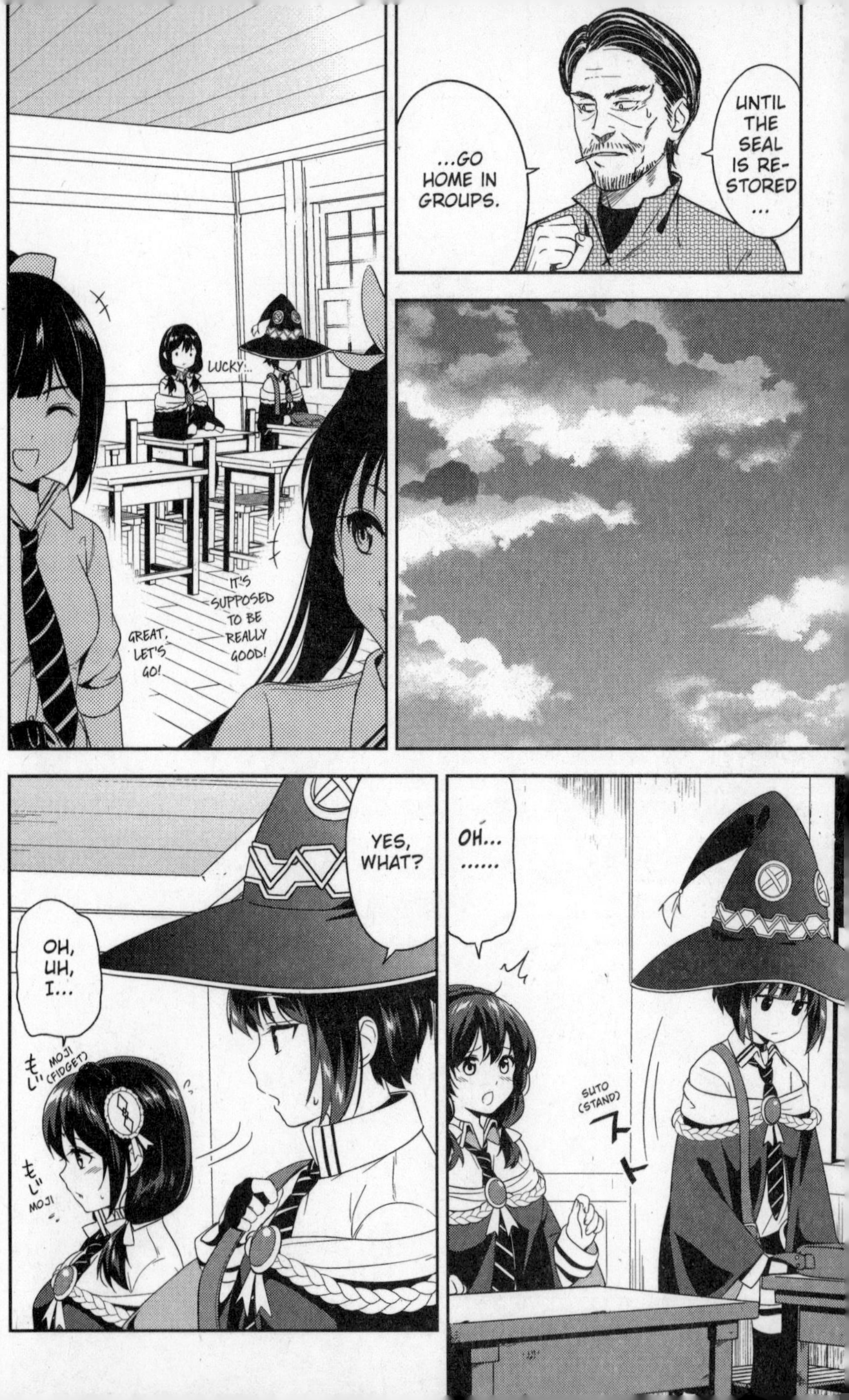
UNTIL THE SEAL IS RE-STORED ...
...GO HOME IN GROUPS.
LUCKY!...
IT'S SUPPOSED TO BE REALLY GOOD!
GREAT, LET'S GO!
OH... ......
スト
SUTO (STAND)
YES, WHAT?
OH, UH, I...
もじ
MOJI (FIDGET)
もじ
MOJI

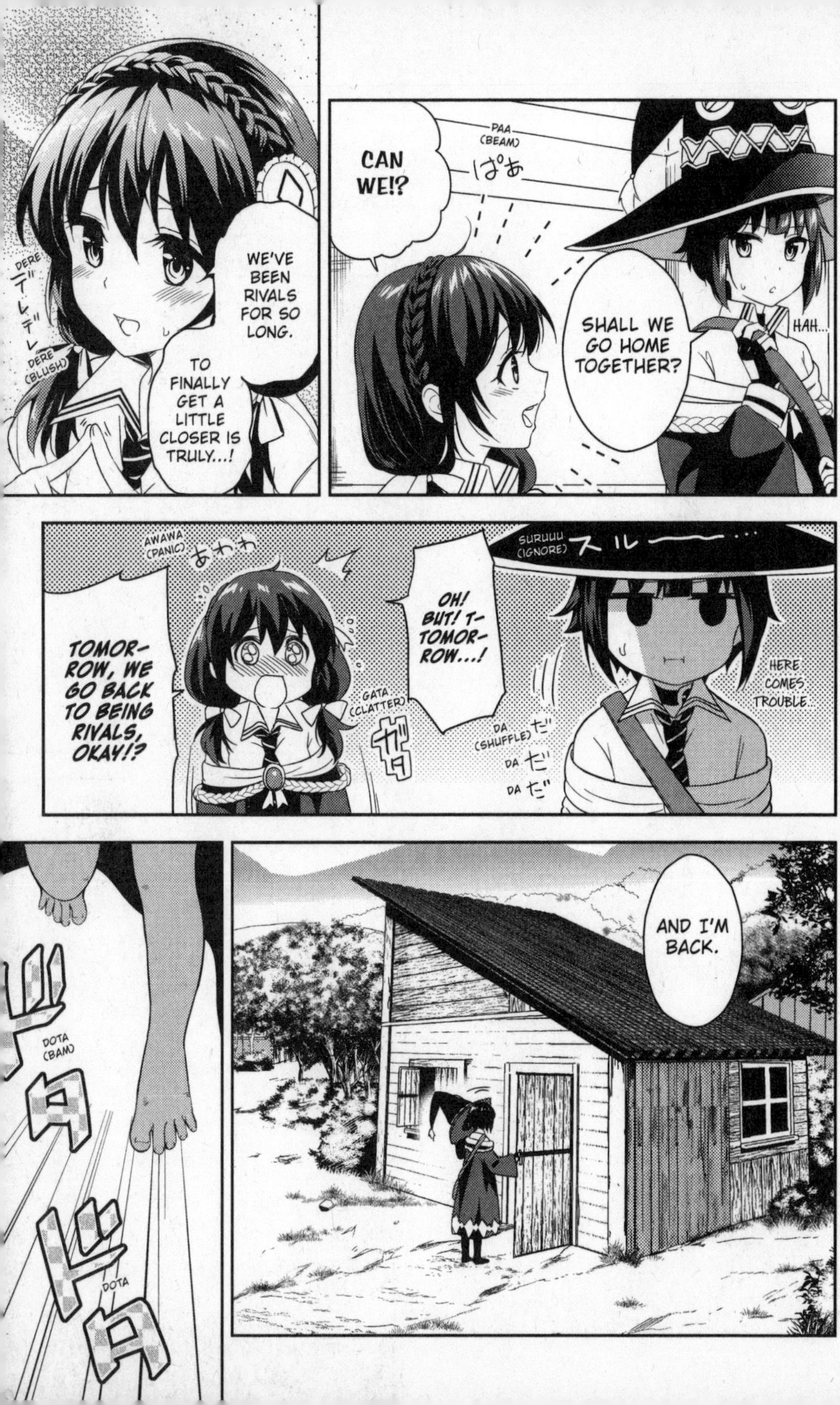

HAH...
SHALL WE GO HOME TOGETHER?
PAA (BEAM)
ぱあ
CAN WE!?
WE'VE BEEN RIVALS FOR SO LONG.
TO FINALLY GET A LITTLE CLOSER IS TRULY...!
DERE DERE (BLUSH)
デレデレ
SURUUU (IGNORE)
スルー…
HERE COMES TROUBLE.
DA (SHUFFLE) だ
DA だ
DA だ
OH! BUT! T-TOMORROW...!
GATA (CLATTER)
ガタ
AWAWA (PANIC)
あわわ
TOMORROW, WE GO BACK TO BEING RIVALS, OKAY!?
AND I'M BACK.
DOTA (BAM)
ドタ
DOTA
ドタ

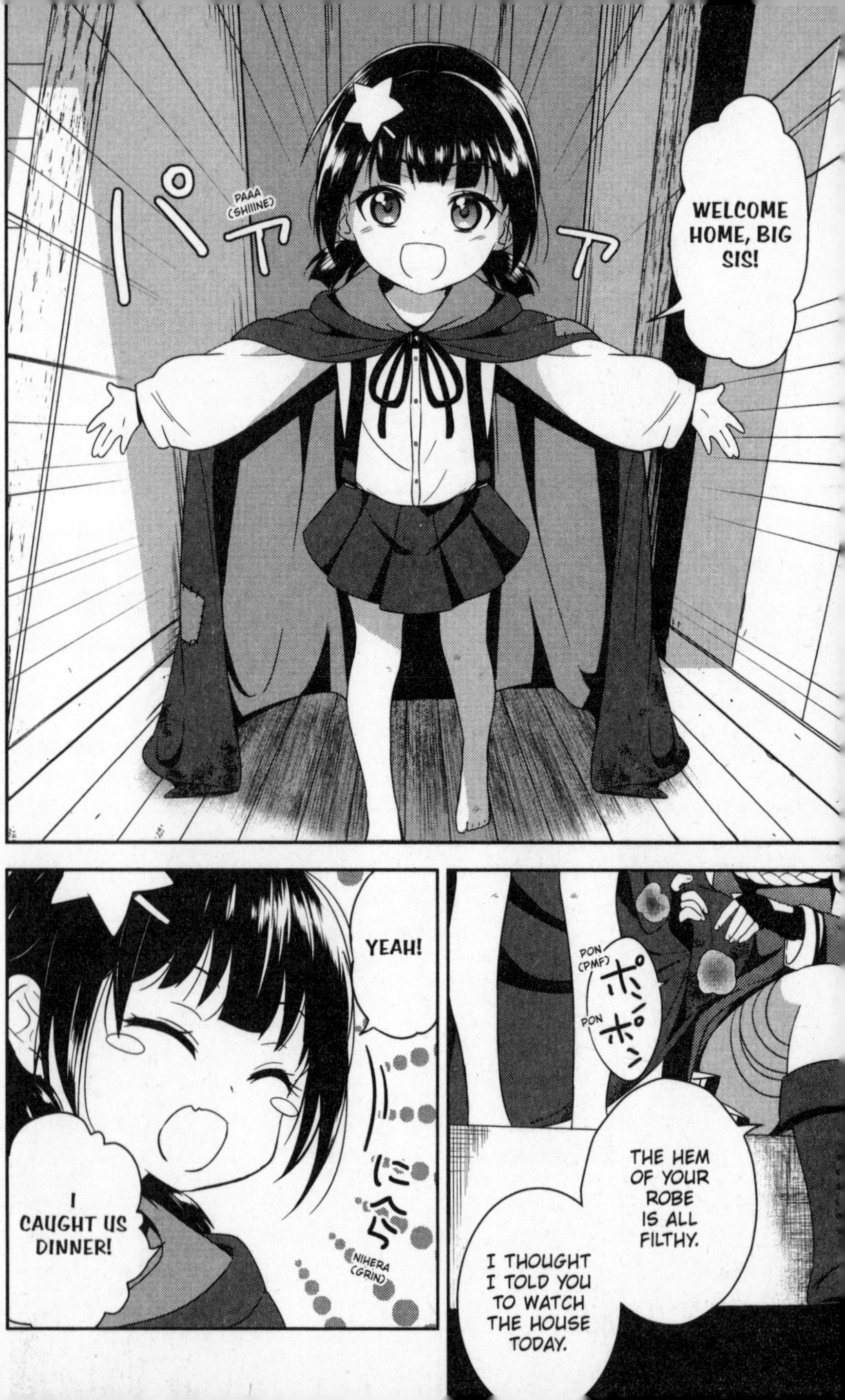
パァァ
PAAA (SHIIINE)
WELCOME HOME, BIG SIS!
ポンポン
PON (PMF)
PON
THE HEM OF YOUR ROBE IS ALL FILTHY.
I THOUGHT I TOLD YOU TO WATCH THE HOUSE TODAY.
YEAH!
にへら
NIHERA (GRIN)
I CAUGHT US DINNER!

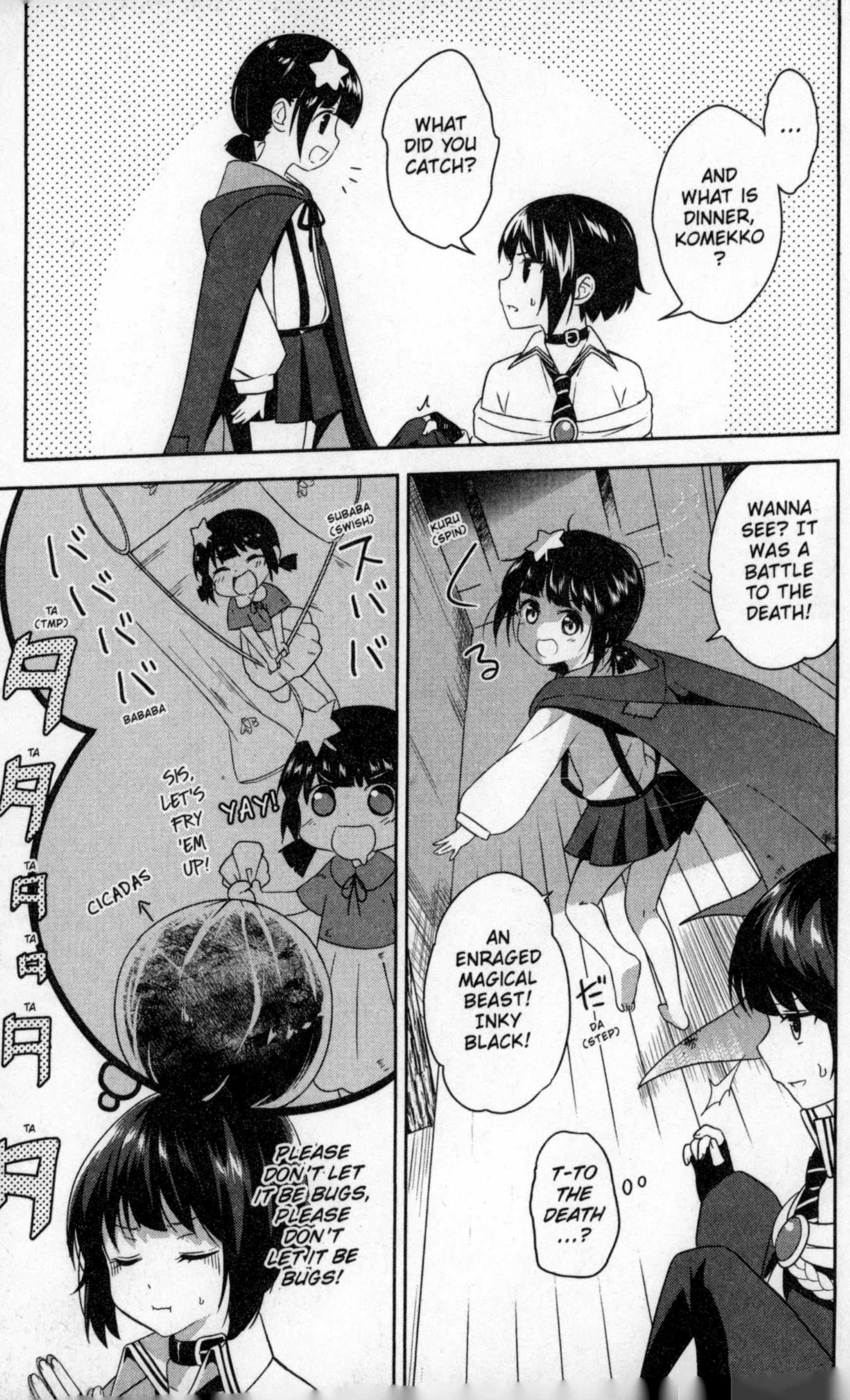
...
AND WHAT IS DINNER, KOMEKKO?
WHAT DID YOU CATCH?
KURU (SPIN)
WANNA SEE? IT WAS A BATTLE TO THE DEATH!
AN ENRAGED MAGICAL BEAST! INKY BLACK!
DA (STEP)
T-TO THE DEATH...?
SUBABA (SWISH)
BABABA
TA (TMP)
YAY!
SIS, LET'S FRY 'EM UP!
CICADAS
TA
TA
TA
TA
TA
PLEASE DON'T LET IT BE BUGS, PLEASE DON'T LET IT BE BUGS!

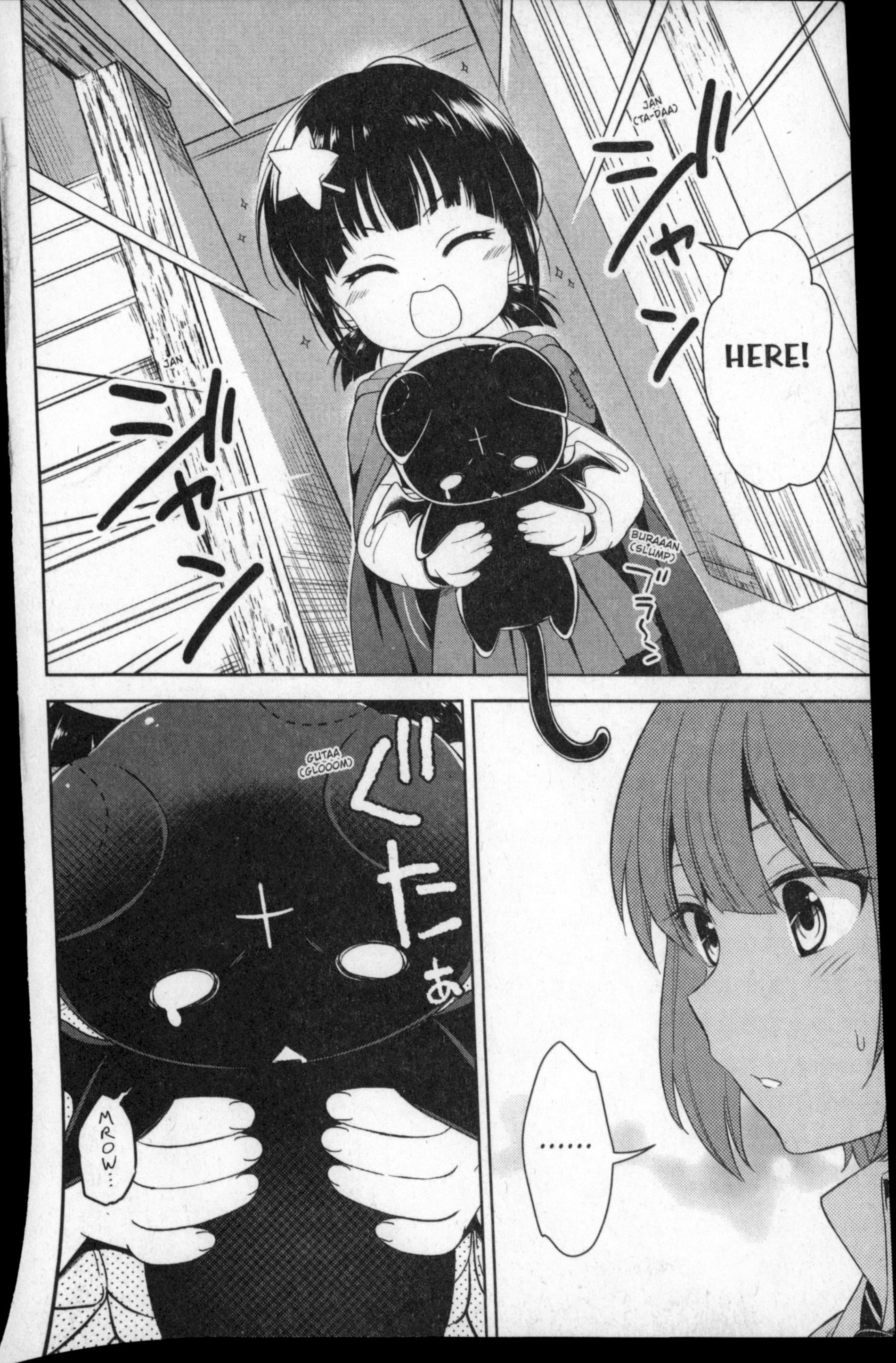
JAN (TA-DAA)
ジャン
HERE!
JAN
ジャン
BURAAAN (SLUMP)
......
GUTAA (GLOOOM)
ぐたぁ
MROW...

KONOSUBA: AN EXPLOSION ON THIS WONDERFUL WORLD!

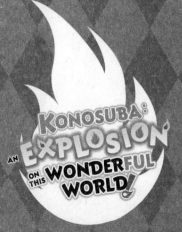

KONOSUBA: AN EXPLOSION ON THIS WONDERFUL WORLD!

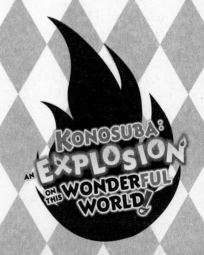

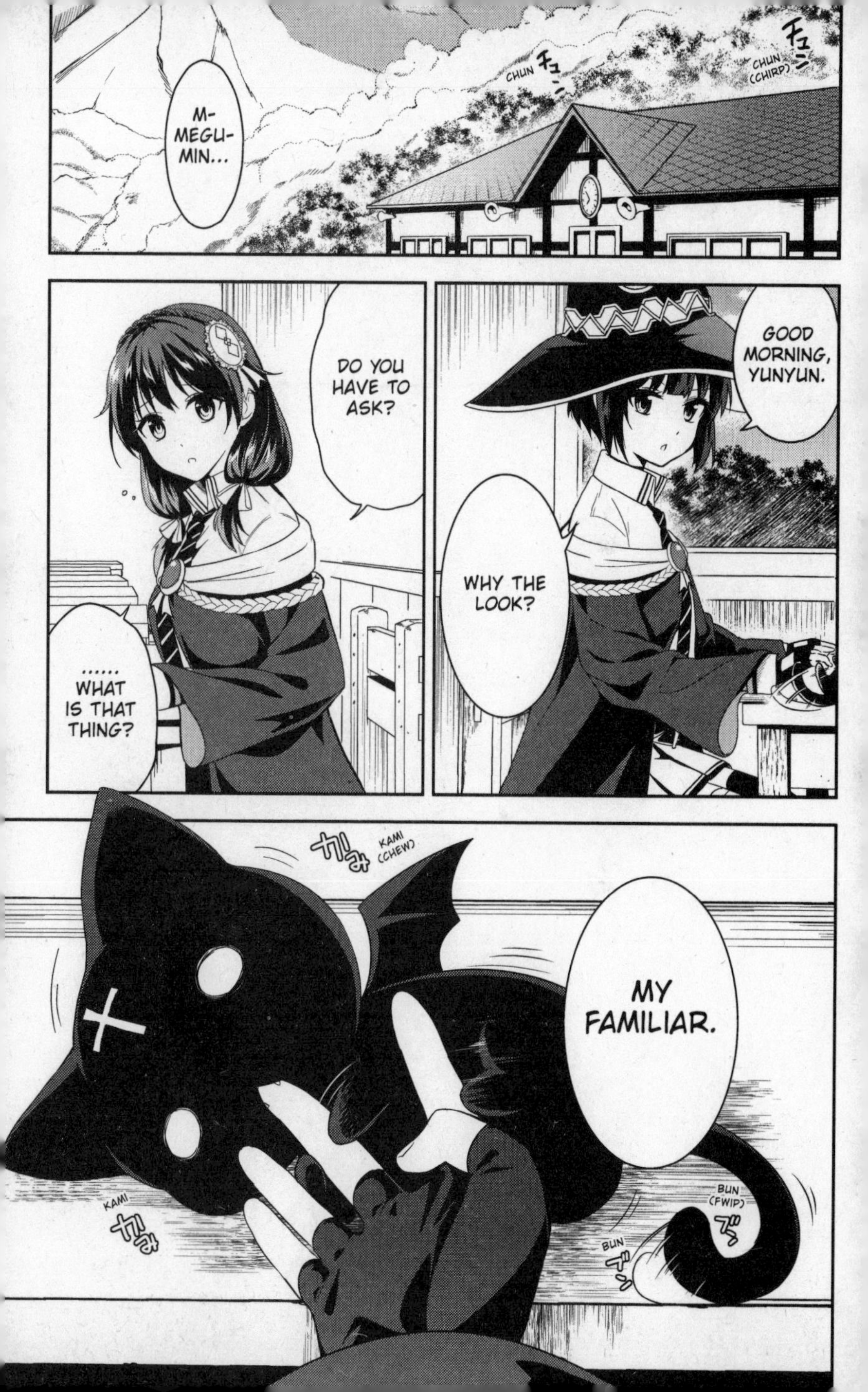

チュン
CHUN (CHIRP)
CHUN
チュン
M-MEGUMIN...
GOOD MORNING, YUNYUN.
WHY THE LOOK?
DO YOU HAVE TO ASK?
...... WHAT IS THAT THING?
かみ
KAMI (CHEW)
MY FAMILIAR.
BUN (FWIP)
ぶん
BUN
ぶん
KAMI
かみ

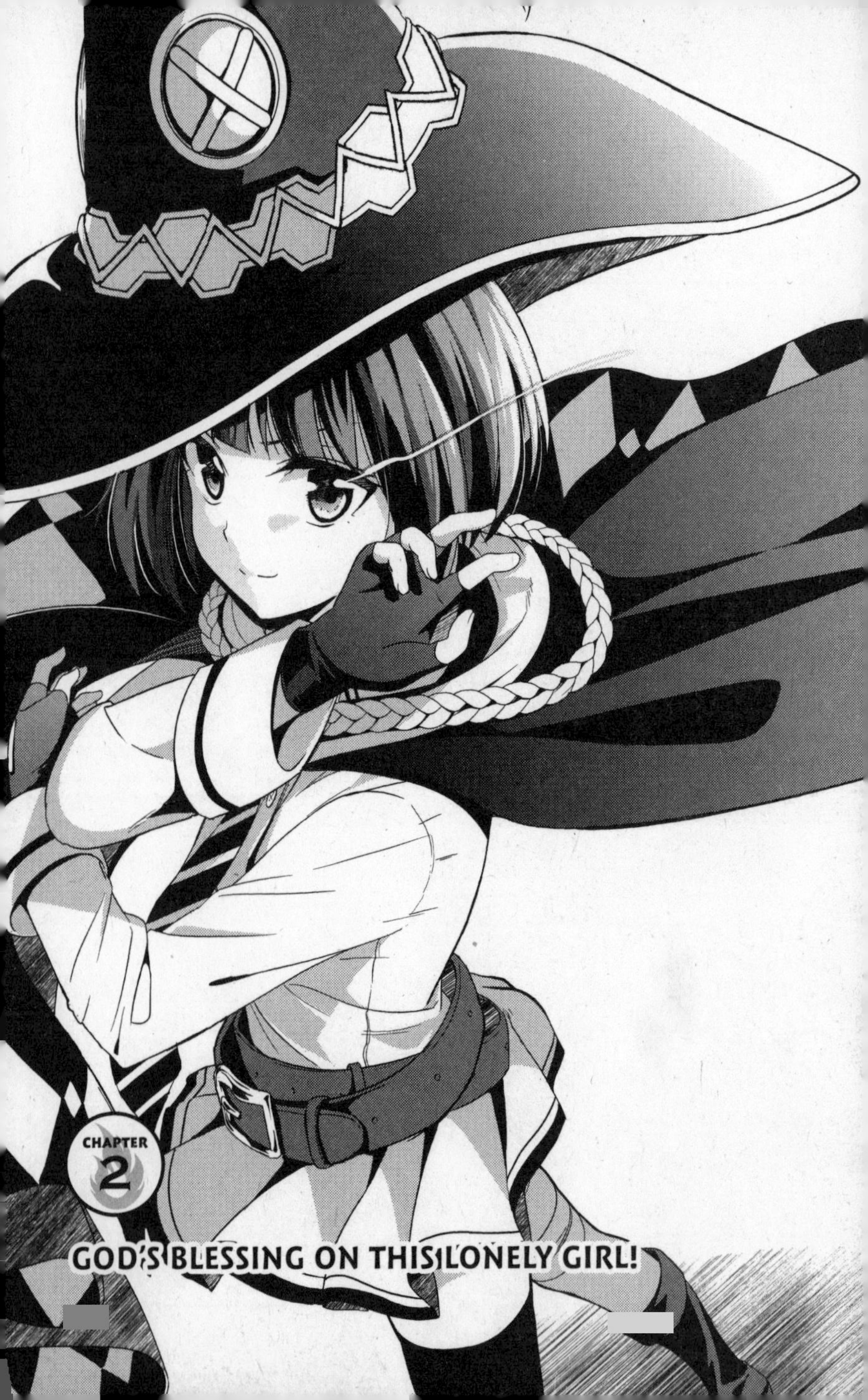
CHAPTER
2
GOD'S BLESSING ON THIS LONELY GIRL!

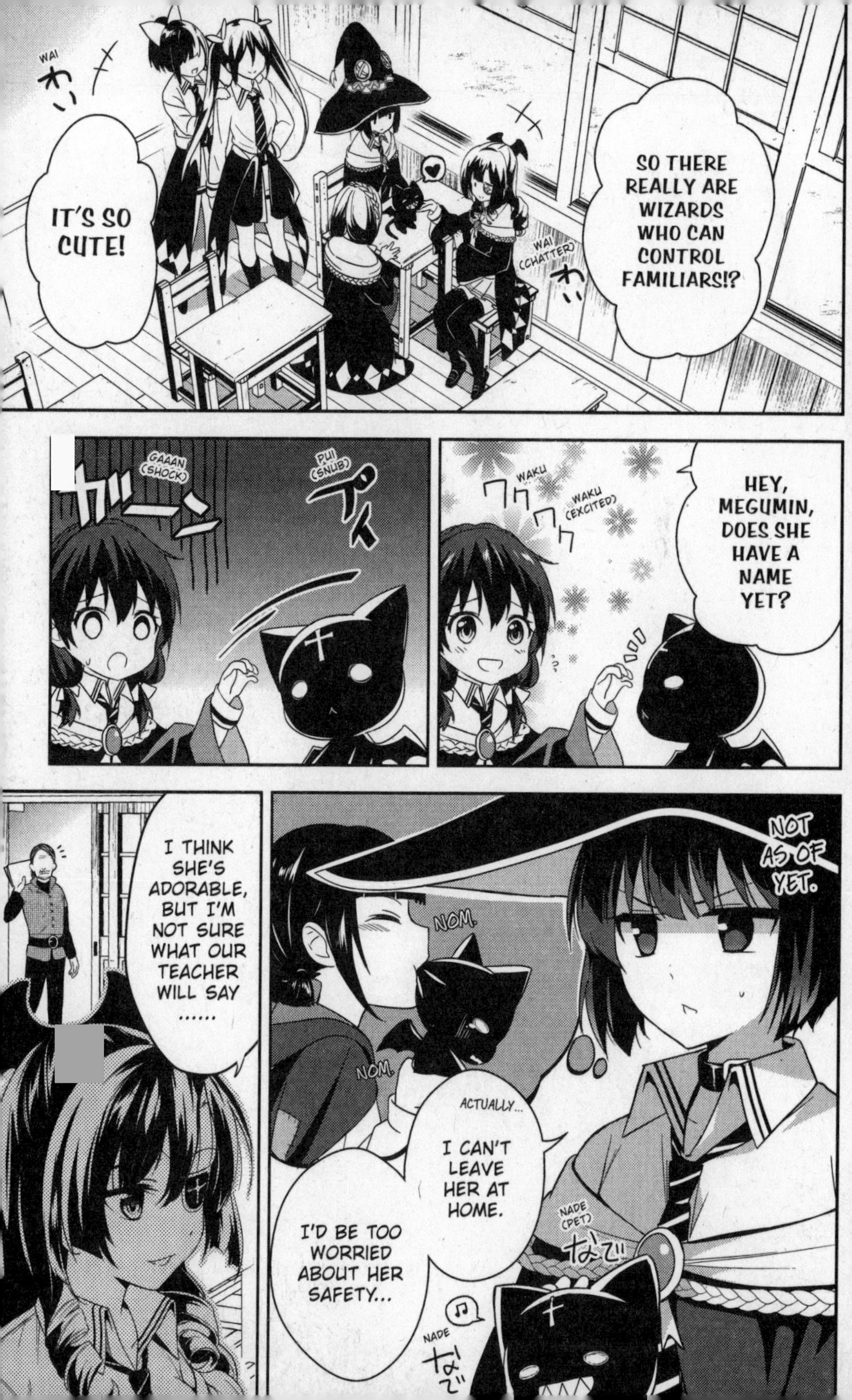
SO THERE REALLY ARE WIZARDS WHO CAN CONTROL FAMILIARS!?
WAI (CHATTER)
わい
WAI
わい
IT'S SO CUTE!
HEY, MEGUMIN, DOES SHE HAVE A NAME YET?
WAKU
ワク
WAKU (EXCITED)
ワク
PUI (SNUB)
プイ
GAAAN (SHOCK)
ガーン
NOT AS OF YET.
NOM.
ACTUALLY...
I CAN'T LEAVE HER AT HOME.
NADE (PET)
なで
I'D BE TOO WORRIED ABOUT HER SAFETY...
NADE
なで
NOM.
I THINK SHE'S ADORABLE, BUT I'M NOT SURE WHAT OUR TEACHER WILL SAY ......

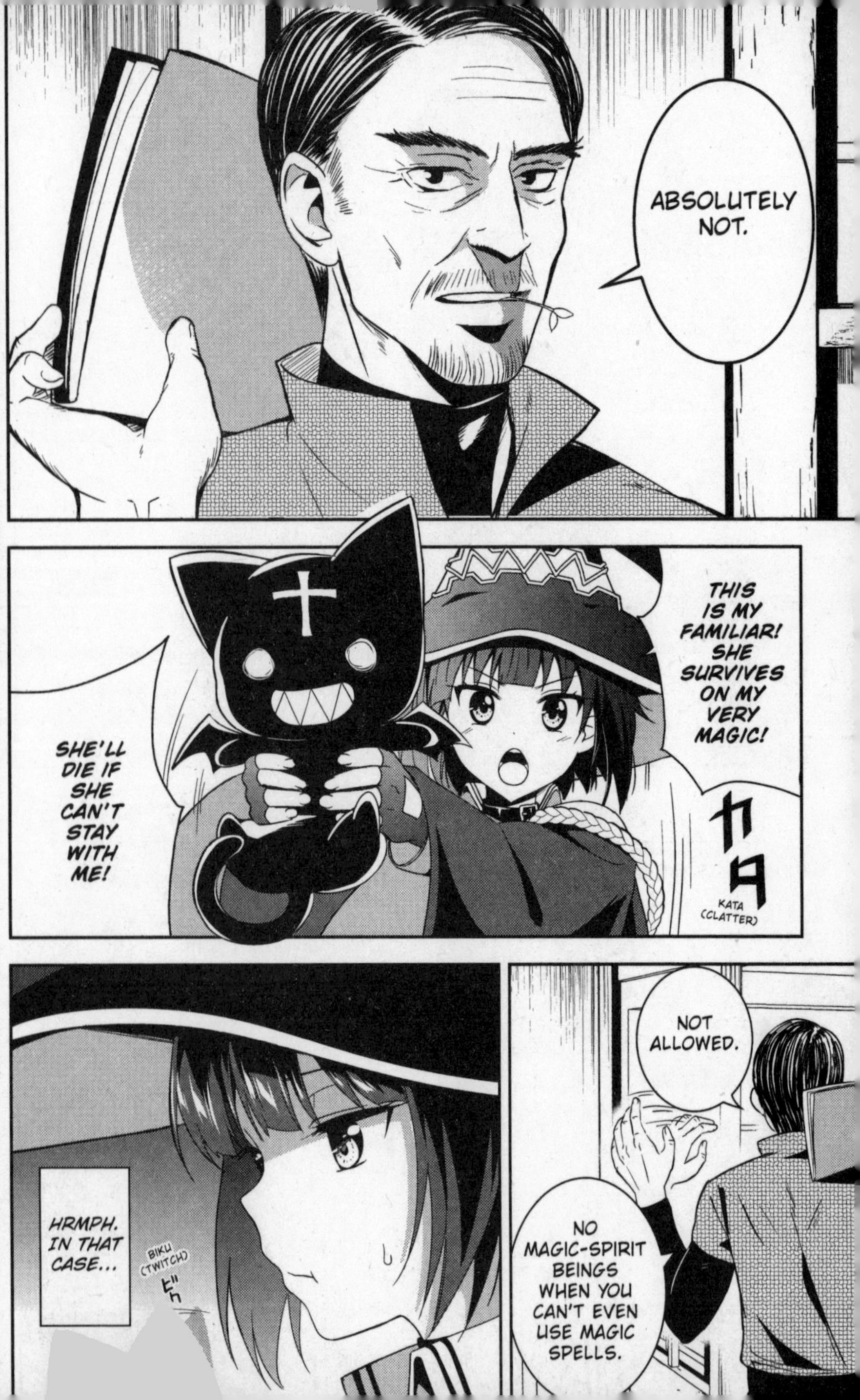
ABSOLUTELY NOT.
THIS IS MY FAMILIAR! SHE SURVIVES ON MY VERY MAGIC!
SHE'LL DIE IF SHE CAN'T STAY WITH ME!
カタ
KATA (CLATTER)
NOT ALLOWED.
NO MAGIC-SPIRIT BEINGS WHEN YOU CAN'T EVEN USE MAGIC SPELLS.
ビク
BIKU (TWITCH)
HRMPH. IN THAT CASE...

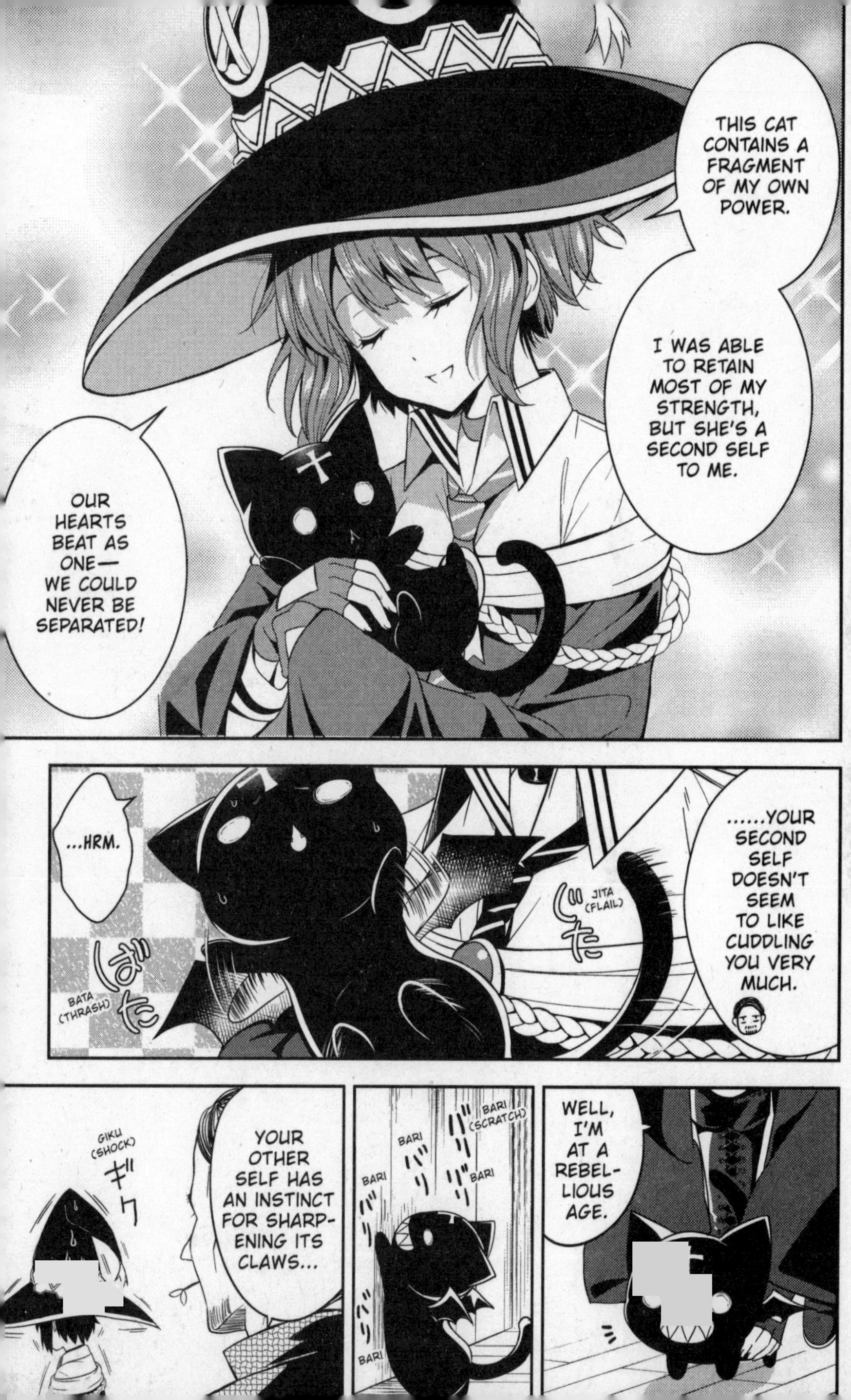
THIS CAT CONTAINS A FRAGMENT OF MY OWN POWER.
I WAS ABLE TO RETAIN MOST OF MY STRENGTH, BUT SHE'S A SECOND SELF TO ME.
OUR HEARTS BEAT AS ONE— WE COULD NEVER BE SEPARATED!
......YOUR SECOND SELF DOESN'T SEEM TO LIKE CUDDLING YOU VERY MUCH.
じた
JITA (FLAIL)
ばた
BATA (THRASH)
...HRM.
WELL, I'M AT A REBEL-LIOUS AGE.
BARI (SCRATCH)
BARI
BARI
BARI
BARI
YOUR OTHER SELF HAS AN INSTINCT FOR SHARP-ENING ITS CLAWS...
ギク
GIKU (SHOCK)

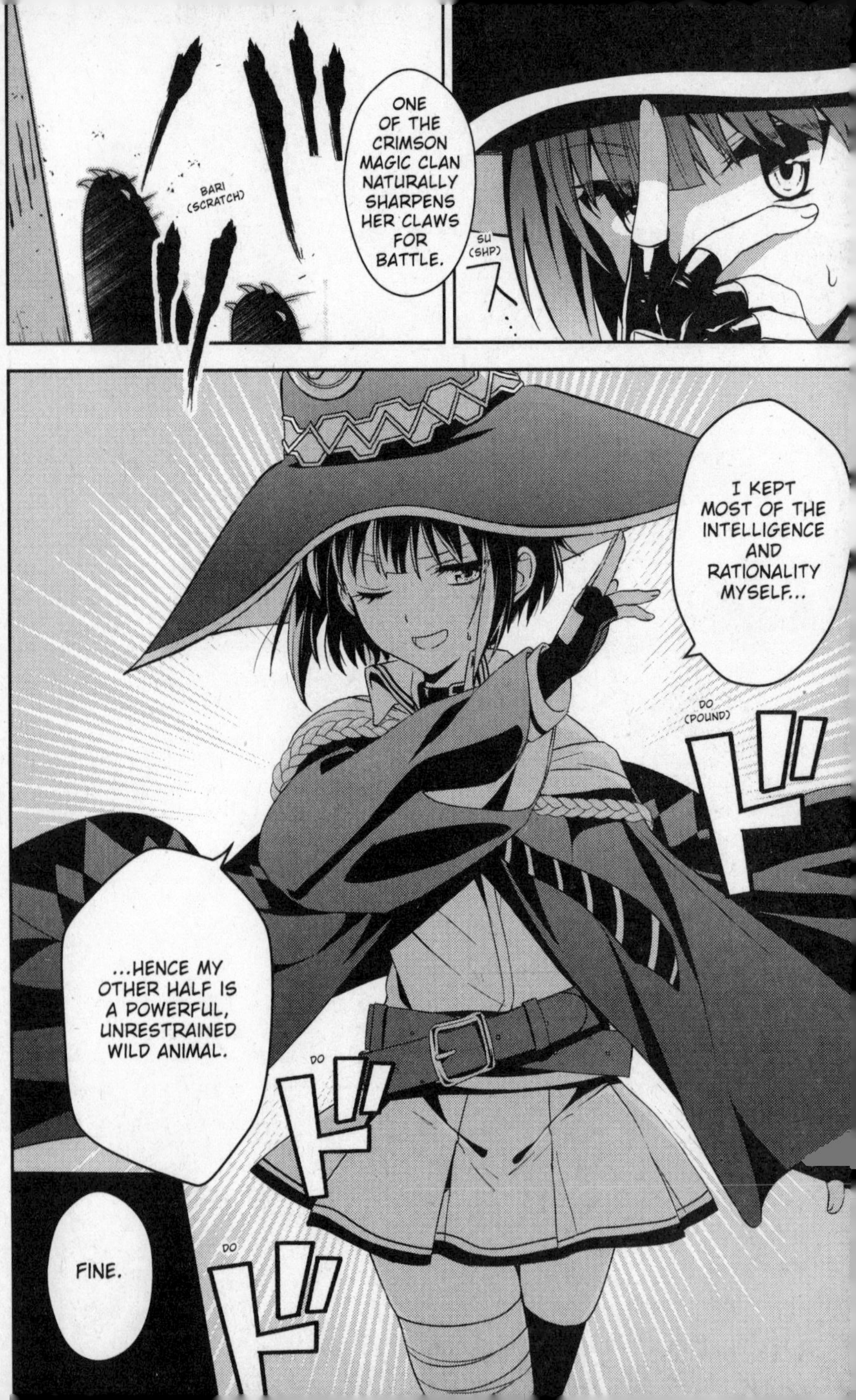
ONE OF THE CRIMSON MAGIC CLAN NATURALLY SHARPENS HER CLAWS FOR BATTLE.
SU (SHP)
BARI (SCRATCH)
I KEPT MOST OF THE INTELLIGENCE AND RATIONALITY MYSELF...
DO (POUND)
...HENCE MY OTHER HALF IS A POWERFUL, UNRESTRAINED WILD ANIMAL.
DO
FINE.
DO

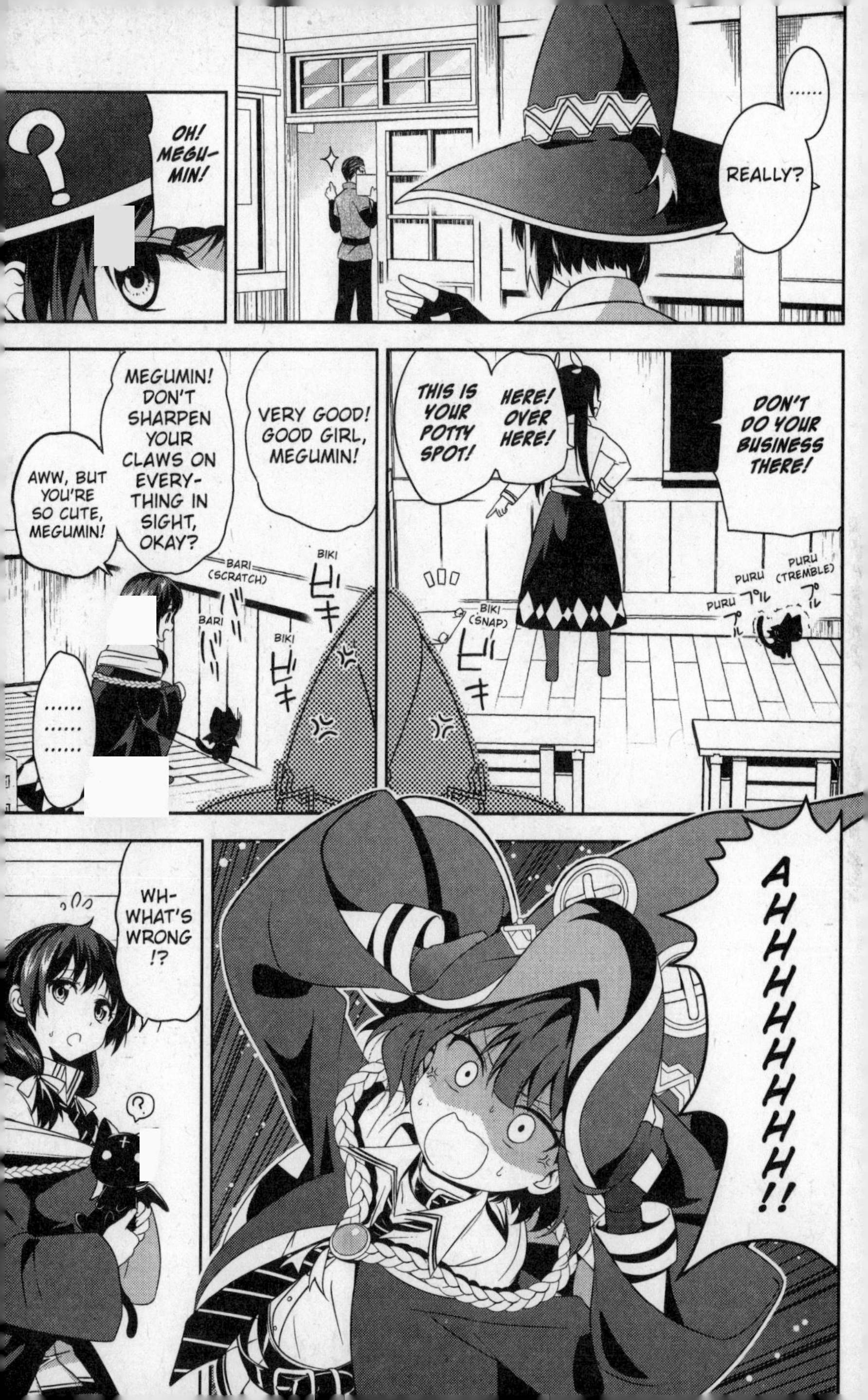
......
REALLY?
OH! MEGU-MIN!
DON'T DO YOUR BUSINESS THERE!
PURU PURU (TREMBLE) PURU
HERE! OVER HERE!
THIS IS YOUR POTTY SPOT!
BIKI (SNAP)
VERY GOOD! GOOD GIRL, MEGUMIN!
BIKI
MEGUMIN! DON'T SHARPEN YOUR CLAWS ON EVERYTHING IN SIGHT, OKAY?
AWW, BUT YOU'RE SO CUTE, MEGUMIN!
BARI (SCRATCH) BARI
BIKI
......
......
......
AHHHHHHHH!!
WH-WHAT'S WRONG!?

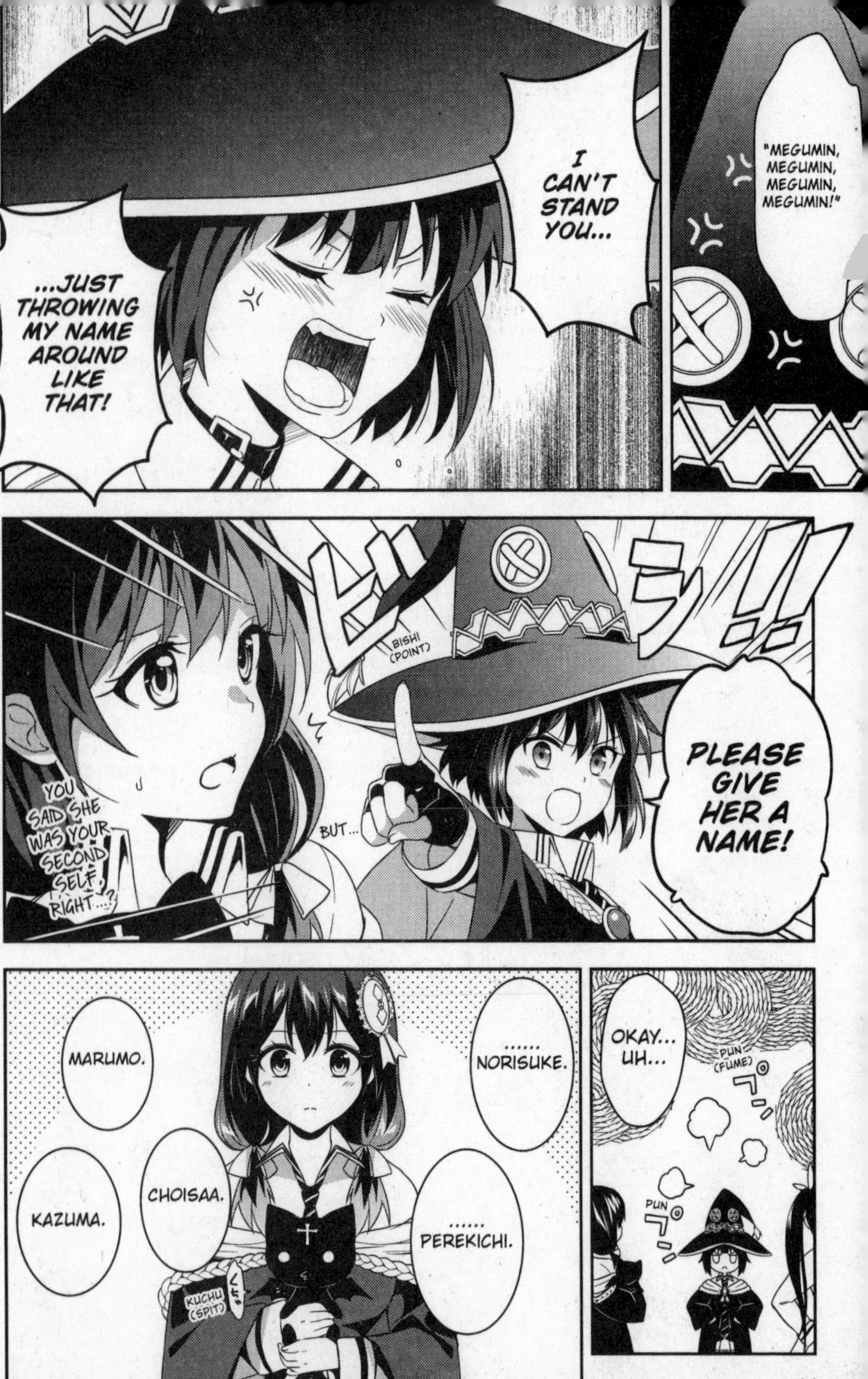
"MEGUMIN, MEGUMIN, MEGUMIN, MEGUMIN!"
I CAN'T STAND YOU...
...JUST THROWING MY NAME AROUND LIKE THAT!
ビシッ!!
BISHI (POINT)
PLEASE GIVE HER A NAME!
BUT...
YOU SAID SHE WAS YOUR SECOND SELF, RIGHT...?
OKAY... UH...
PUN (FUME)
PUN
......NORISUKE.
MARUMO.
......PEREKICHI.
CHOISAA.
KAZUMA.
KUCHU (SPIT)

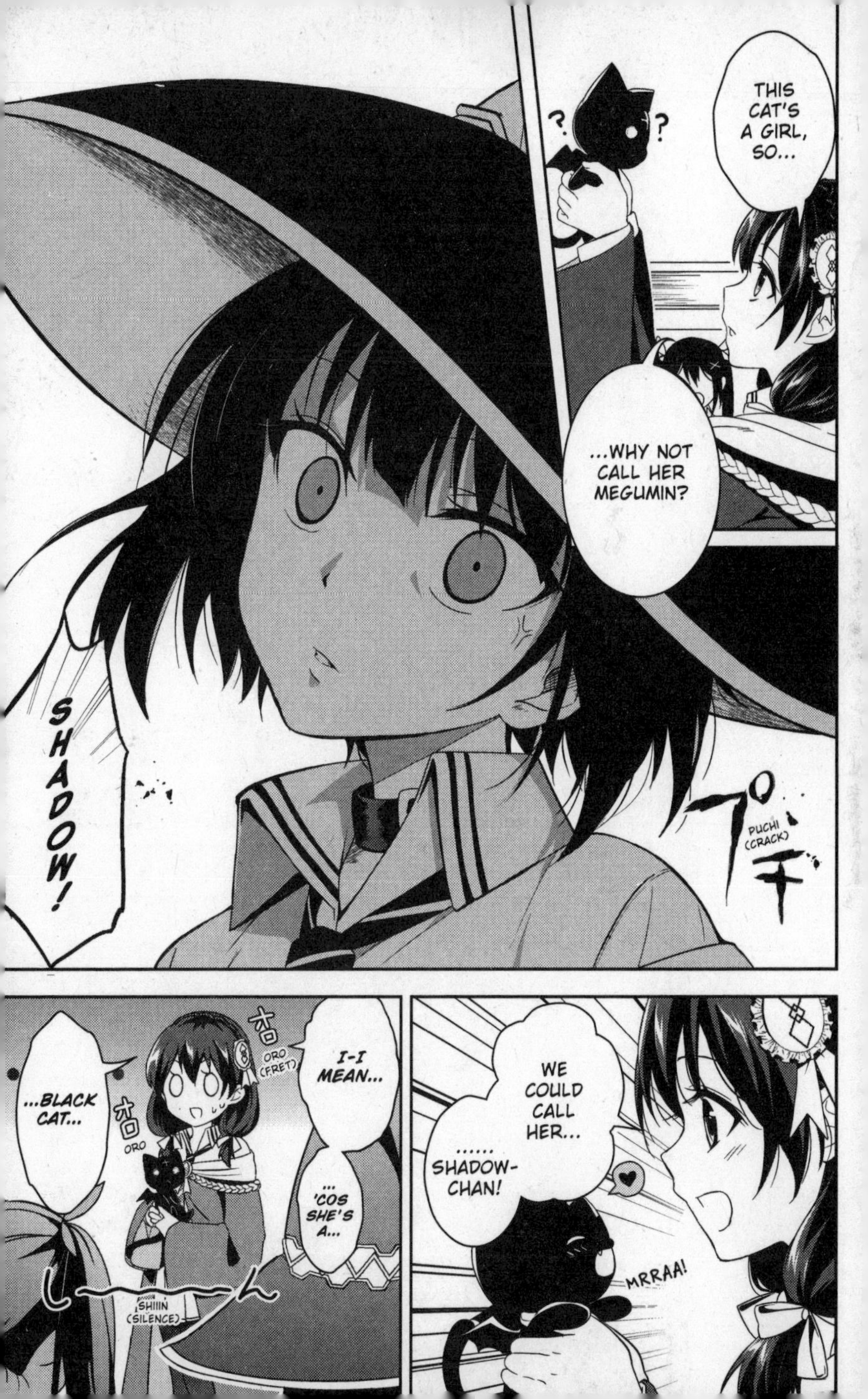
THIS CAT'S A GIRL, SO...
?
?
...WHY NOT CALL HER MEGUMIN?
PUCHI (CRACK)
SHADOW!
WE COULD CALL HER...
......SHADOW-CHAN!
MRRAA!
I-I MEAN...
...'COS SHE'S A...
ORO (FRET)
ORO
...BLACK CAT...
SHIIIN (SILENCE)

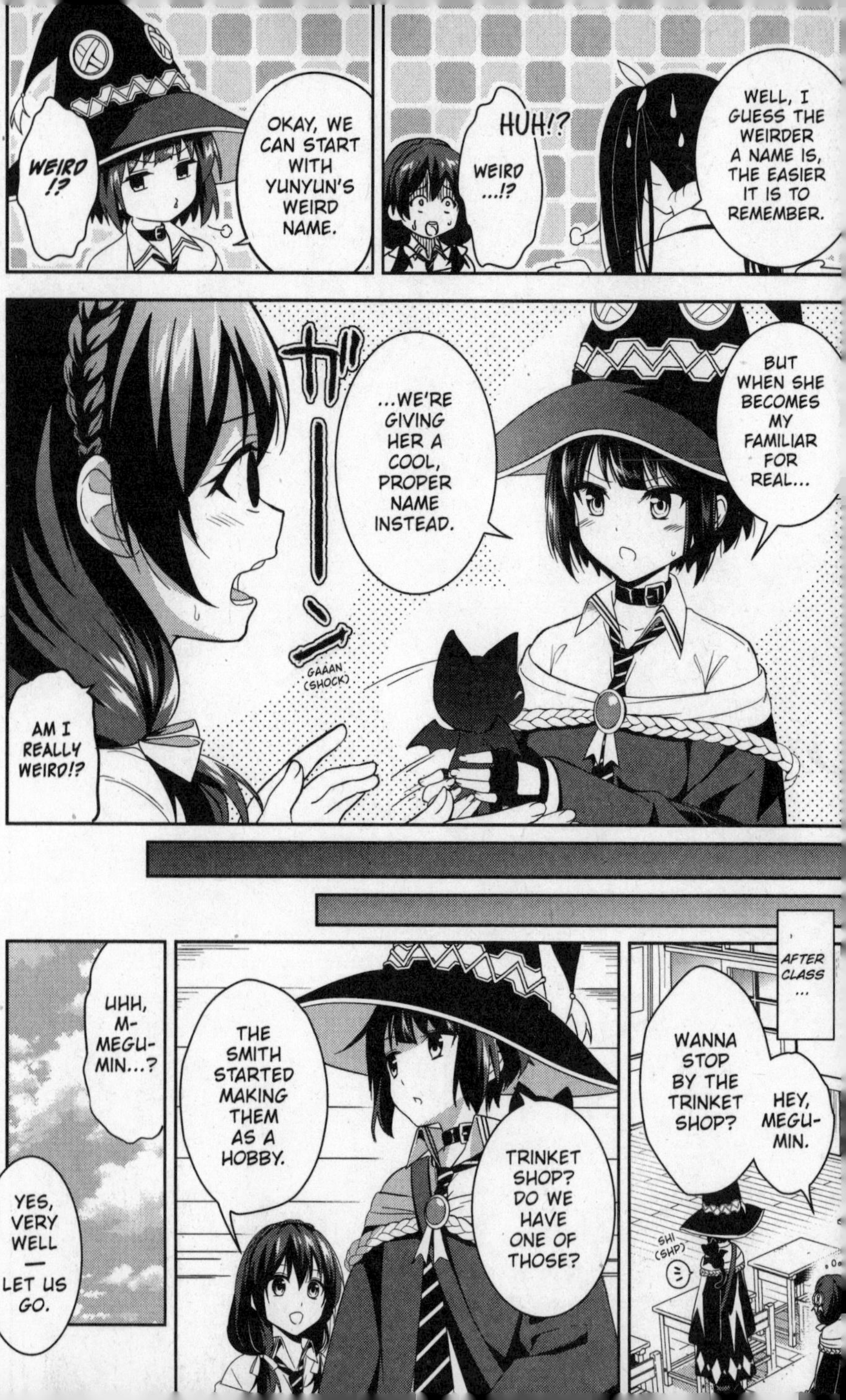
WELL, I GUESS THE WEIRDER A NAME IS, THE EASIER IT IS TO REMEMBER.
HUH!?
WEIRD ...!?
OKAY, WE CAN START WITH YUNYUN'S WEIRD NAME.
WEIRD !?
BUT WHEN SHE BECOMES MY FAMILIAR FOR REAL...
...WE'RE GIVING HER A COOL, PROPER NAME INSTEAD.
GAAAN (SHOCK)
AM I REALLY WEIRD!?
AFTER CLASS...
HEY, MEGUMIN.
WANNA STOP BY THE TRINKET SHOP?
SHI (SHP)
TRINKET SHOP? DO WE HAVE ONE OF THOSE?
THE SMITH STARTED MAKING THEM AS A HOBBY.
UHH, M-MEGUMIN...?
YES, VERY WELL—LET US GO.

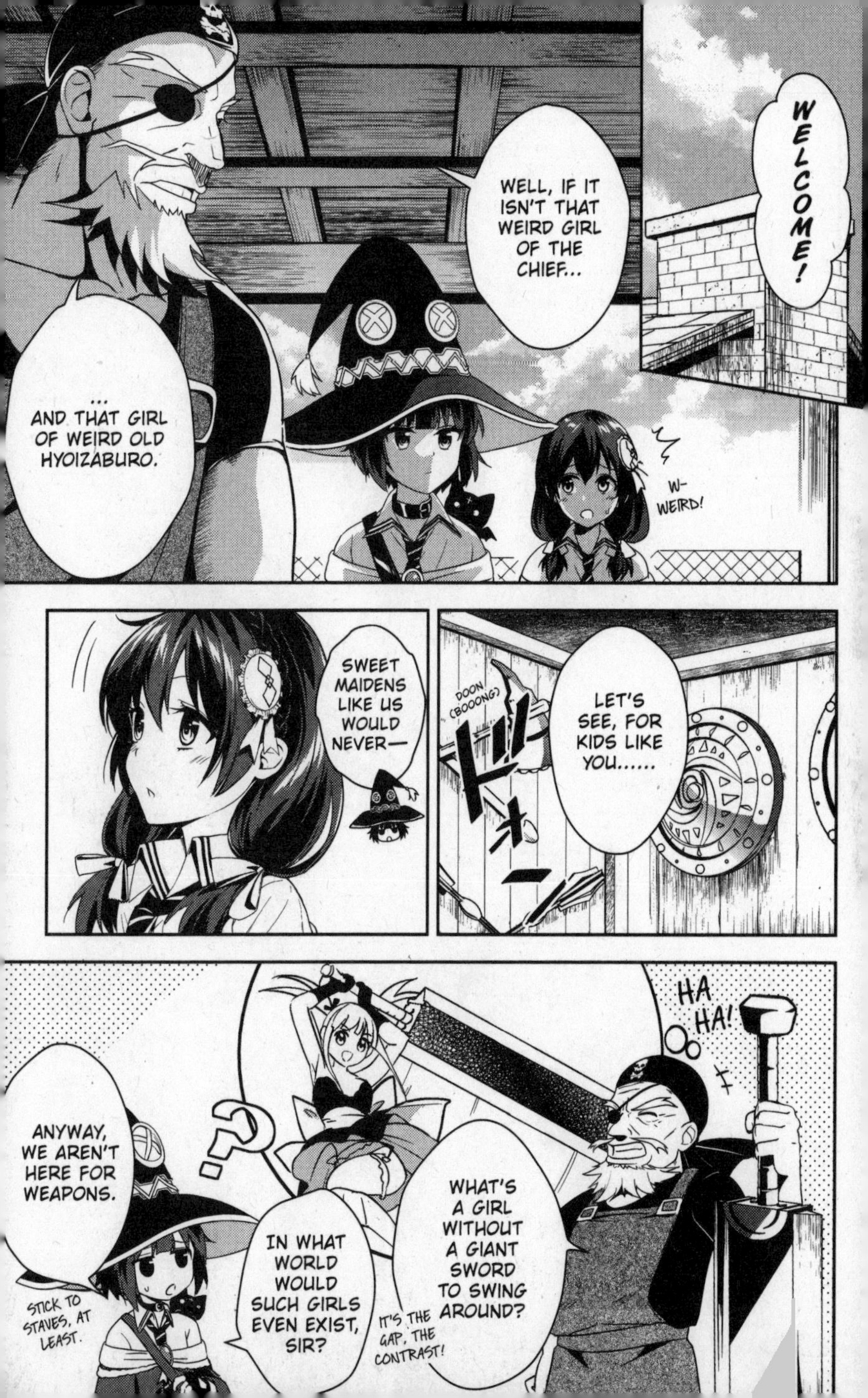
WELCOME!
WELL, IF IT ISN'T THAT WEIRD GIRL OF THE CHIEF...
... AND THAT GIRL OF WEIRD OLD HYOIZABURO.
W-WEIRD!
DOON (BOOONG)
LET'S SEE, FOR KIDS LIKE YOU......
SWEET MAIDENS LIKE US WOULD NEVER—
HA HA!
WHAT'S A GIRL WITHOUT A GIANT SWORD TO SWING AROUND?
IT'S THE GAP, THE CONTRAST!
IN WHAT WORLD WOULD SUCH GIRLS EVEN EXIST, SIR?
ANYWAY, WE AREN'T HERE FOR WEAPONS.
STICK TO STAVES, AT LEAST.

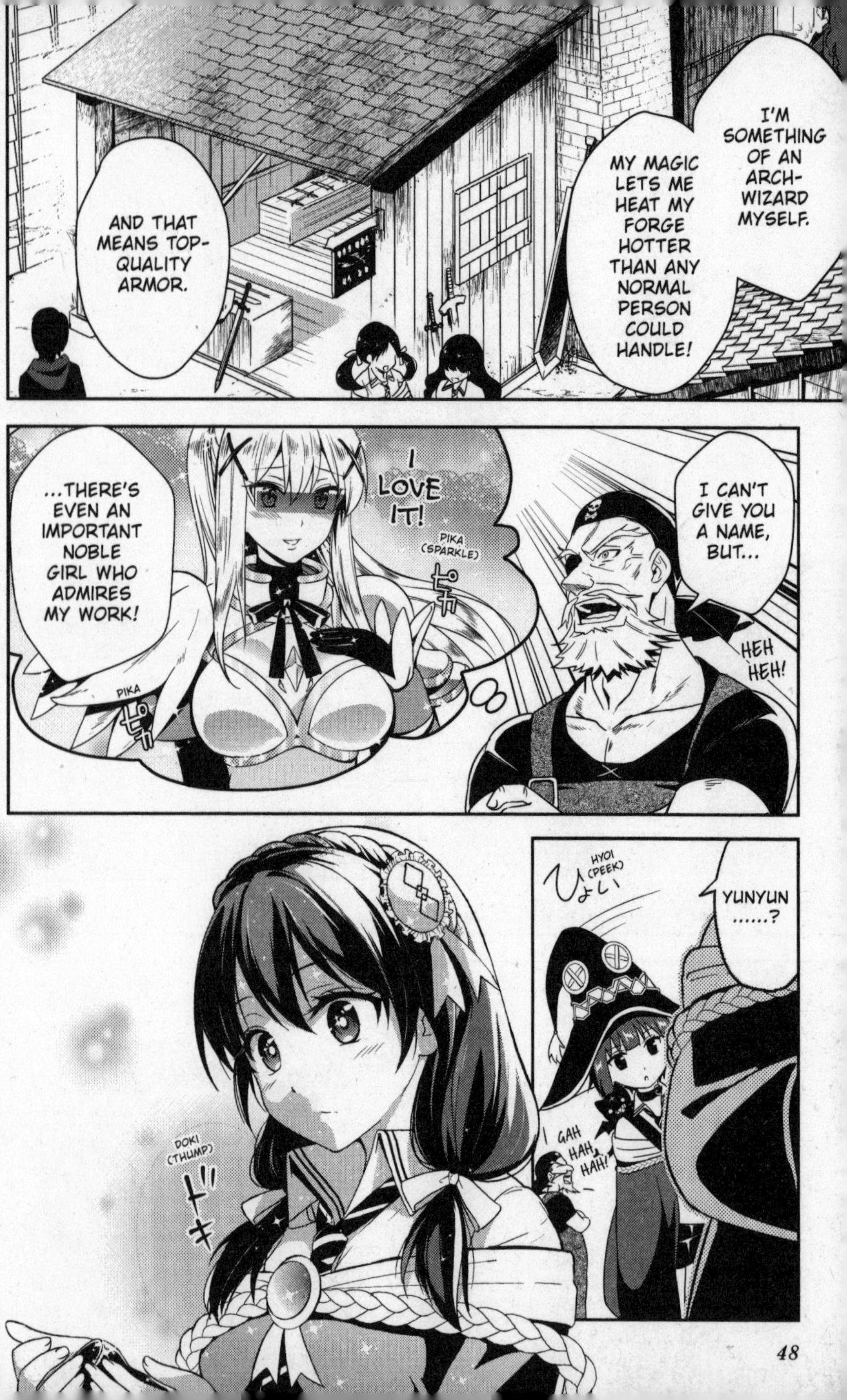
I'M SOMETHING OF AN ARCH-WIZARD MYSELF.
MY MAGIC LETS ME HEAT MY FORGE HOTTER THAN ANY NORMAL PERSON COULD HANDLE!
AND THAT MEANS TOP-QUALITY ARMOR.
I CAN'T GIVE YOU A NAME, BUT...
HEH HEH!
I LOVE IT!
PIKA (SPARKLE)
...THERE'S EVEN AN IMPORTANT NOBLE GIRL WHO ADMIRES MY WORK!
PIKA
YUNYUN ......?
HYOI (PEEK)
GAH HAH, HAH!
DOKI (THUMP)

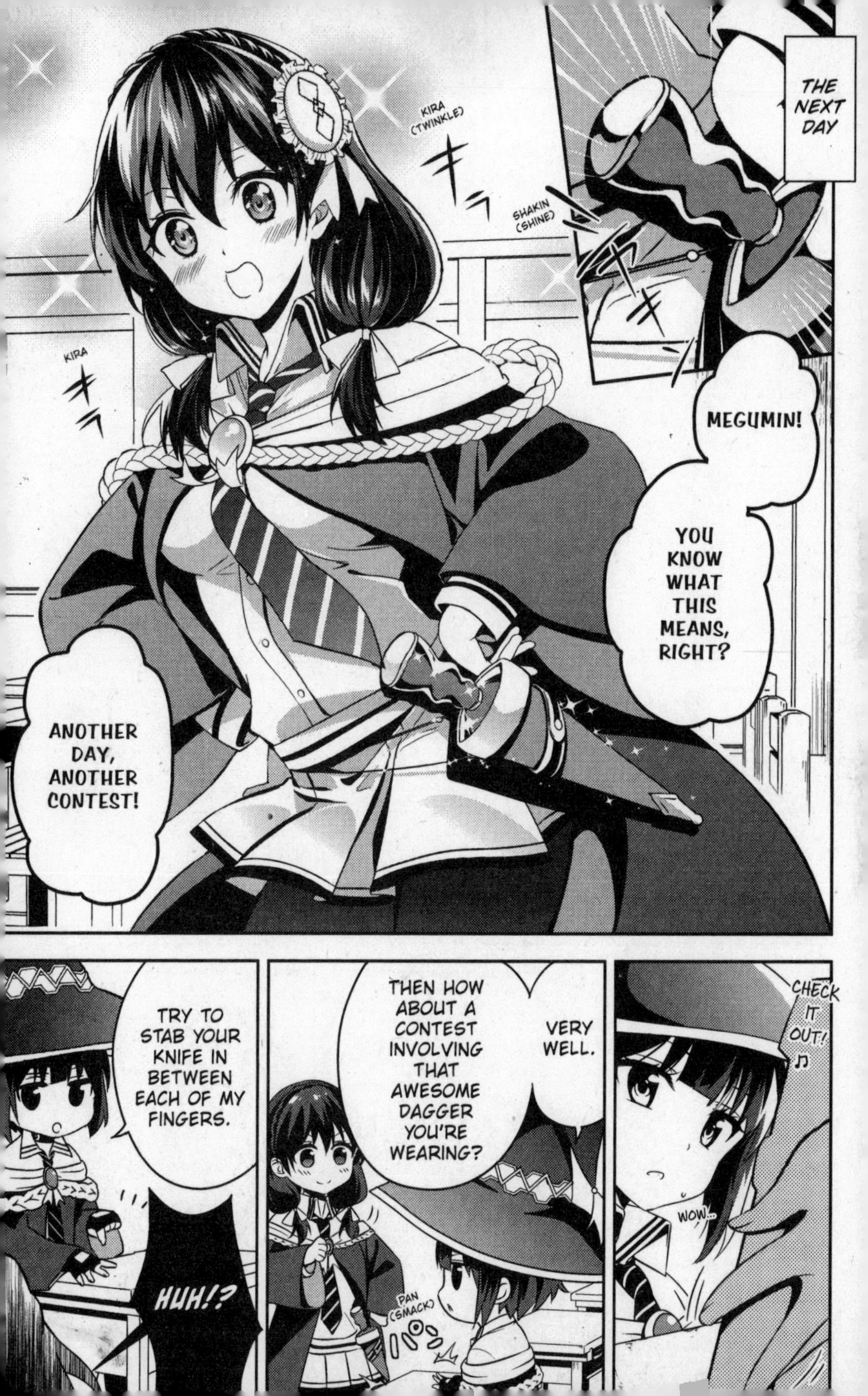
THE NEXT DAY
SHAKIN (SHINE)
MEGUMIN!
YOU KNOW WHAT THIS MEANS, RIGHT?
KIRA (TWINKLE)
KIRA
ANOTHER DAY, ANOTHER CONTEST!
CHECK IT OUT! ♫
WOW...
VERY WELL.
THEN HOW ABOUT A CONTEST INVOLVING THAT AWESOME DAGGER YOU'RE WEARING?
PAN (SMACK)
TRY TO STAB YOUR KNIFE IN BETWEEN EACH OF MY FINGERS.
HUH!?

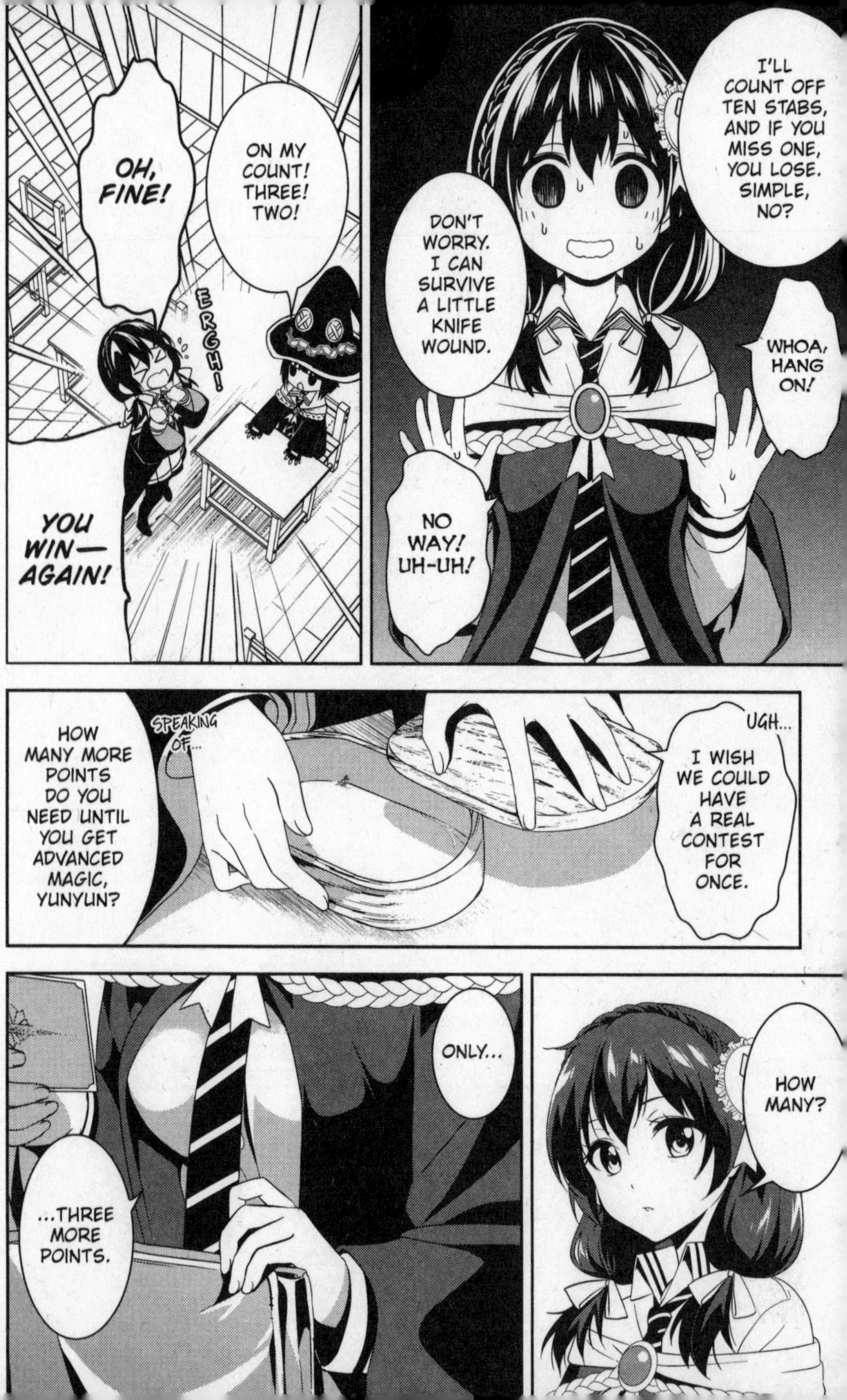

I'LL COUNT OFF TEN STABS, AND IF YOU MISS ONE, YOU LOSE. SIMPLE, NO?
WHOA, HANG ON!
DON'T WORRY. I CAN SURVIVE A LITTLE KNIFE WOUND.
NO WAY! UH-UH!
ON MY COUNT! THREE! TWO!
OH, FINE!
ERGH!
YOU WIN—AGAIN!
UGH... I WISH WE COULD HAVE A REAL CONTEST FOR ONCE.
SPEAKING OF...
HOW MANY MORE POINTS DO YOU NEED UNTIL YOU GET ADVANCED MAGIC, YUNYUN?
HOW MANY?
ONLY...
...THREE MORE POINTS.

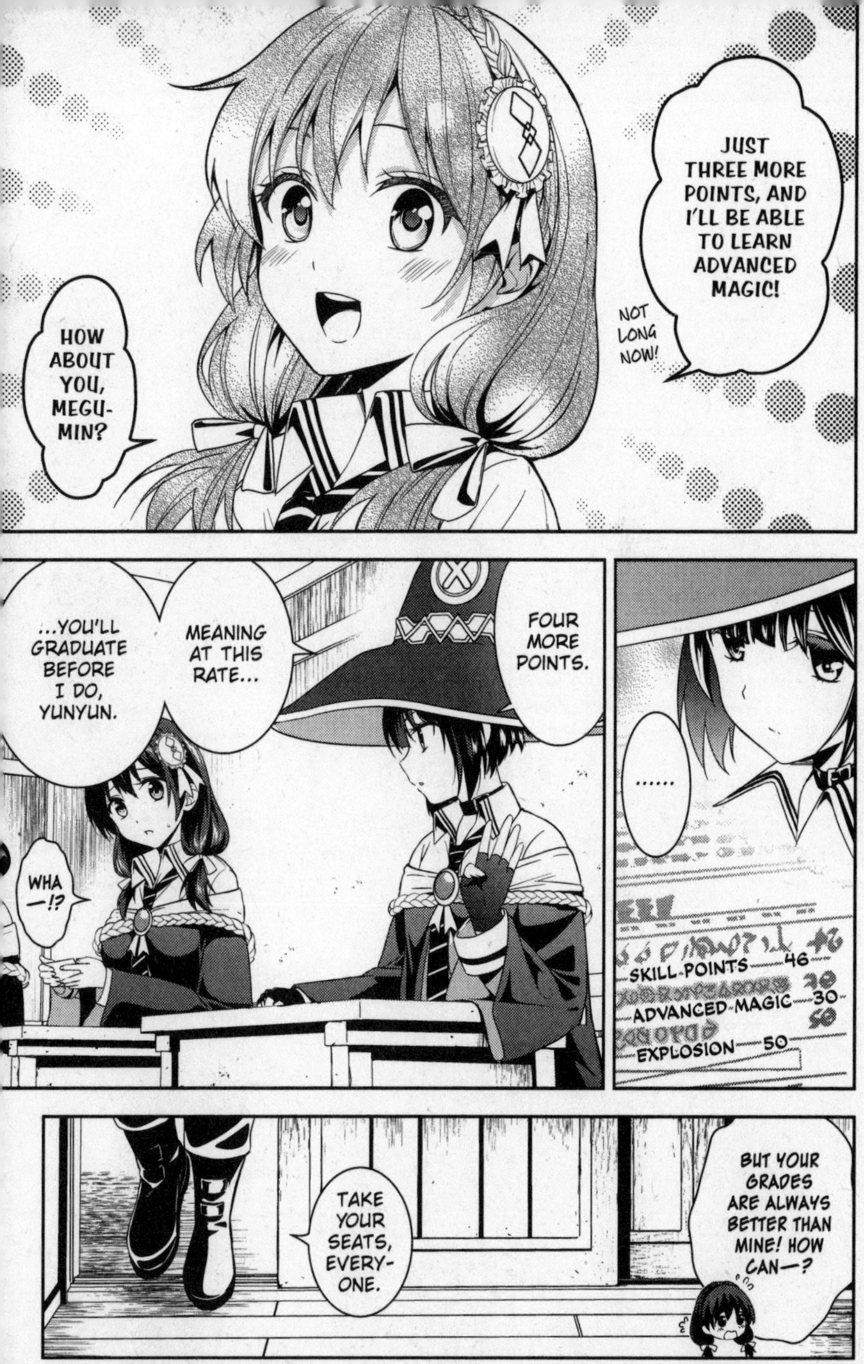
JUST THREE MORE POINTS, AND I'LL BE ABLE TO LEARN ADVANCED MAGIC!
NOT LONG NOW!
HOW ABOUT YOU, MEGU-MIN?
......
SKILL POINTS 46
ADVANCED MAGIC 30
EXPLOSION 50
FOUR MORE POINTS.
MEANING AT THIS RATE...
...YOU'LL GRADUATE BEFORE I DO, YUNYUN.
WHA—!?
BUT YOUR GRADES ARE ALWAYS BETTER THAN MINE! HOW CAN—?
TAKE YOUR SEATS, EVERY-ONE.

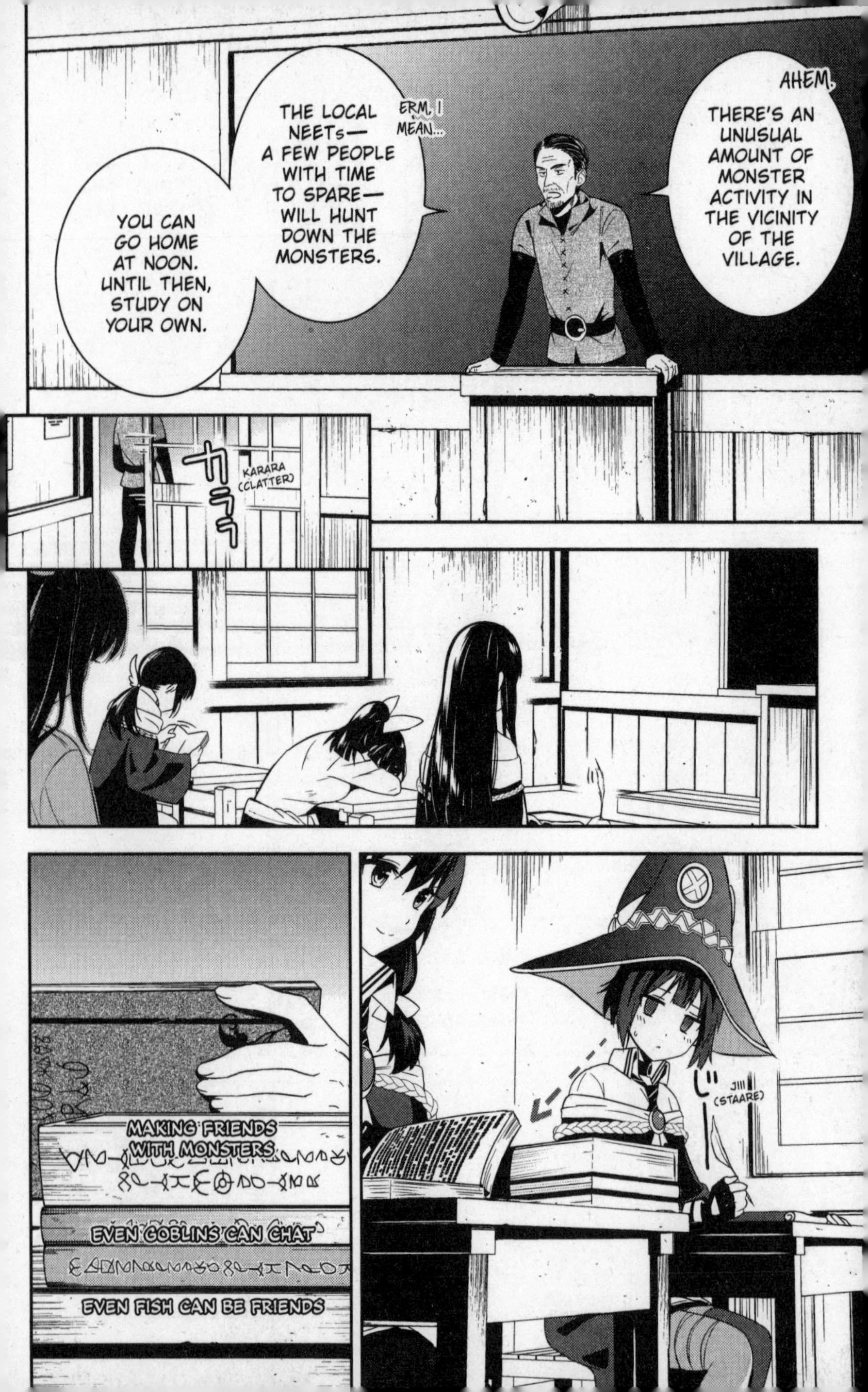
AHEM.
THERE'S AN UNUSUAL AMOUNT OF MONSTER ACTIVITY IN THE VICINITY OF THE VILLAGE.
THE LOCAL NEETs— A FEW PEOPLE WITH TIME TO SPARE— WILL HUNT DOWN THE MONSTERS.
ERM, I MEAN...
YOU CAN GO HOME AT NOON. UNTIL THEN, STUDY ON YOUR OWN.
KARARA (CLATTER)
JIII (STAARE)
MAKING FRIENDS WITH MONSTERS
EVEN GOBLINS CAN CHAT
EVEN FISH CAN BE FRIENDS

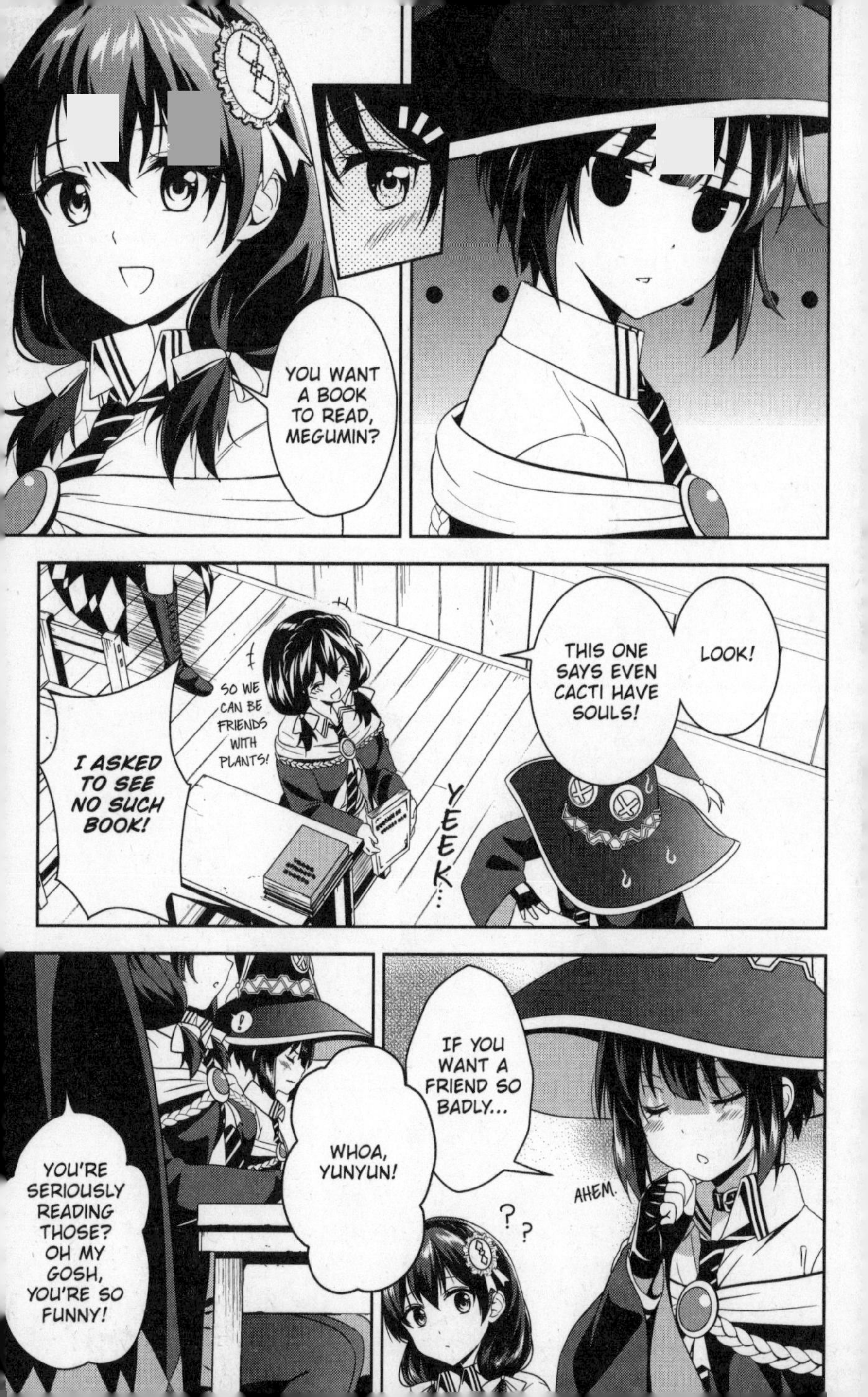
YOU WANT A BOOK TO READ, MEGUMIN?
LOOK!
THIS ONE SAYS EVEN CACTI HAVE SOULS!
YEEK...
SO WE CAN BE FRIENDS WITH PLANTS!
I ASKED TO SEE NO SUCH BOOK!
IF YOU WANT A FRIEND SO BADLY...
AHEM.
??
WHOA, YUNYUN!
YOU'RE SERIOUSLY READING THOSE? OH MY GOSH, YOU'RE SO FUNNY!

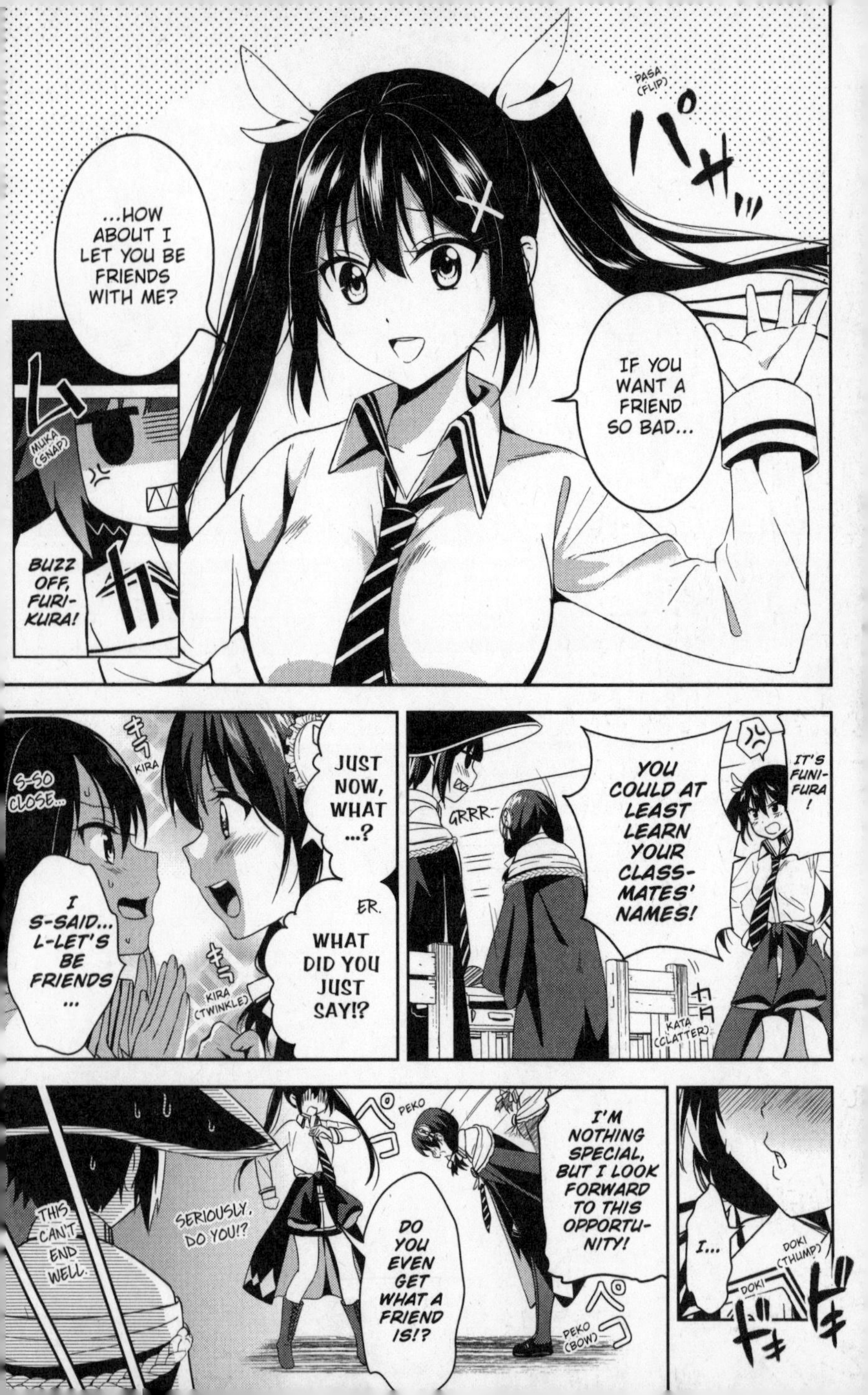
PASA (FLIP)
IF YOU WANT A FRIEND SO BAD...
...HOW ABOUT I LET YOU BE FRIENDS WITH ME?
MUKA (SNAP)
BUZZ OFF, FURI-KURA!
IT'S FUNI-FURA!
YOU COULD AT LEAST LEARN YOUR CLASS-MATES' NAMES!
GRRR.
KATA (CLATTER)
JUST NOW, WHAT ...?
KIRA
S-SO CLOSE...
ER.
WHAT DID YOU JUST SAY!?
KIRA (TWINKLE)
I S-SAID... L-LET'S BE FRIENDS ...
I...
DOKI (THUMP)
DOKI
I'M NOTHING SPECIAL, BUT I LOOK FORWARD TO THIS OPPORTU-NITY!
PEKO
DO YOU EVEN GET WHAT A FRIEND IS!?
PEKO (BOW)
SERIOUSLY, DO YOU!?
THIS CAN'T END WELL.

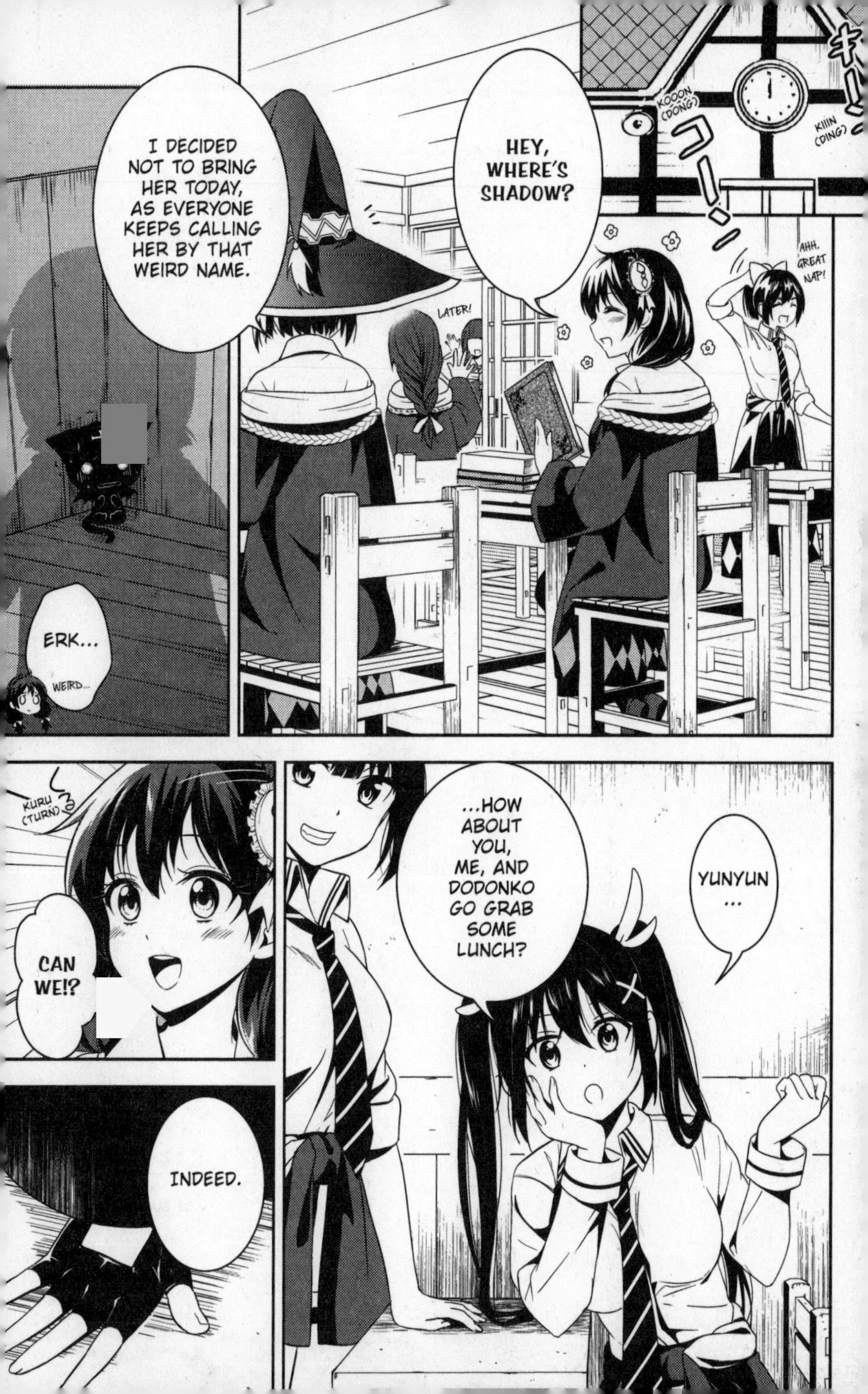
KOOON (DONG)
KIIIN (DING)
AHH, GREAT NAP!
HEY, WHERE'S SHADOW?
LATER!
I DECIDED NOT TO BRING HER TODAY, AS EVERYONE KEEPS CALLING HER BY THAT WEIRD NAME.
ERK...
WEIRD...
YUNYUN...
...HOW ABOUT YOU, ME, AND DODONKO GO GRAB SOME LUNCH?
KURU (TURN)
CAN WE!?
INDEED.

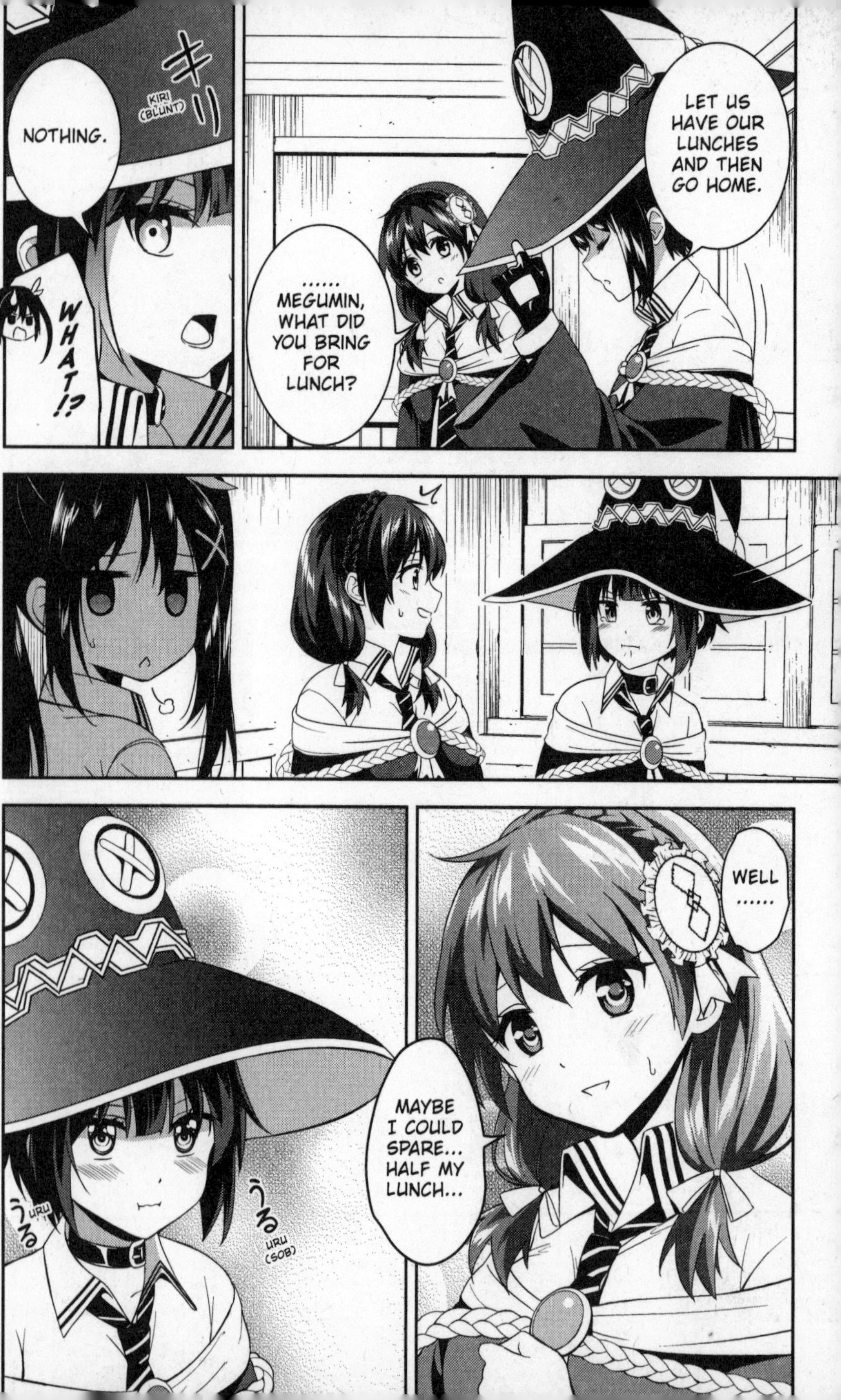
LET US HAVE OUR LUNCHES AND THEN GO HOME.
...... MEGUMIN, WHAT DID YOU BRING FOR LUNCH?
キリ
KIRI (BLUNT)
NOTHING.
WHAT!?
WELL ......
MAYBE I COULD SPARE... HALF MY LUNCH...
うる
URU
うる
URU (SOB)

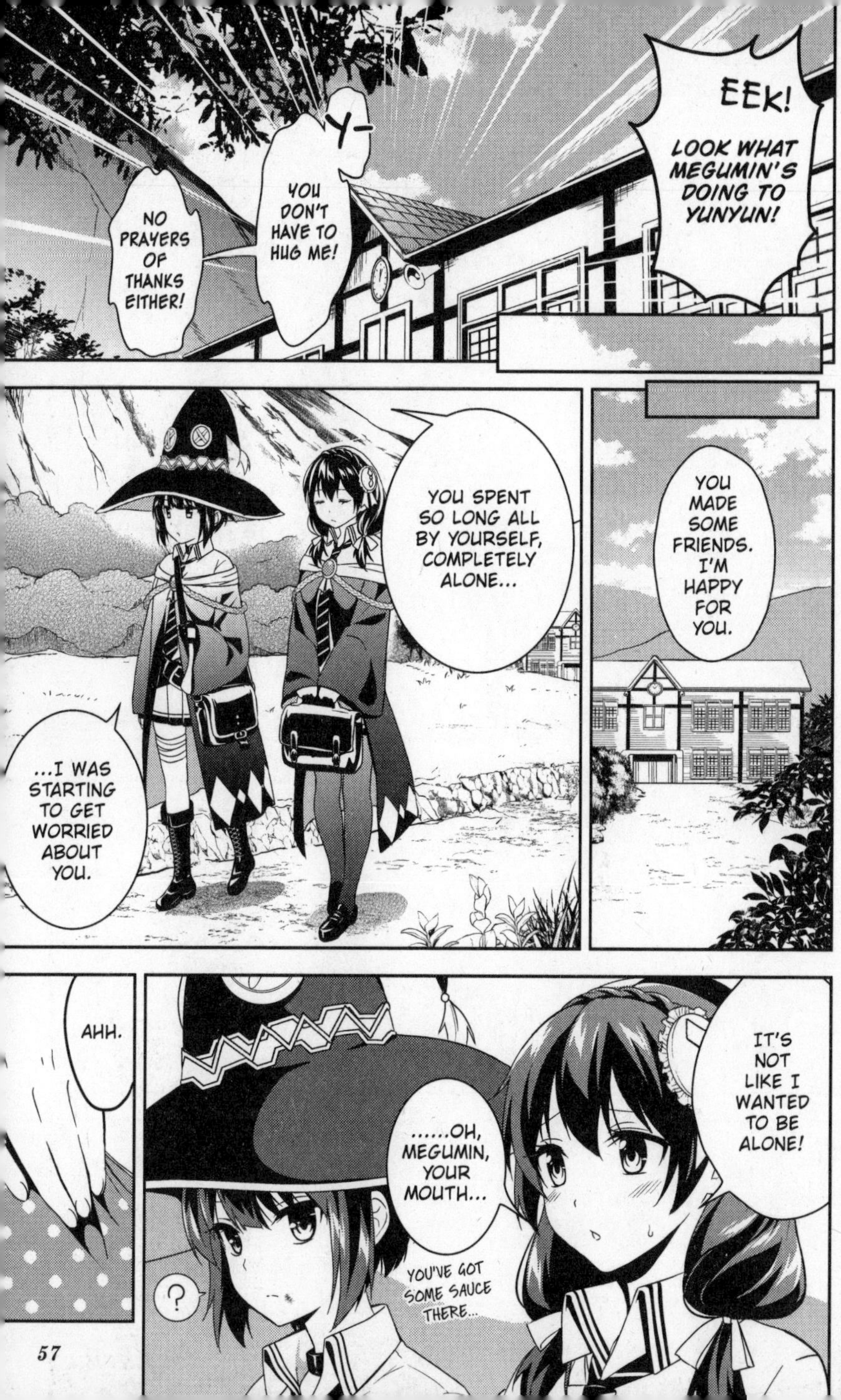
EEK!
LOOK WHAT MEGUMIN'S DOING TO YUNYUN!
Y-
YOU DON'T HAVE TO HUG ME!
NO PRAYERS OF THANKS EITHER!
YOU MADE SOME FRIENDS. I'M HAPPY FOR YOU.
YOU SPENT SO LONG ALL BY YOURSELF, COMPLETELY ALONE...
...I WAS STARTING TO GET WORRIED ABOUT YOU.
IT'S NOT LIKE I WANTED TO BE ALONE!
......OH, MEGUMIN, YOUR MOUTH...
YOU'VE GOT SOME SAUCE THERE...
?
AHH.

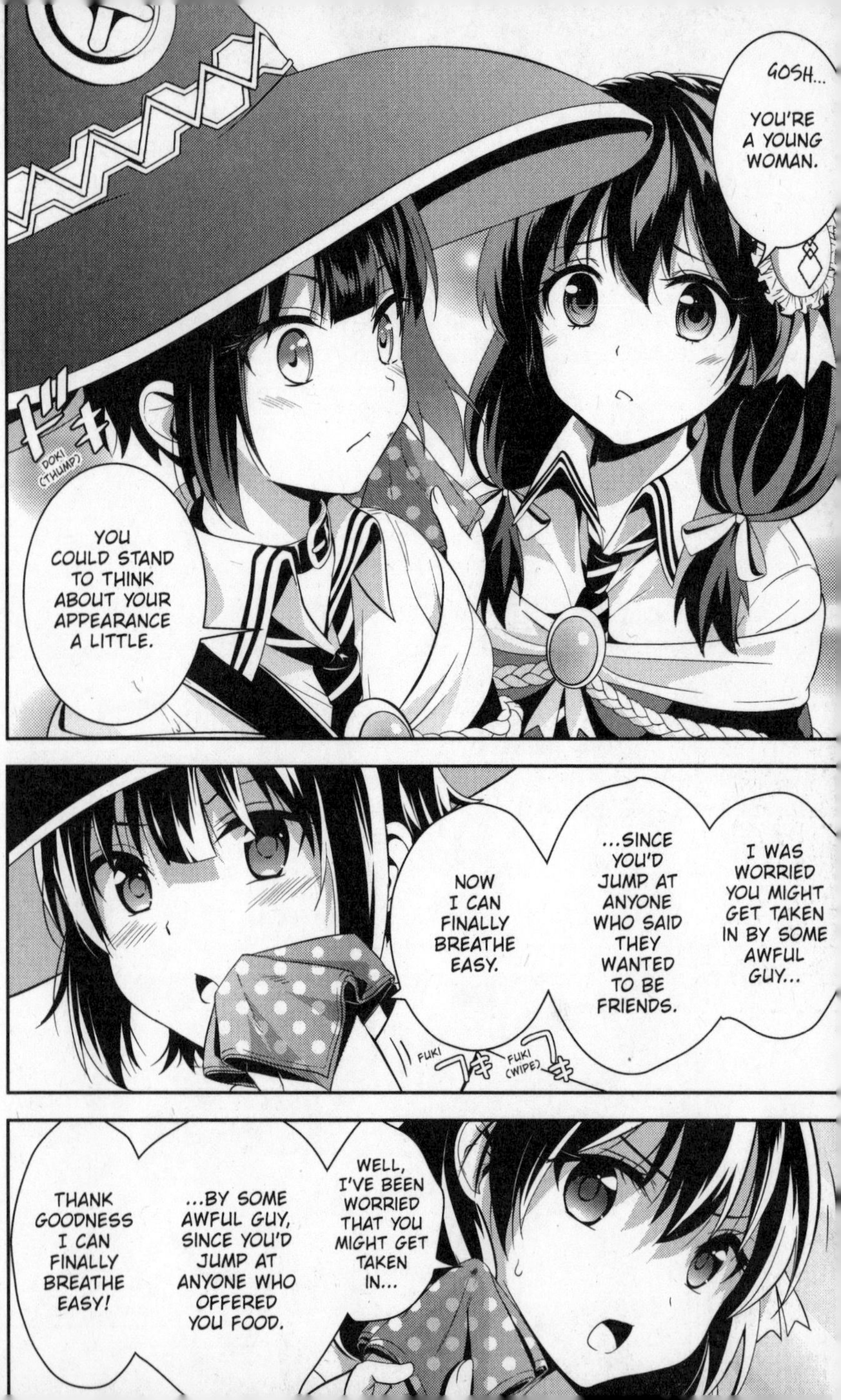
GOSH... YOU'RE A YOUNG WOMAN.
DOKI (THUMP)
YOU COULD STAND TO THINK ABOUT YOUR APPEARANCE A LITTLE.
I WAS WORRIED YOU MIGHT GET TAKEN IN BY SOME AWFUL GUY...
...SINCE YOU'D JUMP AT ANYONE WHO SAID THEY WANTED TO BE FRIENDS.
NOW I CAN FINALLY BREATHE EASY.
FUKI
FUKI (WIPE)
WELL, I'VE BEEN WORRIED THAT YOU MIGHT GET TAKEN IN...
...BY SOME AWFUL GUY, SINCE YOU'D JUMP AT ANYONE WHO OFFERED YOU FOOD.
THANK GOODNESS I CAN FINALLY BREATHE EASY!

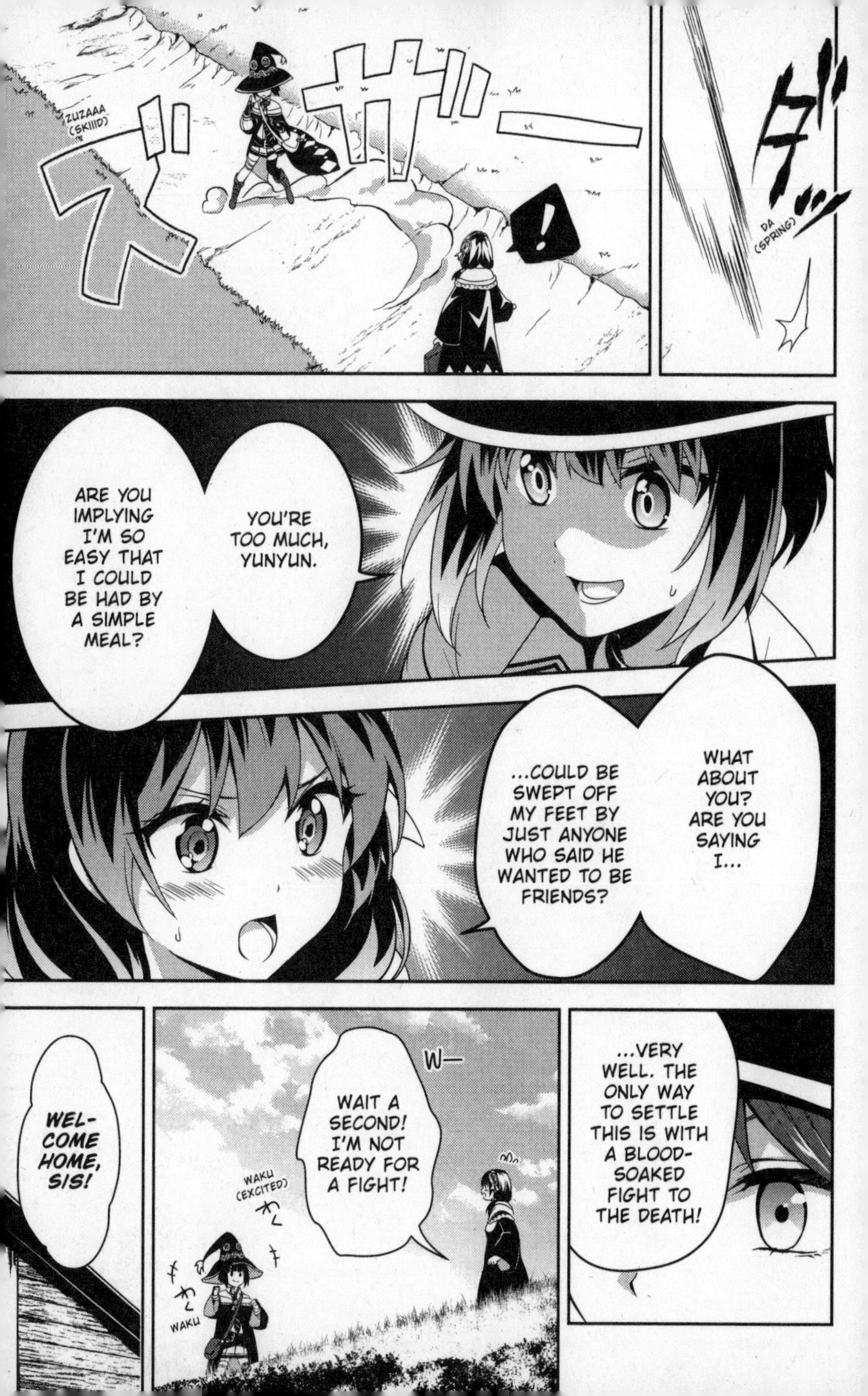
DA (SPRING)
ZUZAAA (SKIIID)
!
YOU'RE TOO MUCH, YUNYUN.
ARE YOU IMPLYING I'M SO EASY THAT I COULD BE HAD BY A SIMPLE MEAL?
WHAT ABOUT YOU? ARE YOU SAYING I...
...COULD BE SWEPT OFF MY FEET BY JUST ANYONE WHO SAID HE WANTED TO BE FRIENDS?
...VERY WELL. THE ONLY WAY TO SETTLE THIS IS WITH A BLOOD-SOAKED FIGHT TO THE DEATH!
W—
WAIT A SECOND! I'M NOT READY FOR A FIGHT!
WAKU (EXCITED)
WAKU
WEL-COME HOME, SIS!

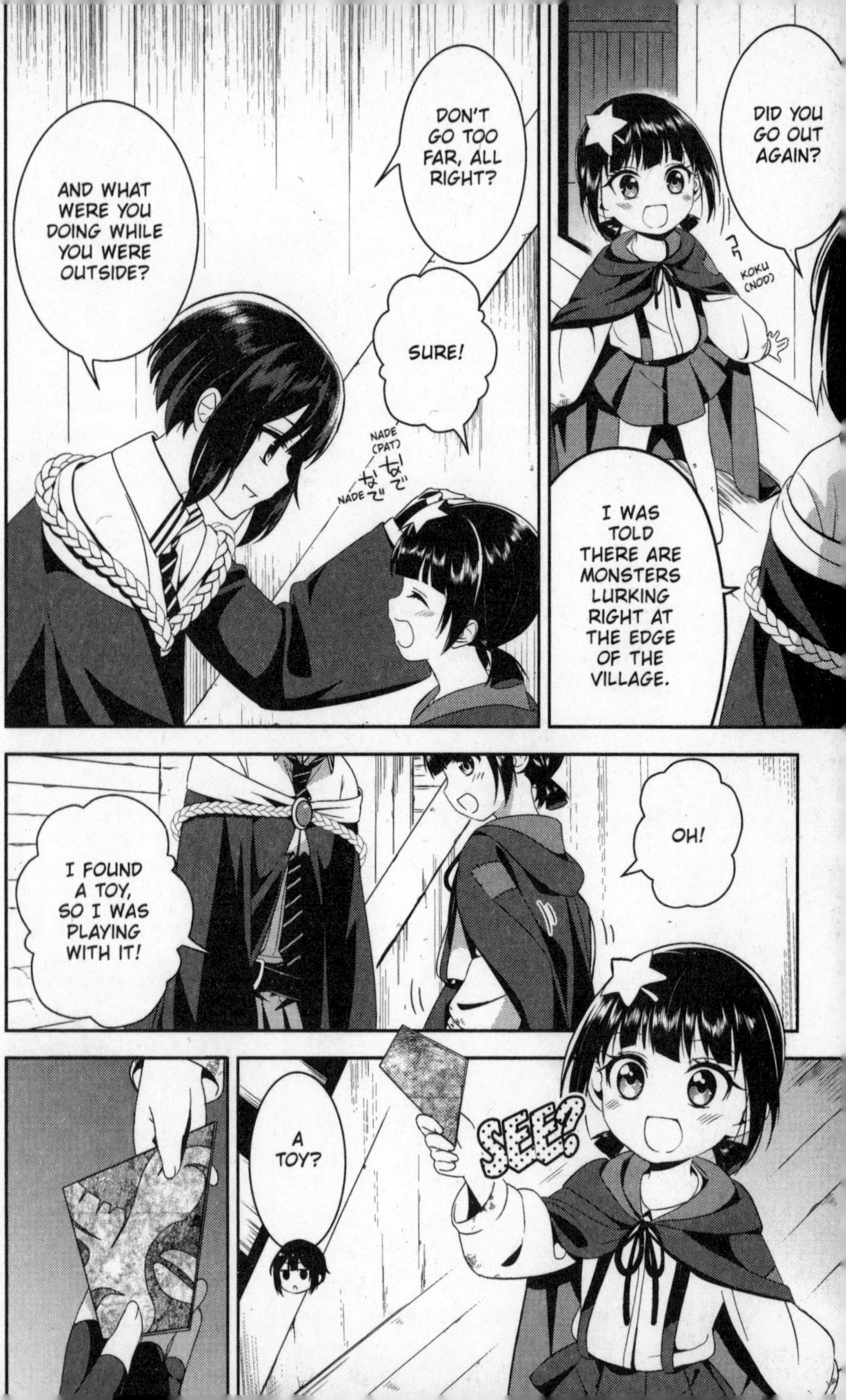
DID YOU GO OUT AGAIN?
コク
KOKU (NOD)
I WAS TOLD THERE ARE MONSTERS LURKING RIGHT AT THE EDGE OF THE VILLAGE.
DON'T GO TOO FAR, ALL RIGHT?
SURE!
なでなで
NADE (PAT) NADE
AND WHAT WERE YOU DOING WHILE YOU WERE OUTSIDE?
OH!
I FOUND A TOY, SO I WAS PLAYING WITH IT!
SEE?
A TOY?

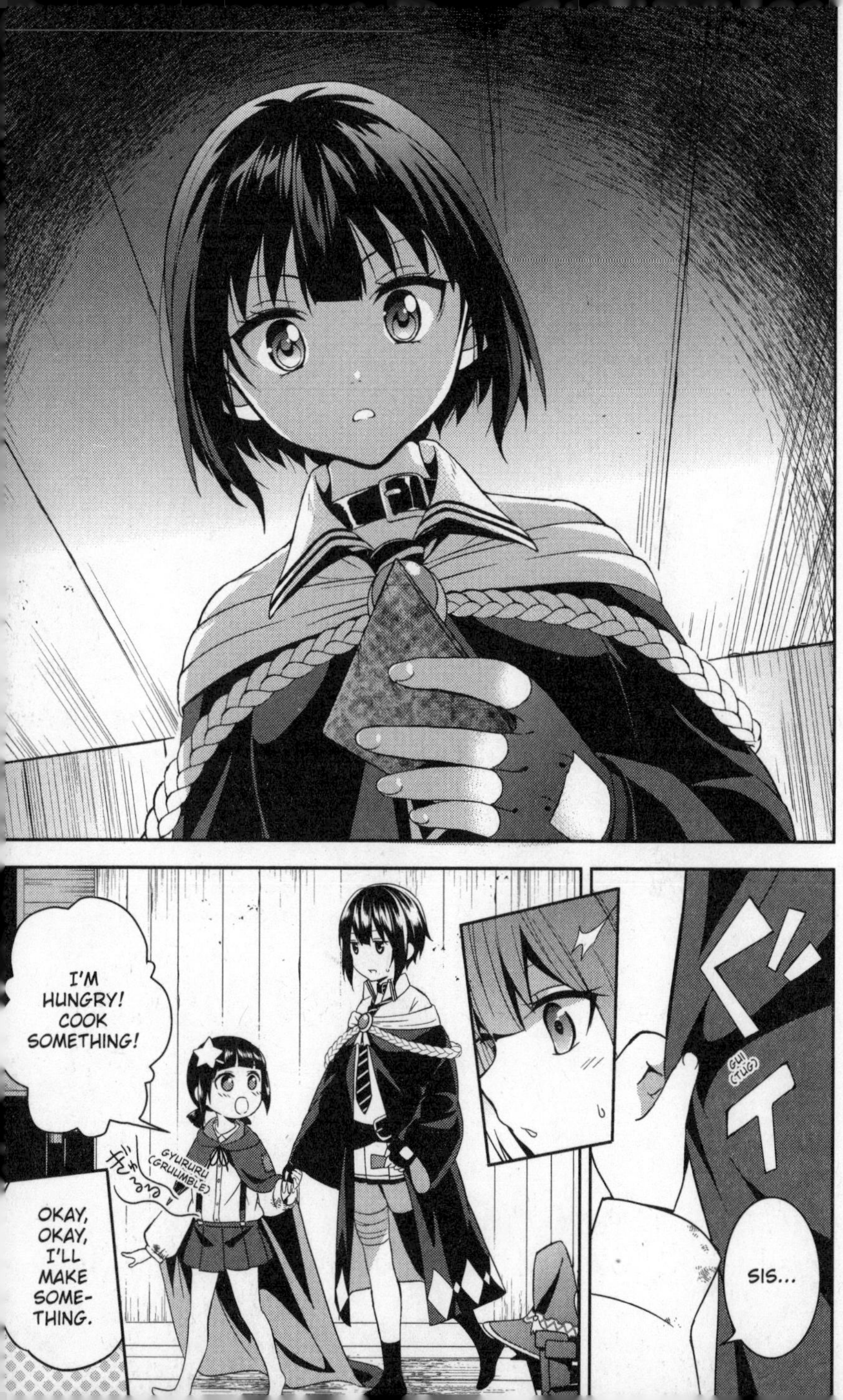
GUI (TUG)
SIS...
I'M HUNGRY! COOK SOMETHING!
GYURURU (GRUUMBLE)
OKAY, OKAY, I'LL MAKE SOME-THING.

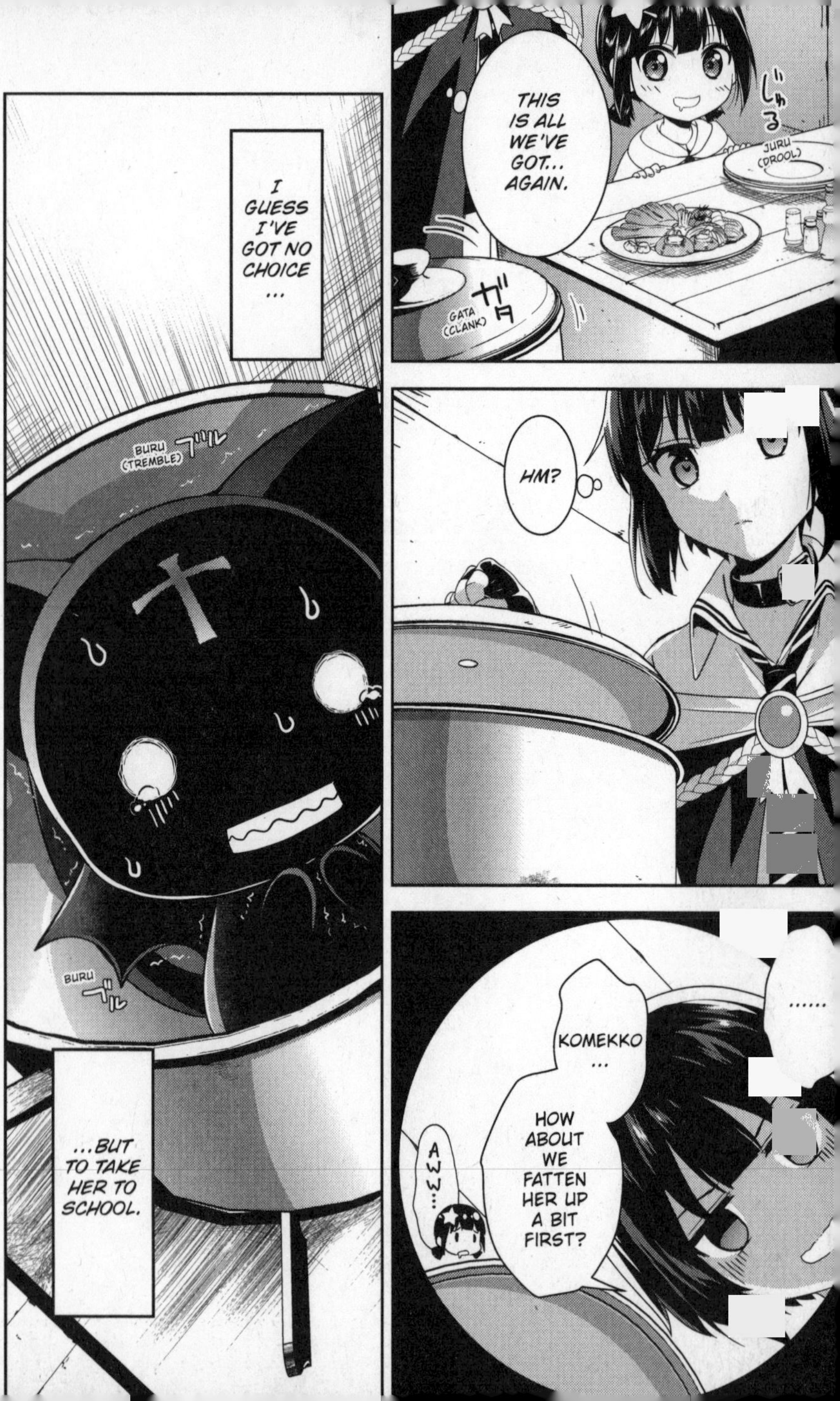
じゅる
JURU (DROOL)
THIS IS ALL WE'VE GOT... AGAIN.
ガタ
GATA (CLANK)
HM?
......
KOMEKKO...
HOW ABOUT WE FATTEN HER UP A BIT FIRST?
AWW...
I GUESS I'VE GOT NO CHOICE...
ブル
BURU (TREMBLE)
BURU
ブル
...BUT TO TAKE HER TO SCHOOL.

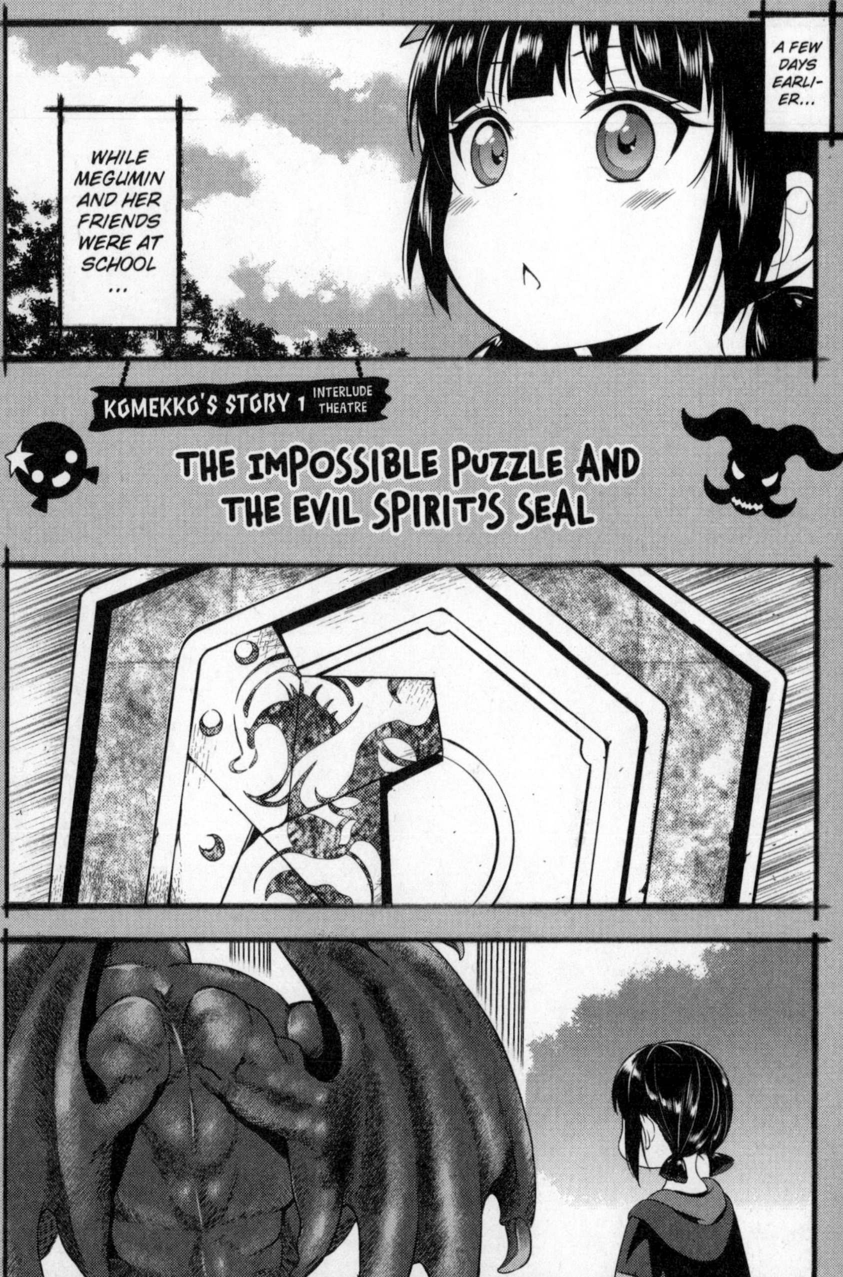
A FEW DAYS EARLIER...
WHILE MEGUMIN AND HER FRIENDS WERE AT SCHOOL...
KOMEKKO'S STORY 1 INTERLUDE THEATRE
THE IMPOSSIBLE PUZZLE AND THE EVIL SPIRIT'S SEAL

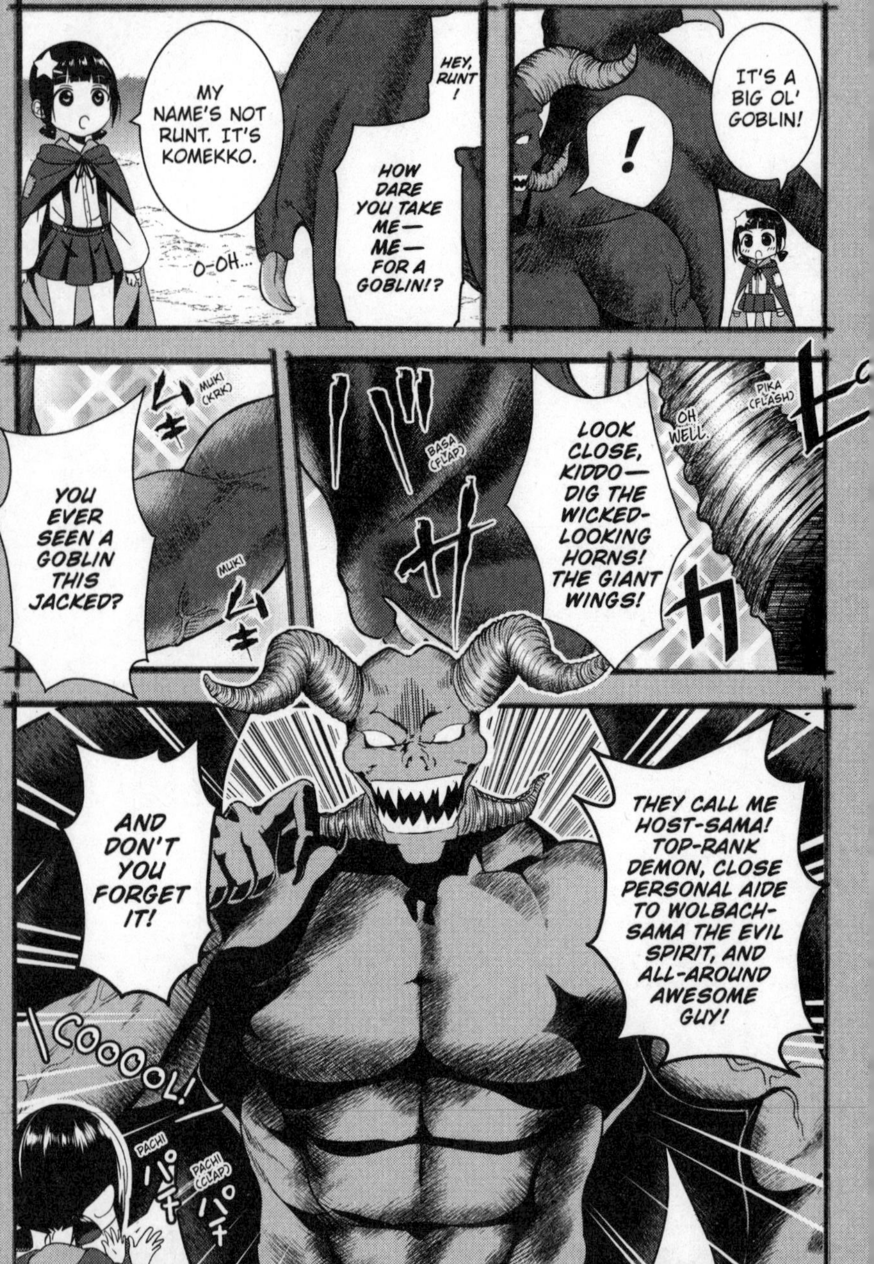
IT'S A BIG OL' GOBLIN!
!
HEY, RUNT!
HOW DARE YOU TAKE ME—ME—FOR A GOBLIN!?
MY NAME'S NOT RUNT. IT'S KOMEKKO.
O-OH...
PIKA (FLASH)
OH WELL.
LOOK CLOSE, KIDDO—DIG THE WICKED-LOOKING HORNS! THE GIANT WINGS!
BASA (FLAP)
MUKI (KRK)
YOU EVER SEEN A GOBLIN THIS JACKED?
MUKI
THEY CALL ME HOST-SAMA! TOP-RANK DEMON, CLOSE PERSONAL AIDE TO WOLBACH-SAMA THE EVIL SPIRIT, AND ALL-AROUND AWESOME GUY!
AND DON'T YOU FORGET IT!
COOOOL!
PACHI
PACHI (CLAP)

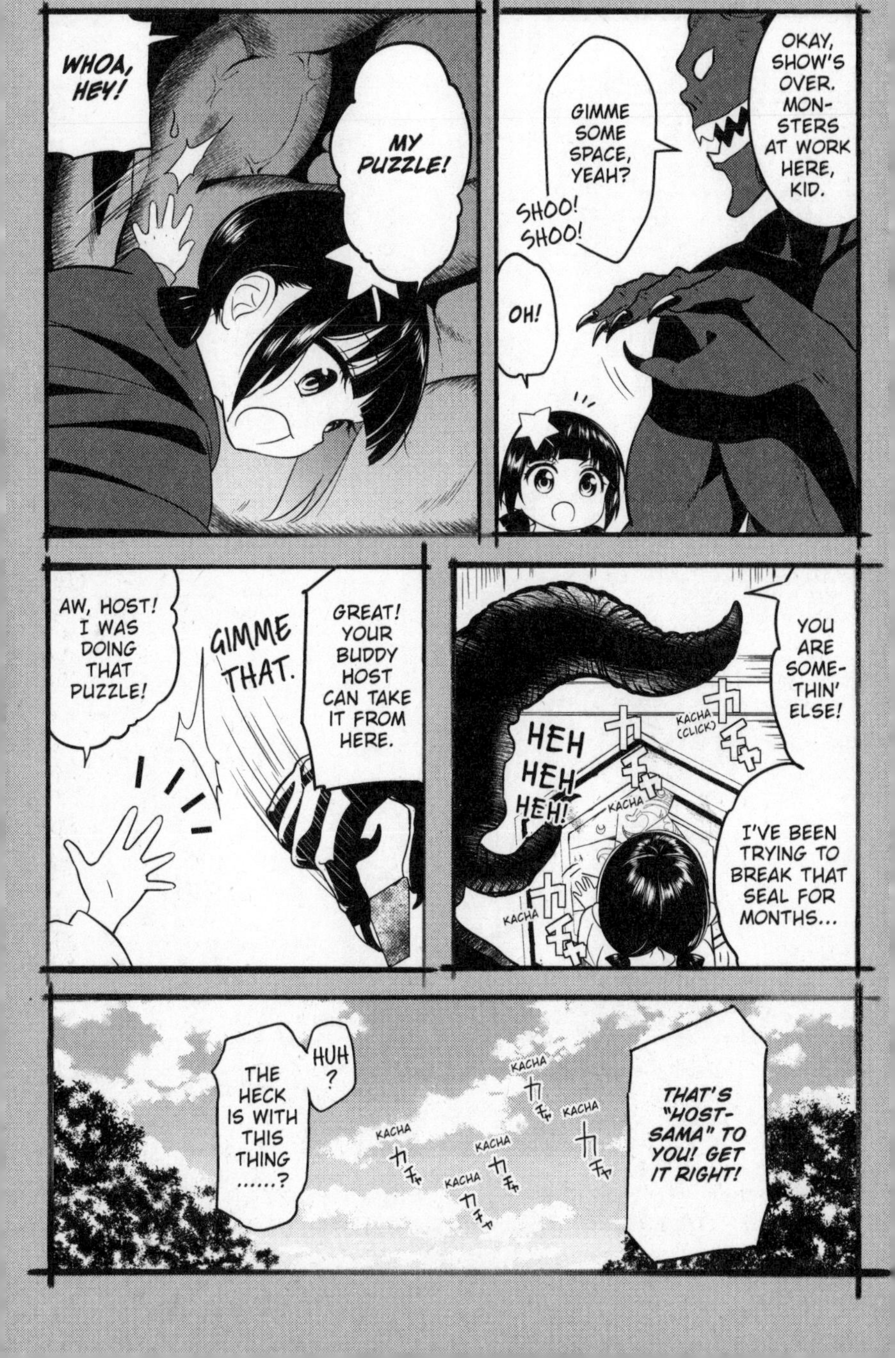
OKAY, SHOW'S OVER. MONSTERS AT WORK HERE, KID.
GIMME SOME SPACE, YEAH?
SHOO! SHOO!
OH!
WHOA, HEY!
MY PUZZLE!
YOU ARE SOMETHIN' ELSE!
KACHA (CLICK)
HEH HEH HEH!
KACHA
KACHA
I'VE BEEN TRYING TO BREAK THAT SEAL FOR MONTHS...
GREAT! YOUR BUDDY HOST CAN TAKE IT FROM HERE.
GIMME THAT.
AW, HOST! I WAS DOING THAT PUZZLE!
THAT'S "HOST-SAMA" TO YOU! GET IT RIGHT!
KACHA
KACHA
KACHA
KACHA
KACHA
HUH?
THE HECK IS WITH THIS THING ......?

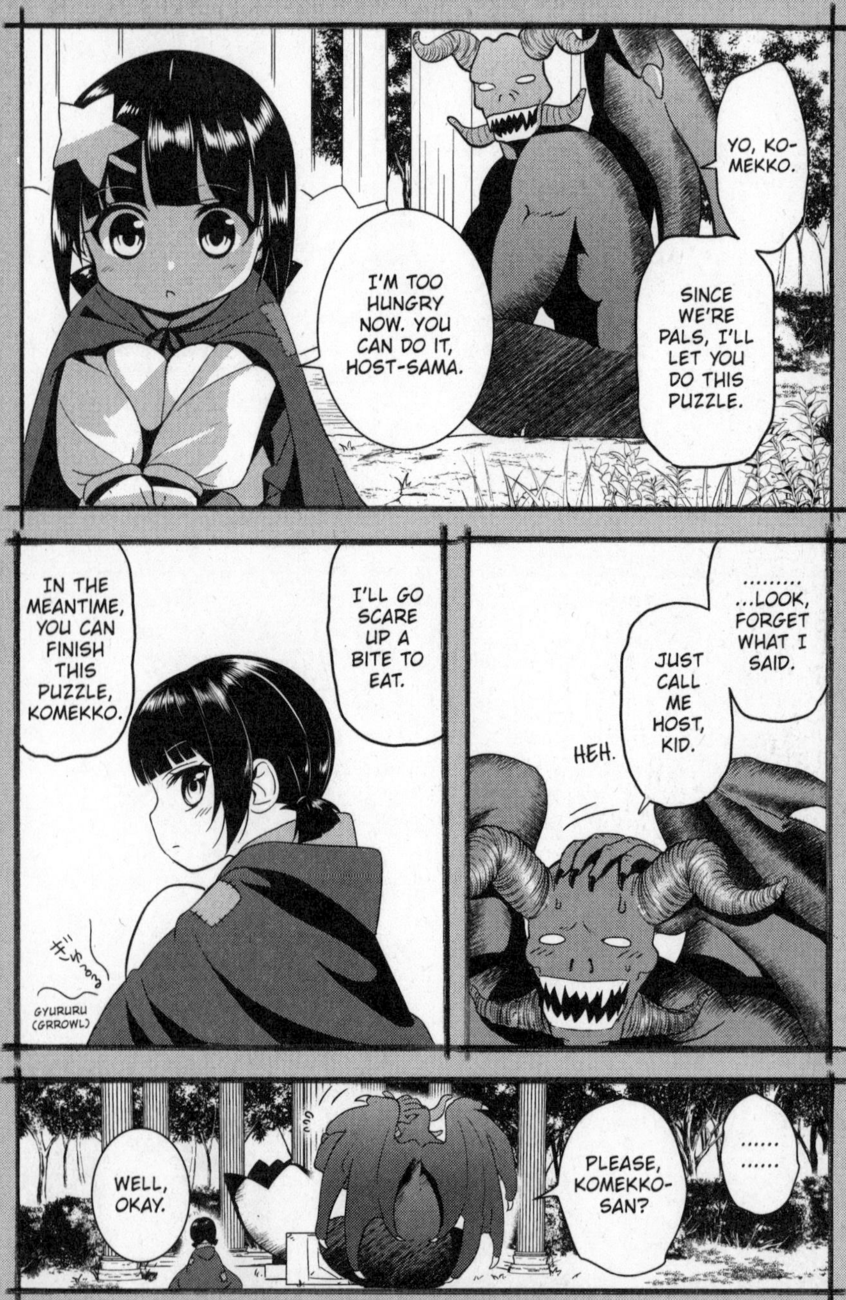
YO, KO-MEKKO.
SINCE WE'RE PALS, I'LL LET YOU DO THIS PUZZLE.
I'M TOO HUNGRY NOW. YOU CAN DO IT, HOST-SAMA.
....LOOK, FORGET WHAT I SAID.
JUST CALL ME HOST, KID.
HEH.
I'LL GO SCARE UP A BITE TO EAT.
IN THE MEANTIME, YOU CAN FINISH THIS PUZZLE, KOMEKKO.
GYURURU (GRROWL)
....
PLEASE, KOMEKKO-SAN?
WELL, OKAY.

KONOSUBA: AN EXPLOSION ON THIS WONDERFUL WORLD!

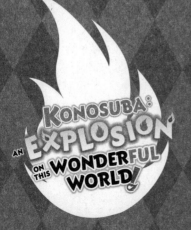

KONOSUBA: AN EXPLOSION ON THIS WONDERFUL WORLD!

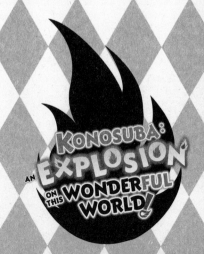

HFF.
HFF.
NGH!
むに
MUNI (SMOOSH)
S—
ブル
BURU (TREMBLE)
BURU
ブル
STOP ...

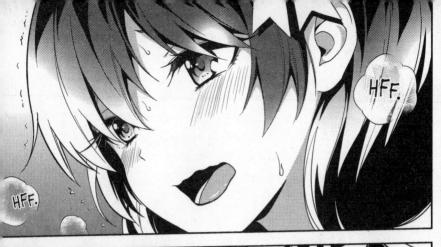

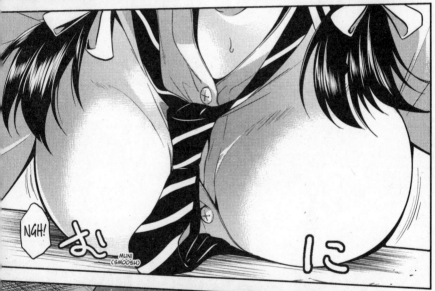

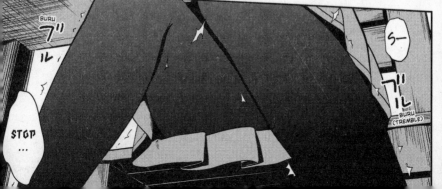

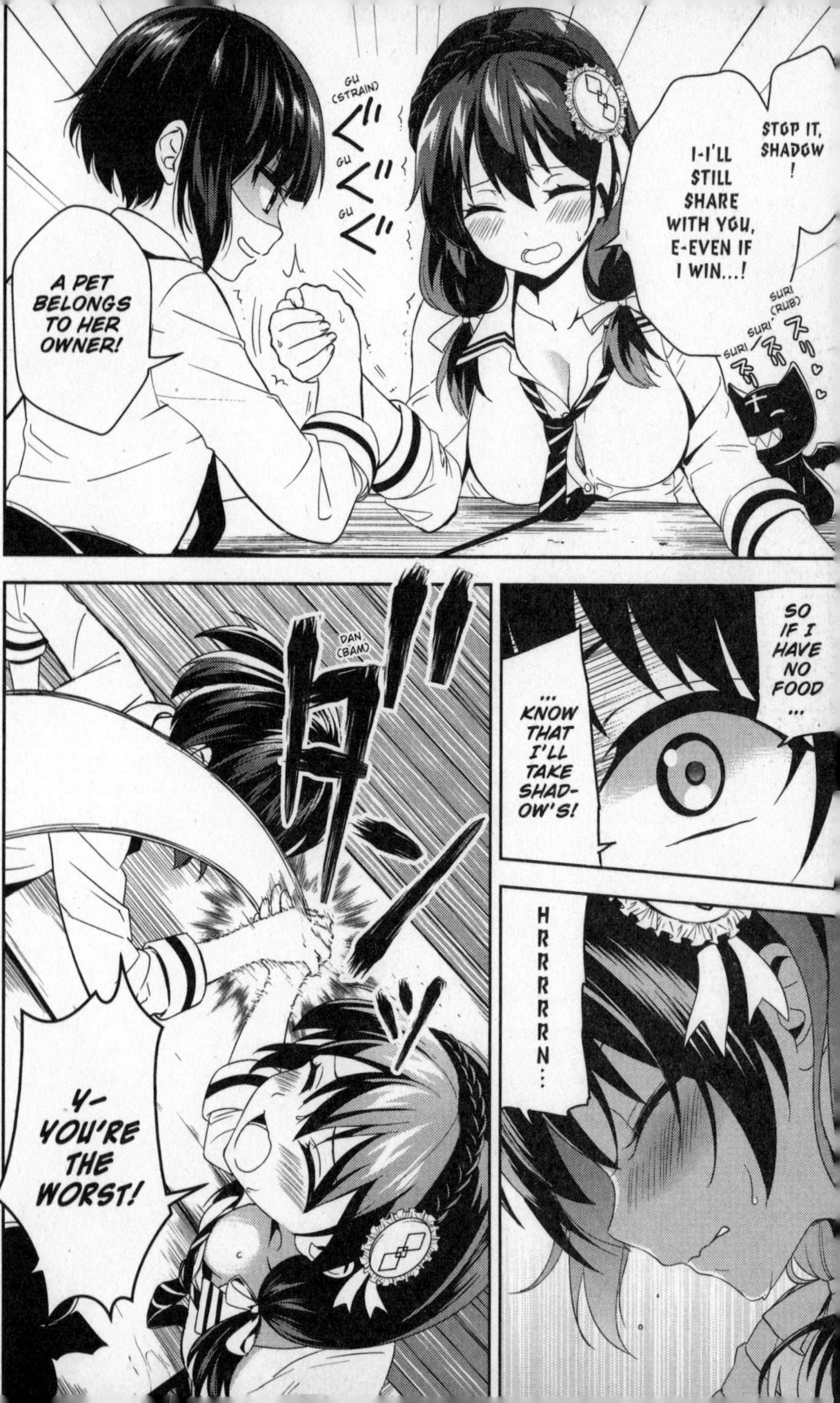
STOP IT, SHADOW!
I-I'LL STILL SHARE WITH YOU, E-EVEN IF I WIN...!
SURI (RUB)
SURI
SURI
GU (STRAIN)
GU
GU
A PET BELONGS TO HER OWNER!
SO IF I HAVE NO FOOD...
...KNOW THAT I'LL TAKE SHADOW'S!
HRRRRRRN...
DAN (BAM)
Y-YOU'RE THE WORST!

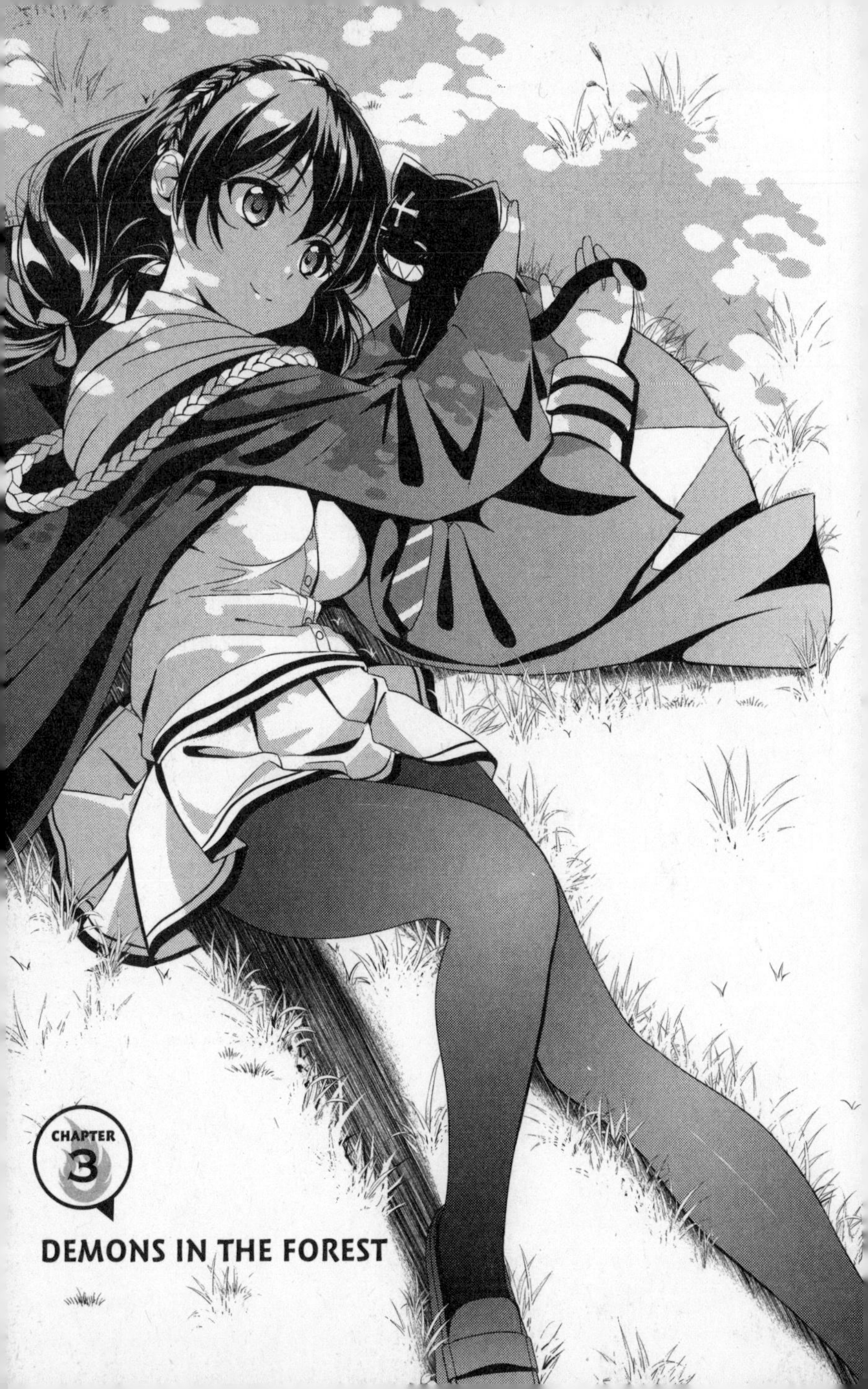
CHAPTER
3
DEMONS IN THE FOREST

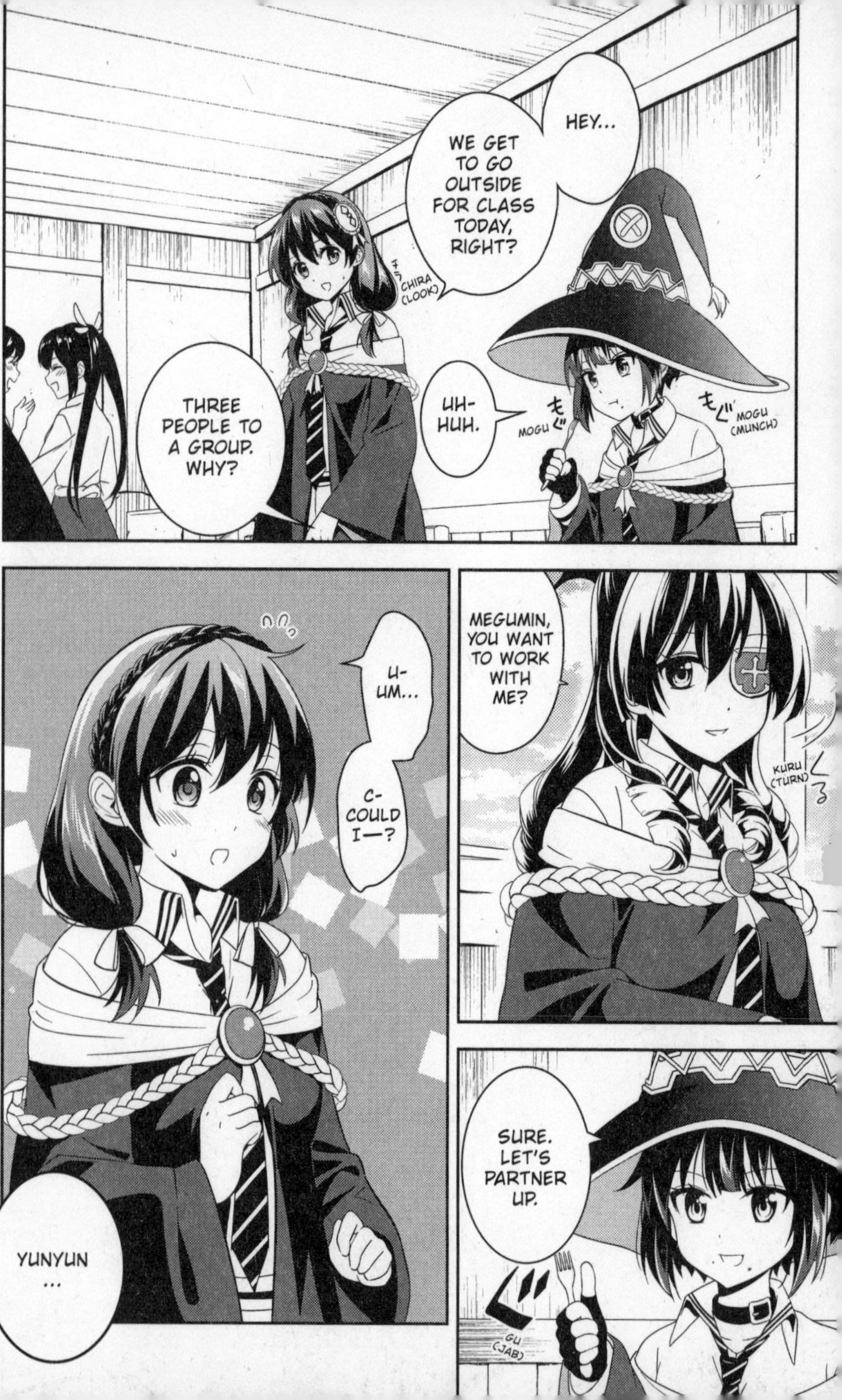
HEY...
WE GET TO GO OUTSIDE FOR CLASS TODAY, RIGHT?
CHIRA (LOOK)
もぐ
MOGU (MUNCH)
UH-HUH.
もぐ
MOGU
THREE PEOPLE TO A GROUP. WHY?
MEGUMIN, YOU WANT TO WORK WITH ME?
くる
KURU (TURN)
SURE. LET'S PARTNER UP.
GU (JAB)
U-UM...
C-COULD I—?
YUNYUN ...

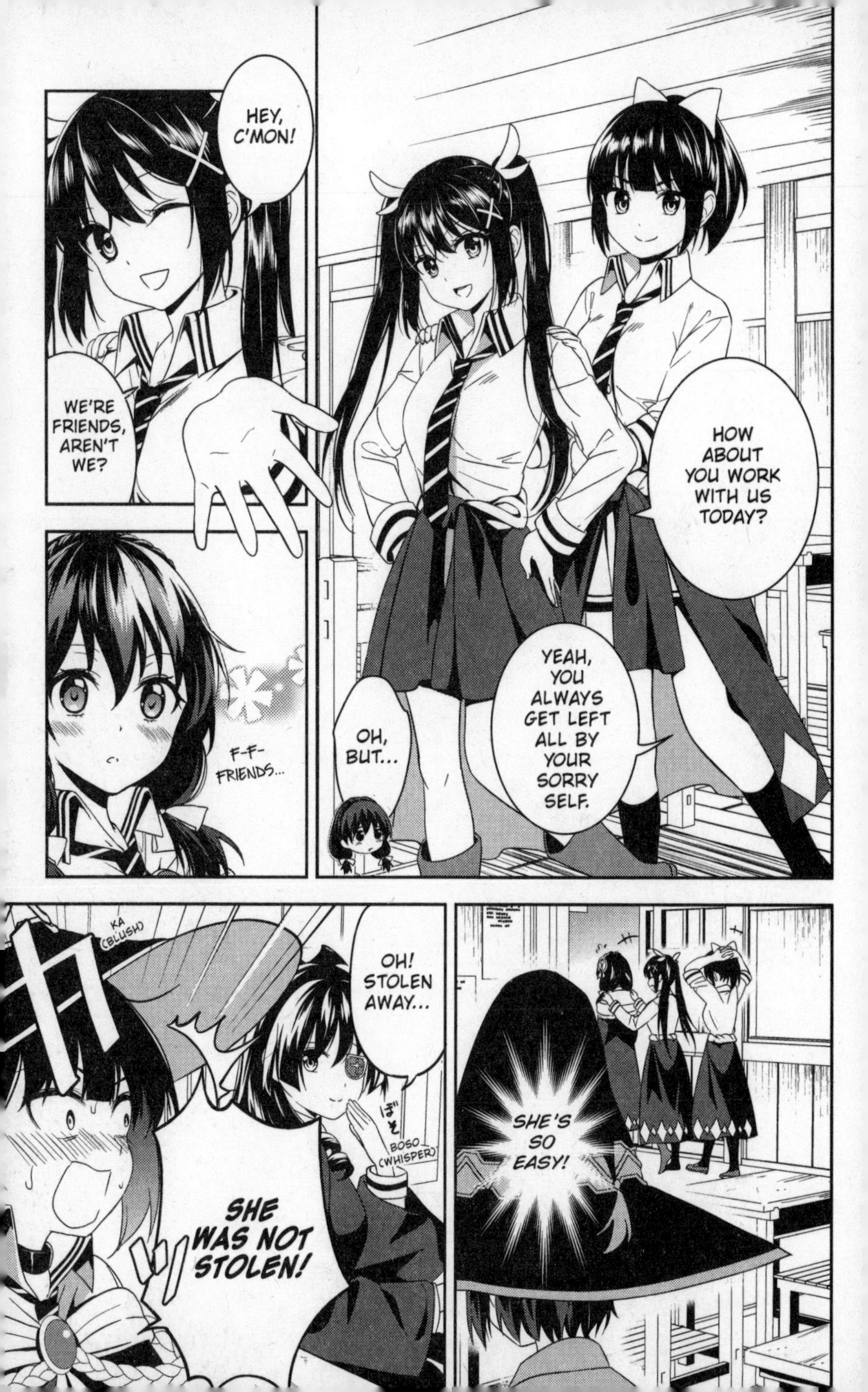
HOW ABOUT YOU WORK WITH US TODAY?
YEAH, YOU ALWAYS GET LEFT ALL BY YOUR SORRY SELF.
OH, BUT...
HEY, C'MON!
WE'RE FRIENDS, AREN'T WE?
F-F-FRIENDS...
SHE'S SO EASY!
OH! STOLEN AWAY...
BOSO (WHISPER)
KA (BLUSH)
SHE WAS NOT STOLEN!

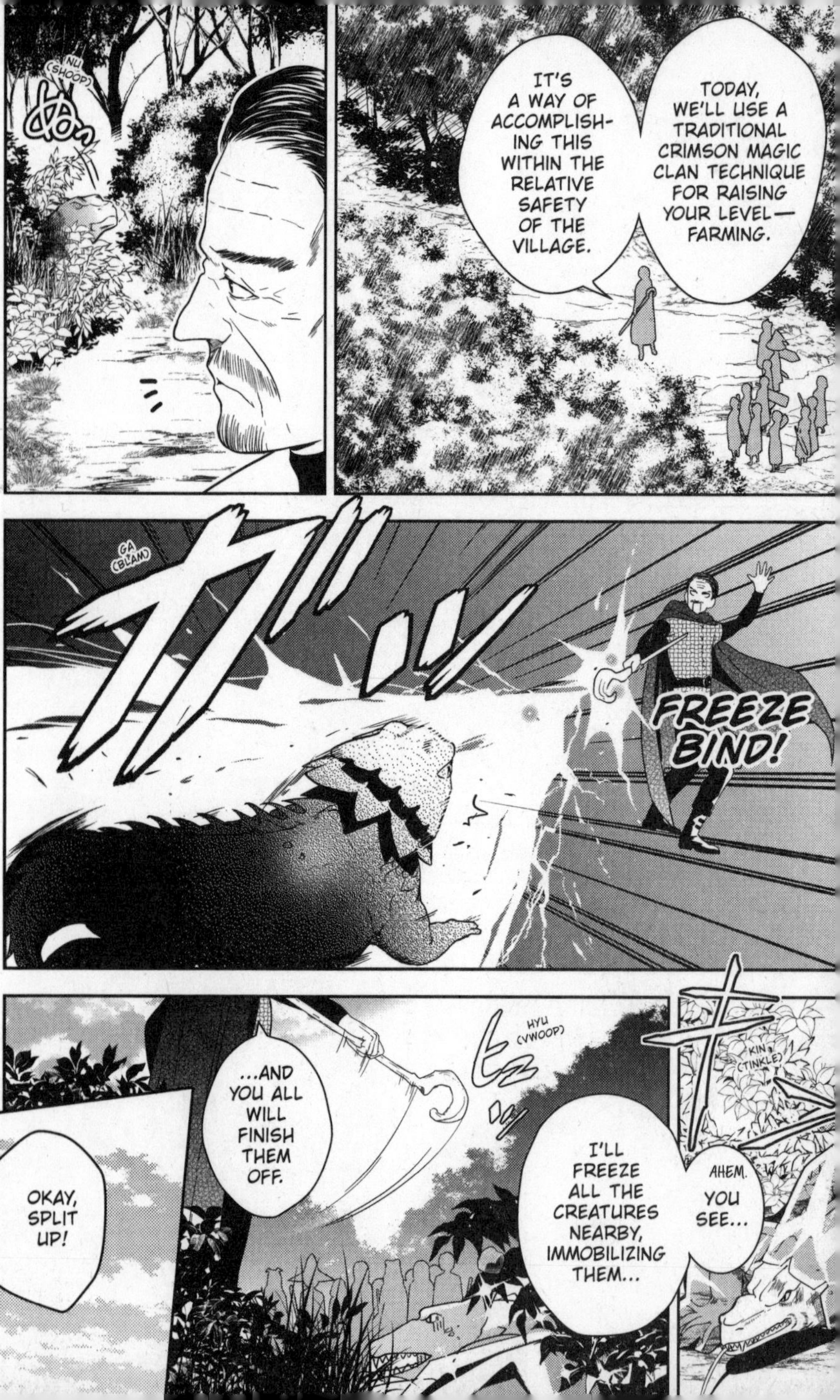
TODAY, WE'LL USE A TRADITIONAL CRIMSON MAGIC CLAN TECHNIQUE FOR RAISING YOUR LEVEL— FARMING.
IT'S A WAY OF ACCOMPLISHING THIS WITHIN THE RELATIVE SAFETY OF THE VILLAGE.
NU (SHOOP)
FREEZE BIND!
GA (BLAM)
KIN (TINKLE)
AHEM. YOU SEE...
I'LL FREEZE ALL THE CREATURES NEARBY, IMMOBILIZING THEM...
HYU (VWOOP)
...AND YOU ALL WILL FINISH THEM OFF.
OKAY, SPLIT UP!

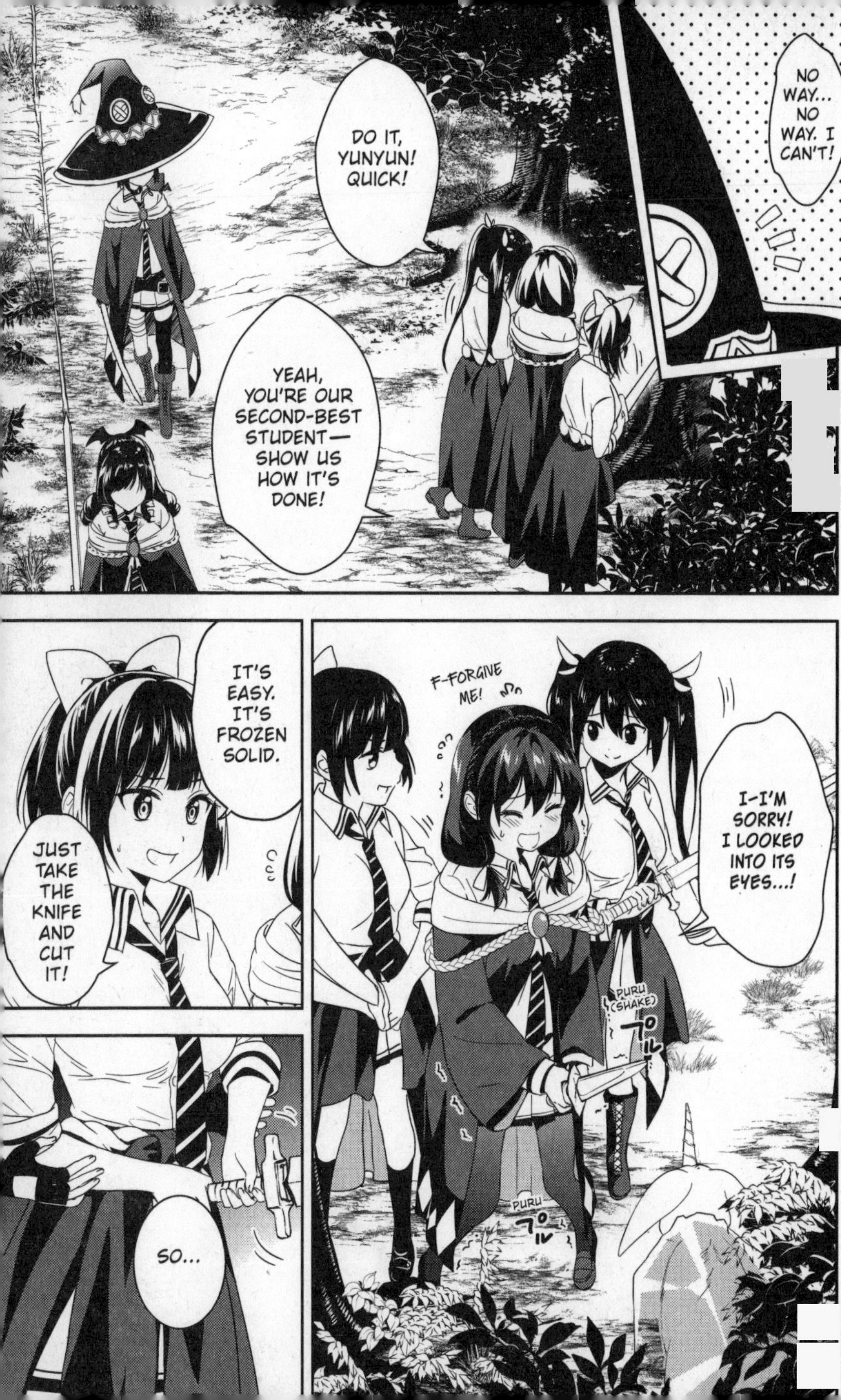
NO WAY... NO WAY. I CAN'T!
DO IT, YUNYUN! QUICK!
YEAH, YOU'RE OUR SECOND-BEST STUDENT—SHOW US HOW IT'S DONE!
I-I'M SORRY! I LOOKED INTO ITS EYES...!
F-FORGIVE ME!
PURU (SHAKE)
PURU
IT'S EASY. IT'S FROZEN SOLID.
JUST TAKE THE KNIFE AND CUT IT!
SO...

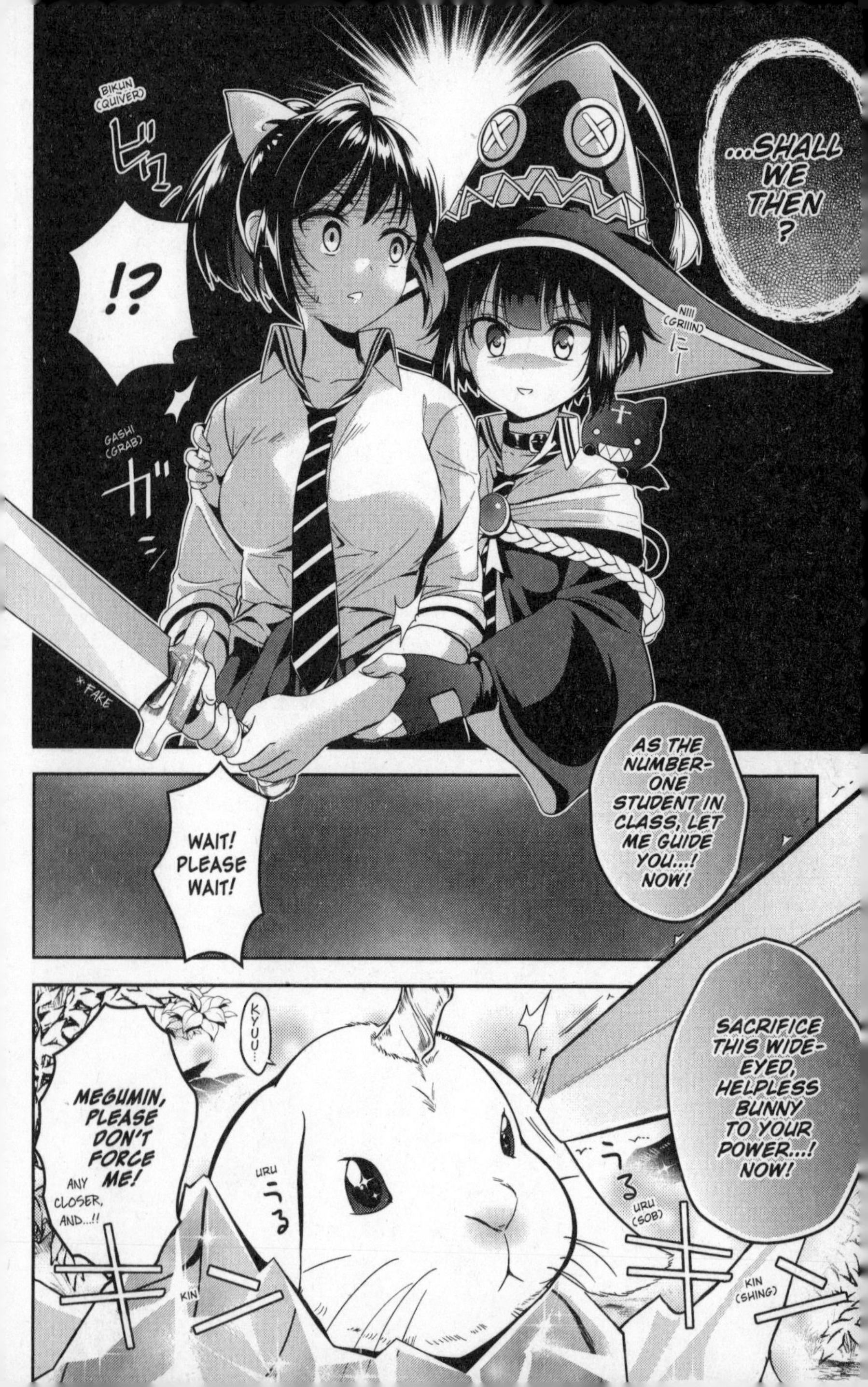
...SHALL WE THEN?
NIII (GRIIIN)
にー
BIKUN (QUIVER)
ビクン
!?
GASHI (GRAB)
ガッ
* FAKE
AS THE NUMBER-ONE STUDENT IN CLASS, LET ME GUIDE YOU...! NOW!
WAIT! PLEASE WAIT!
SACRIFICE THIS WIDE-EYED, HELPLESS BUNNY TO YOUR POWER...! NOW!
KYUU...
URU (SOB)
うる
KIN (SHING)
MEGUMIN, PLEASE DON'T FORCE ME!
ANY CLOSER, AND...!!
URU
うる
KIN

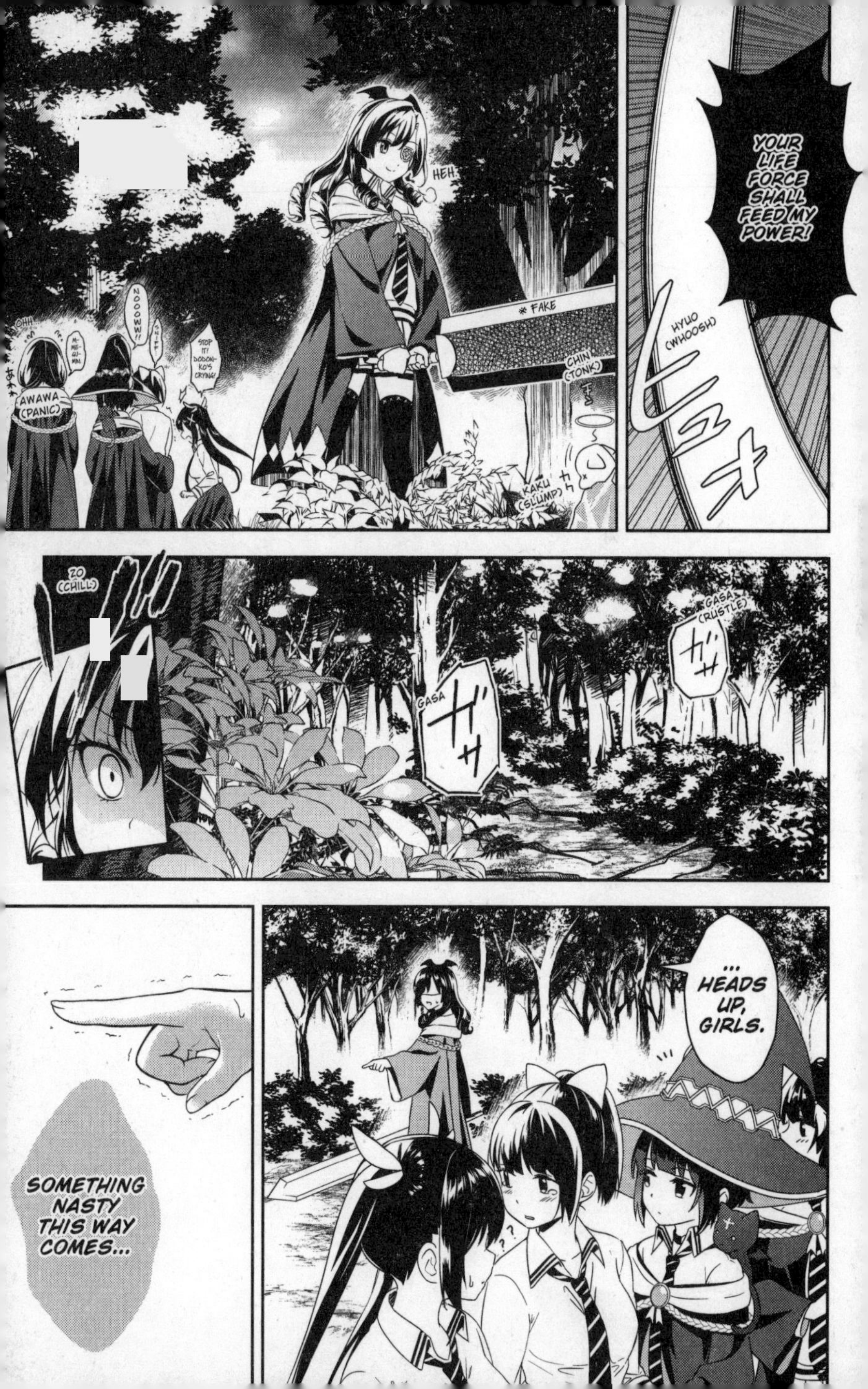
YOUR LIFE FORCE SHALL FEED MY POWER!
HYUO (WHOOSH)
HEH.
※ FAKE
CHIN (TONK)
KAKU (SLUMP)
STOP IT! DODONKO'S CRYING!
SNIFF
NOOOOWW!!
M-ME-GU-MIN
OHH...
AWAWA (PANIC)
ZO (CHILL)
GASA (RUSTLE)
GASA
... HEADS UP, GIRLS.
SOMETHING NASTY THIS WAY COMES...

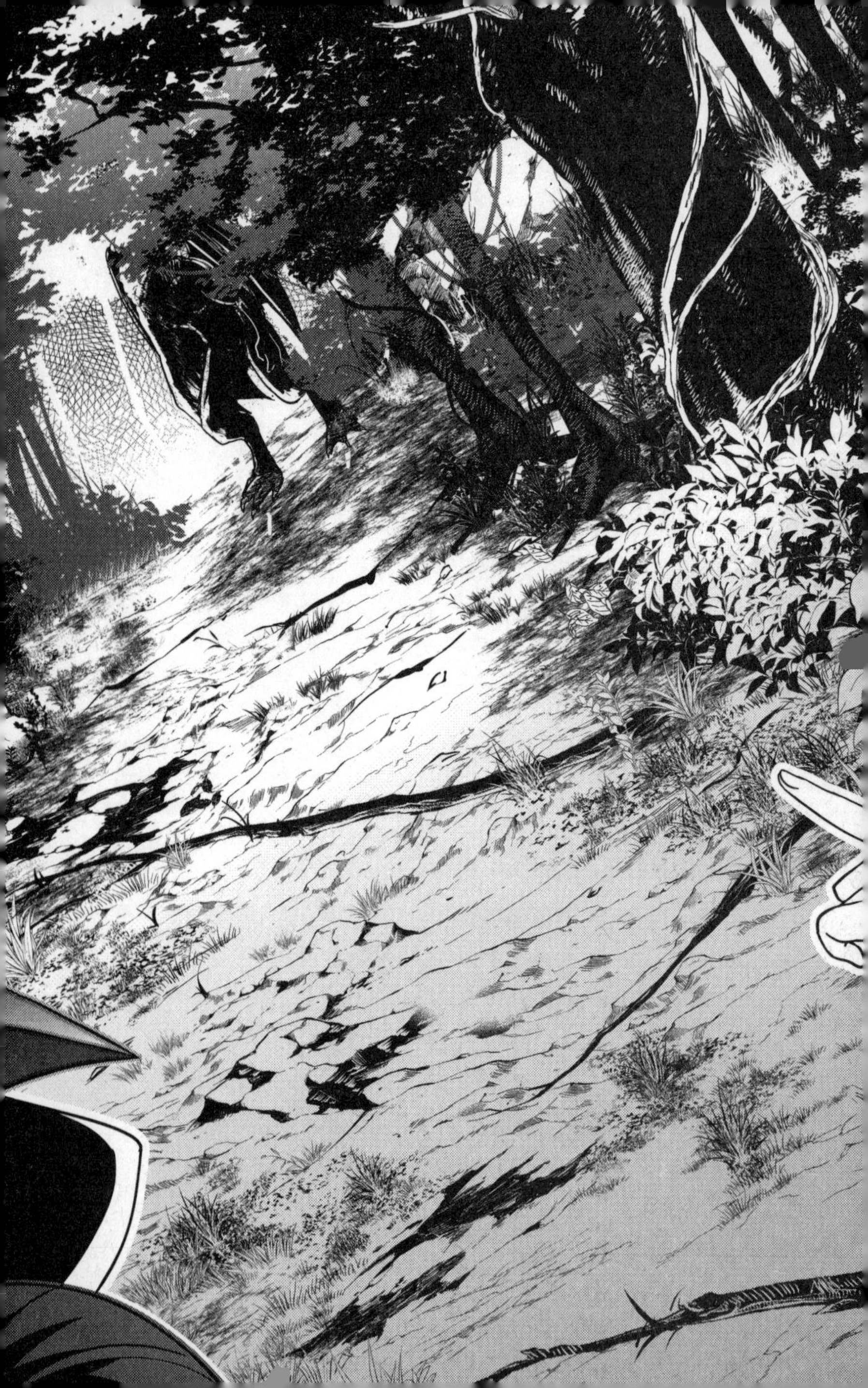

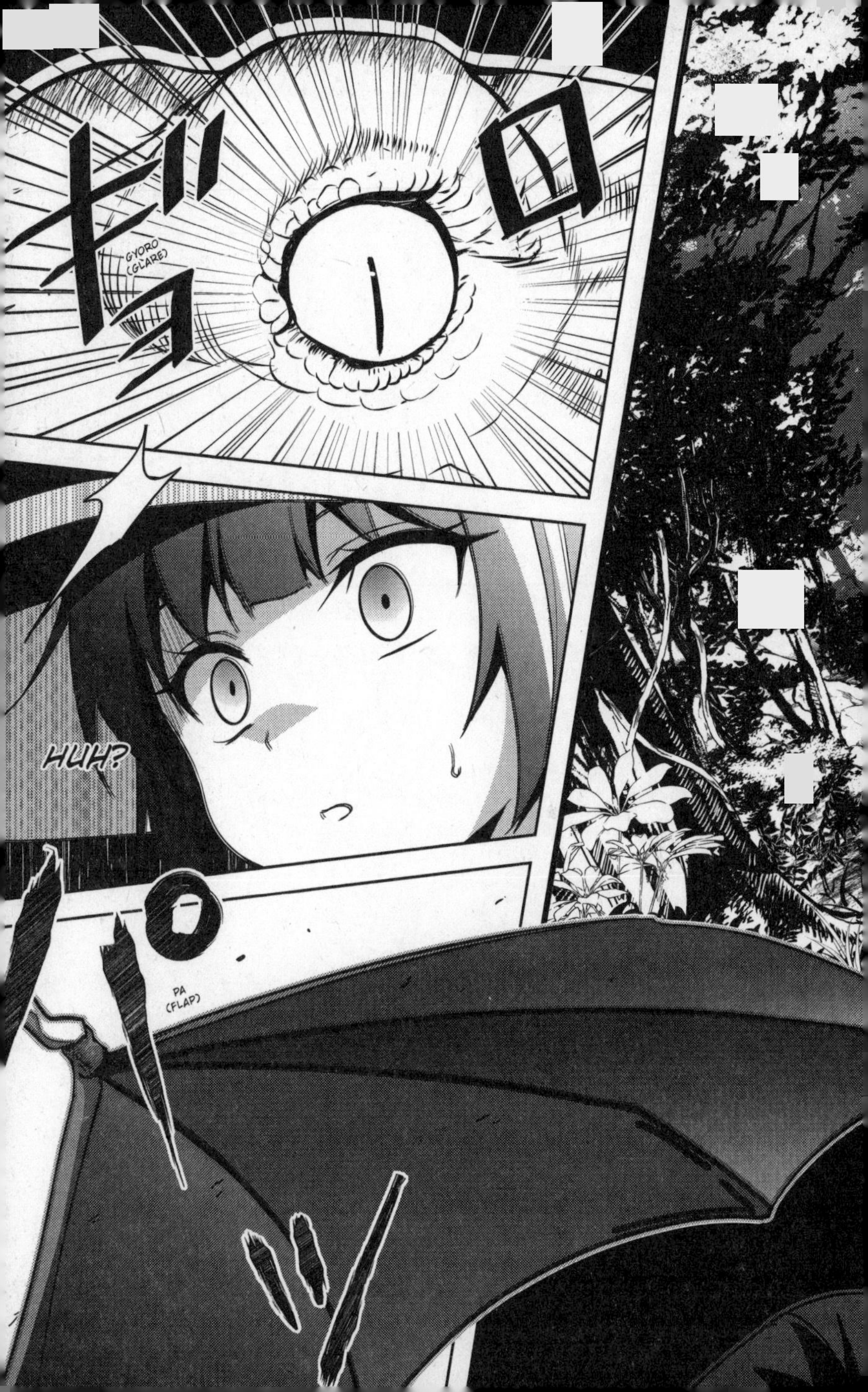
GYORO
(GLARE)
HUH?
PA
(FLAP)

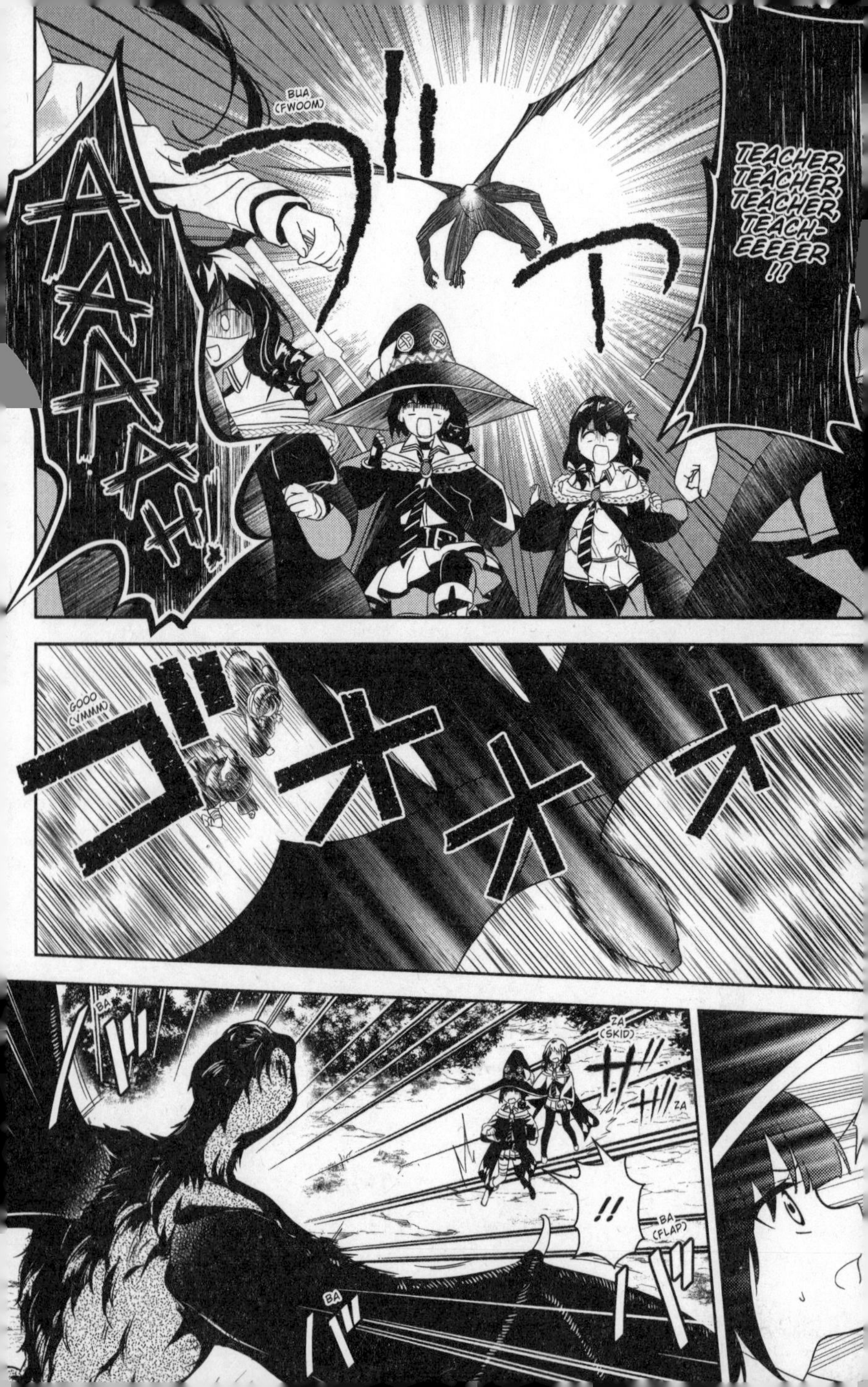
TEACHER, TEACHER, TEACHER, TEACH-EEEEER!!
BUA (FWOOM)
AAAAH!
GOOO (VMMM)
ZA (SKID)
ZA
!!
BA (FLAP)
BA
BA

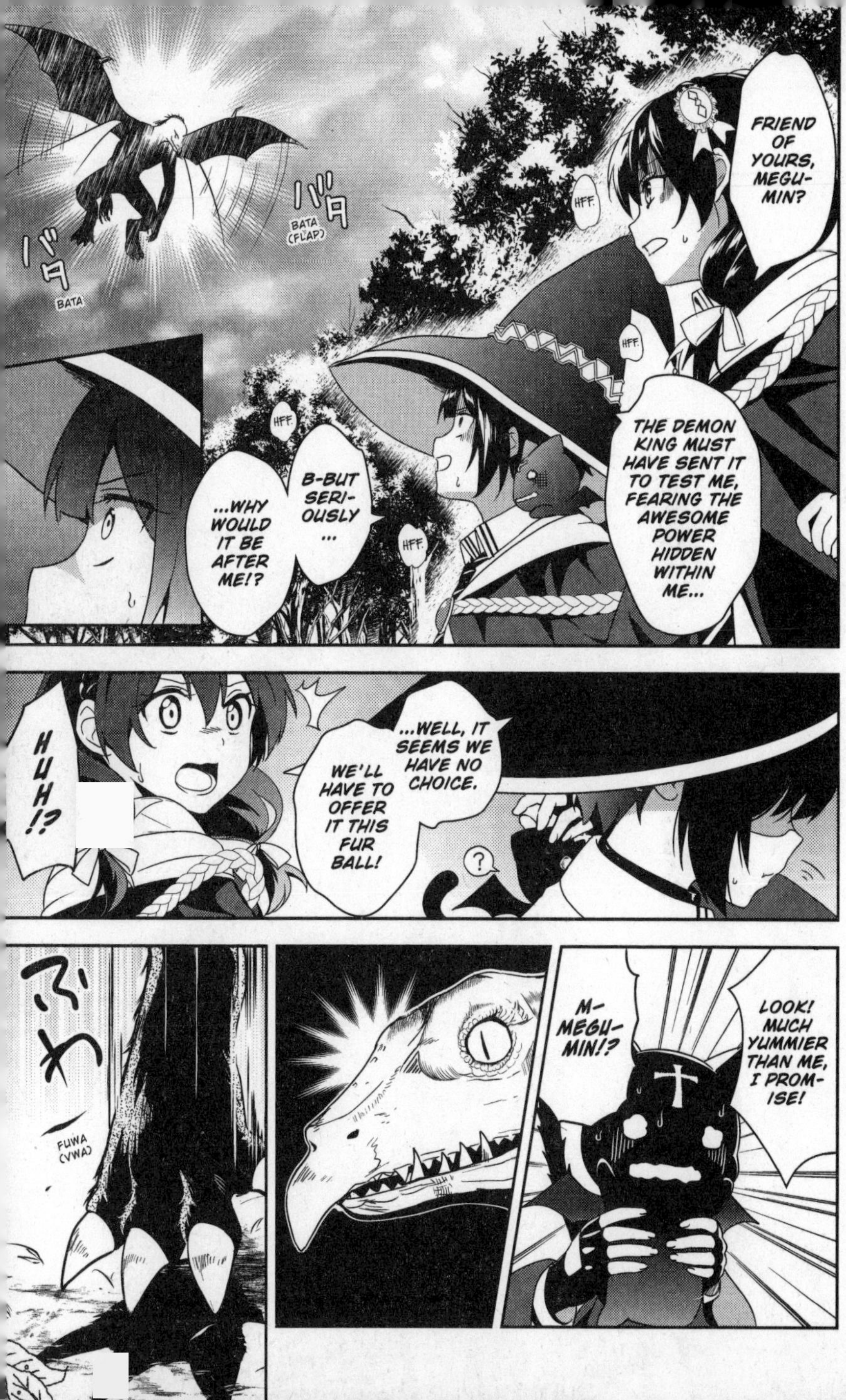
FRIEND OF YOURS, MEGUMIN?
HFF.
バタ
BATA (FLAP)
バタ
BATA
HFF.
THE DEMON KING MUST HAVE SENT IT TO TEST ME, FEARING THE AWESOME POWER HIDDEN WITHIN ME...
HFF.
B-BUT SERIOUSLY...
HFF.
...WHY WOULD IT BE AFTER ME!?
...WELL, IT SEEMS WE HAVE NO CHOICE.
WE'LL HAVE TO OFFER IT THIS FUR BALL!
?
HUH!?
LOOK! MUCH YUMMIER THAN ME, I PROMISE!
M-MEGUMIN!?
ふわ
FUWA (VWA)

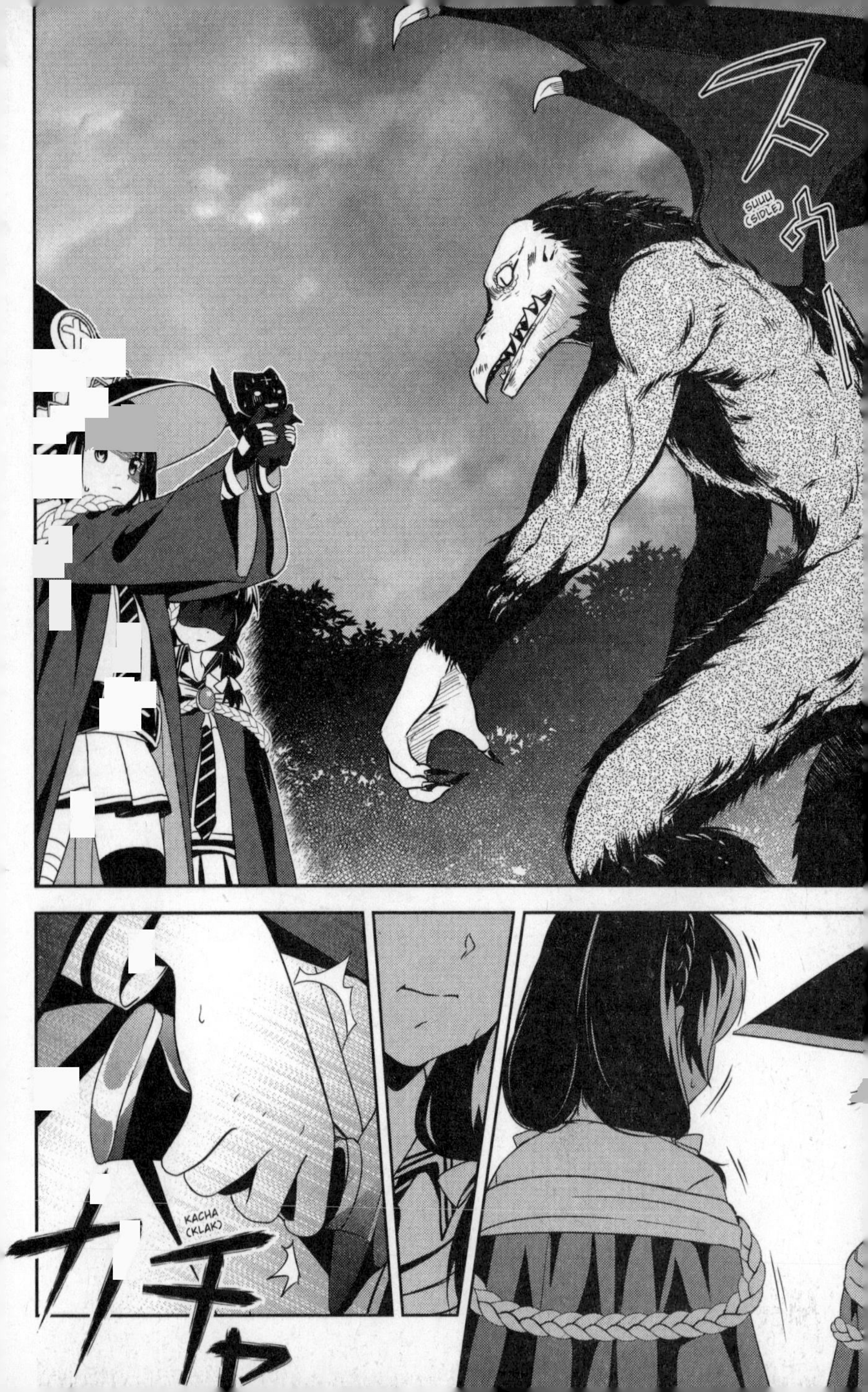

SUUU (SIDLE)
KACHA (KLAK)

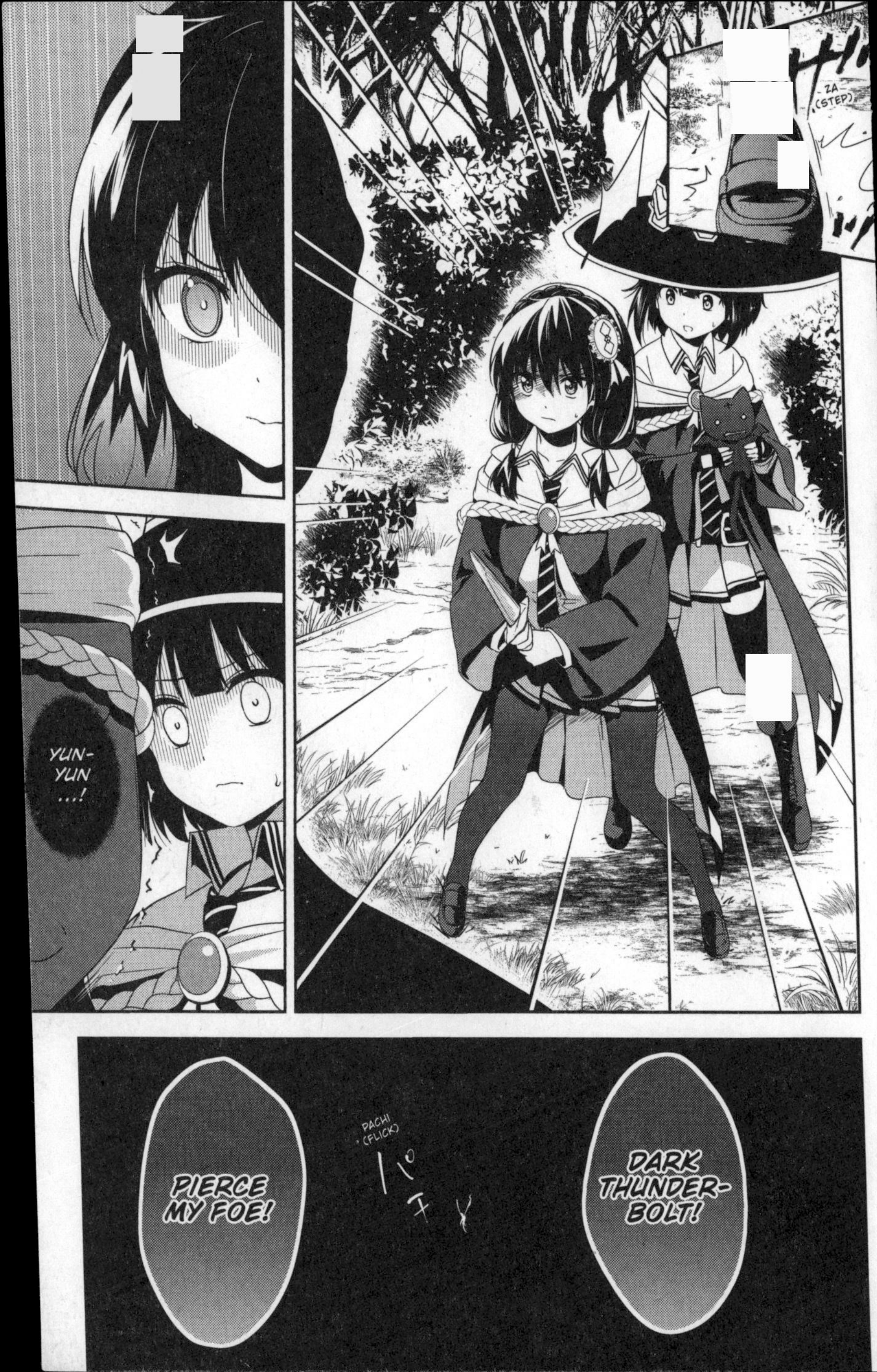
ZA (STEP)
YUN-YUN ...!
DARK THUNDER-BOLT!
PACHI (FLICK)
PIERCE MY FOE!

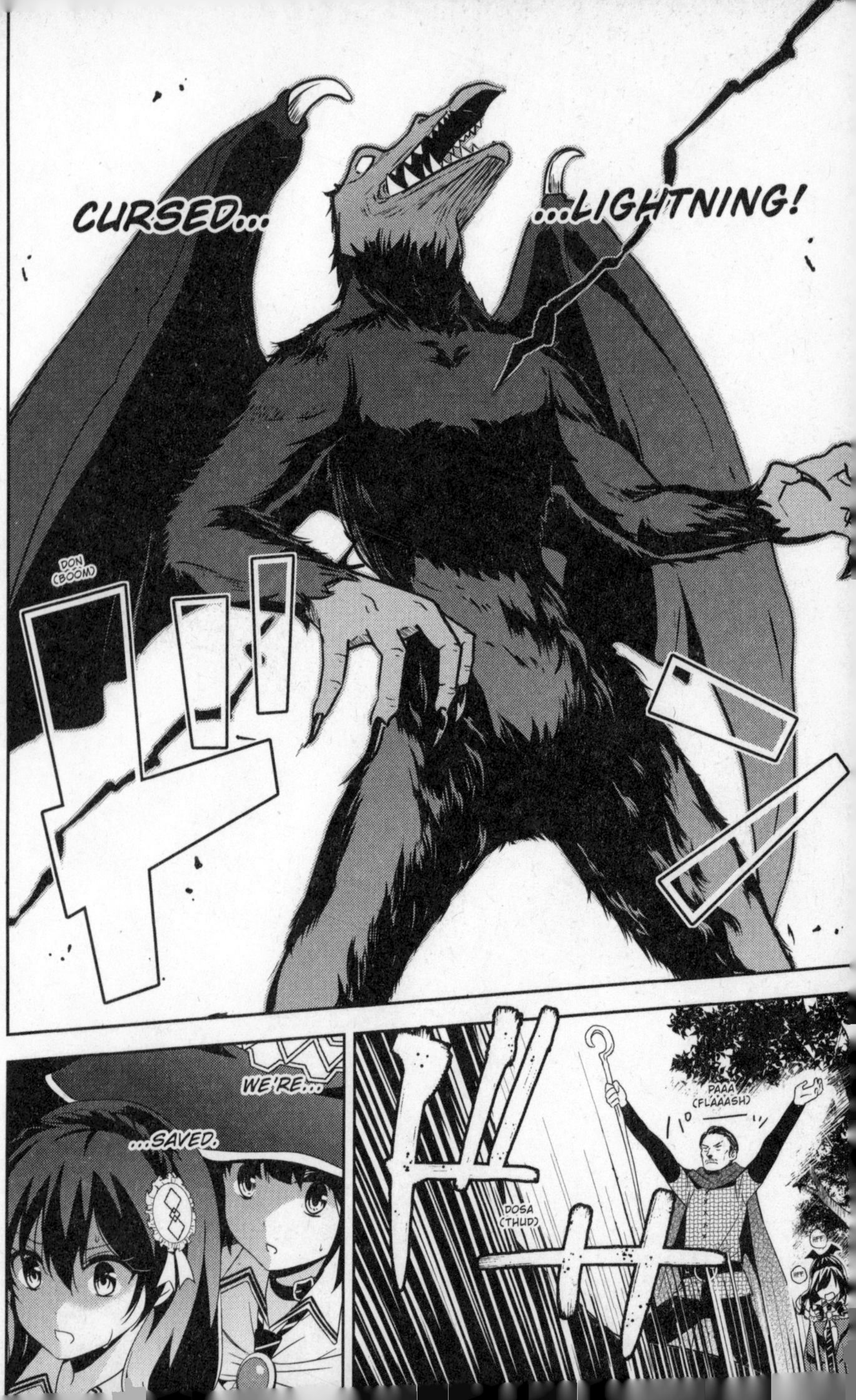
CURSED...
...LIGHTNING!
DON (BOOM)
PAAA (FLAAASH)
DOSA (THUD)
HFF
HFF
WE'RE...
...SAVED.

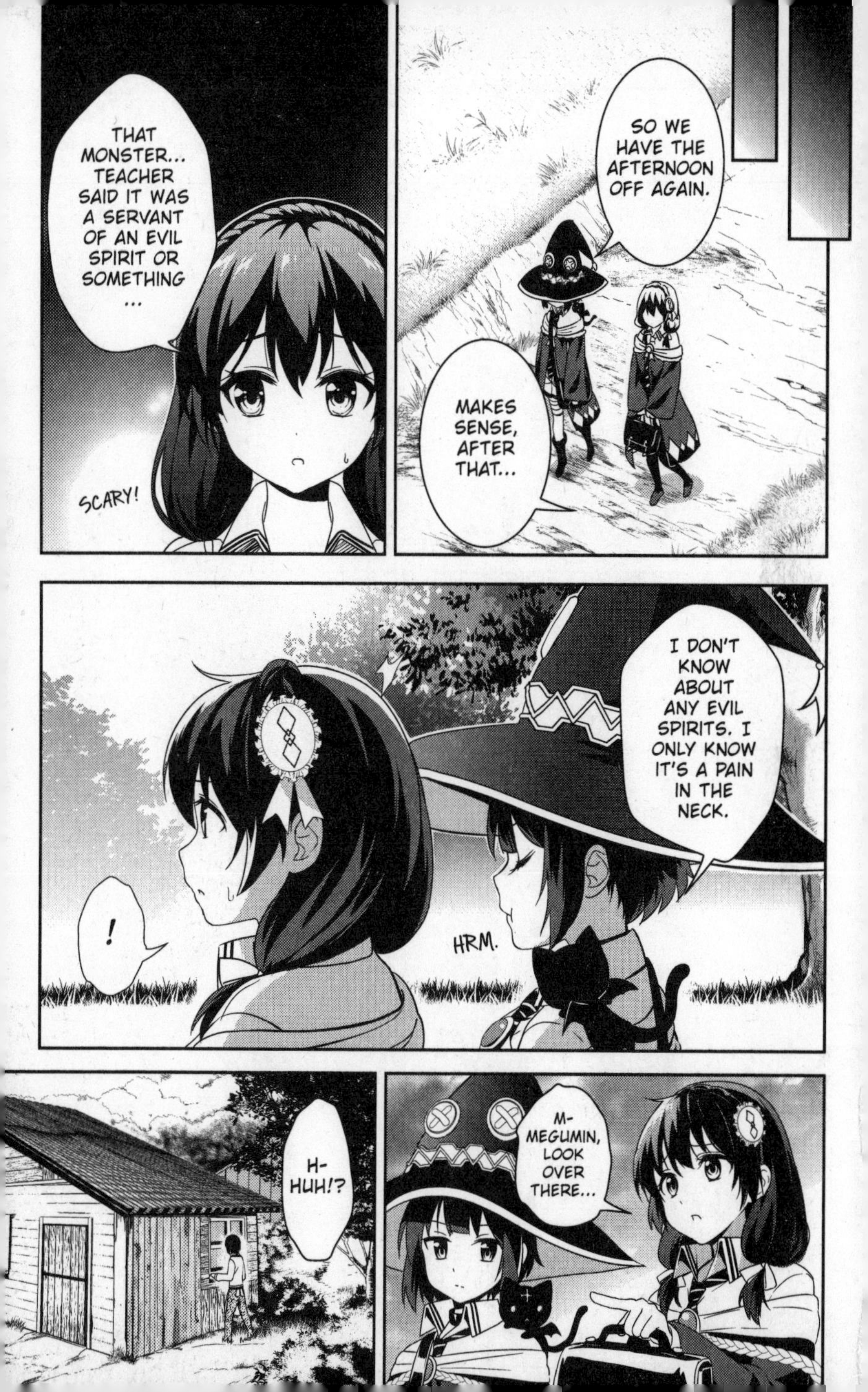
SO WE HAVE THE AFTERNOON OFF AGAIN.
MAKES SENSE, AFTER THAT...
THAT MONSTER... TEACHER SAID IT WAS A SERVANT OF AN EVIL SPIRIT OR SOMETHING...
SCARY!
I DON'T KNOW ABOUT ANY EVIL SPIRITS. I ONLY KNOW IT'S A PAIN IN THE NECK.
HRM.
!
M-MEGUMIN, LOOK OVER THERE...
H-HUH!?

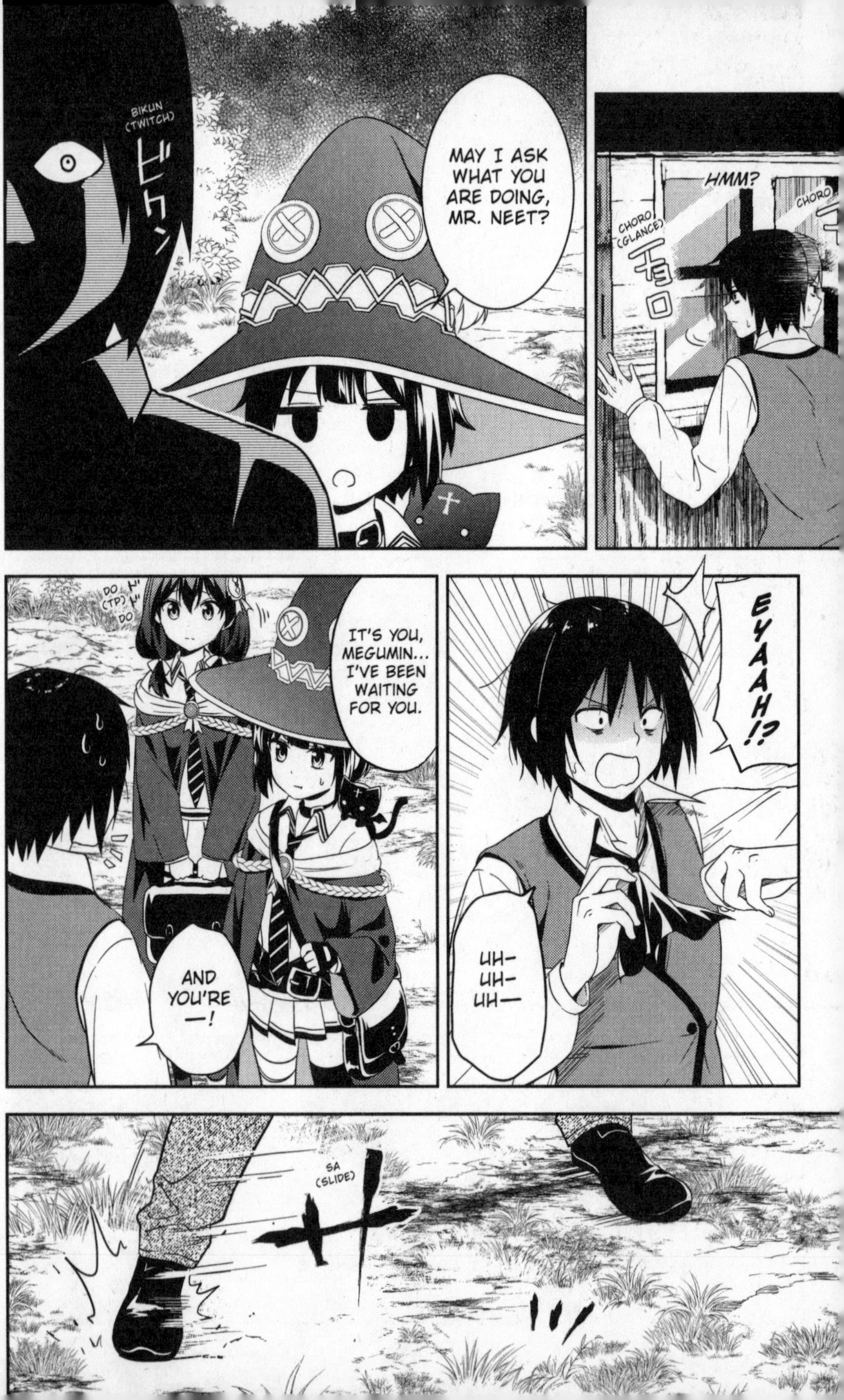
HMM?
CHORO
CHORO (GLANCE)
チョロ
BIKUN (TWITCH)
ビクン
MAY I ASK WHAT YOU ARE DOING, MR. NEET?
EYAAAH!?
UH- UH- UH—
IT'S YOU, MEGUMIN... I'VE BEEN WAITING FOR YOU.
DO (TP) DO
AND YOU'RE —!
SA (SLIDE)

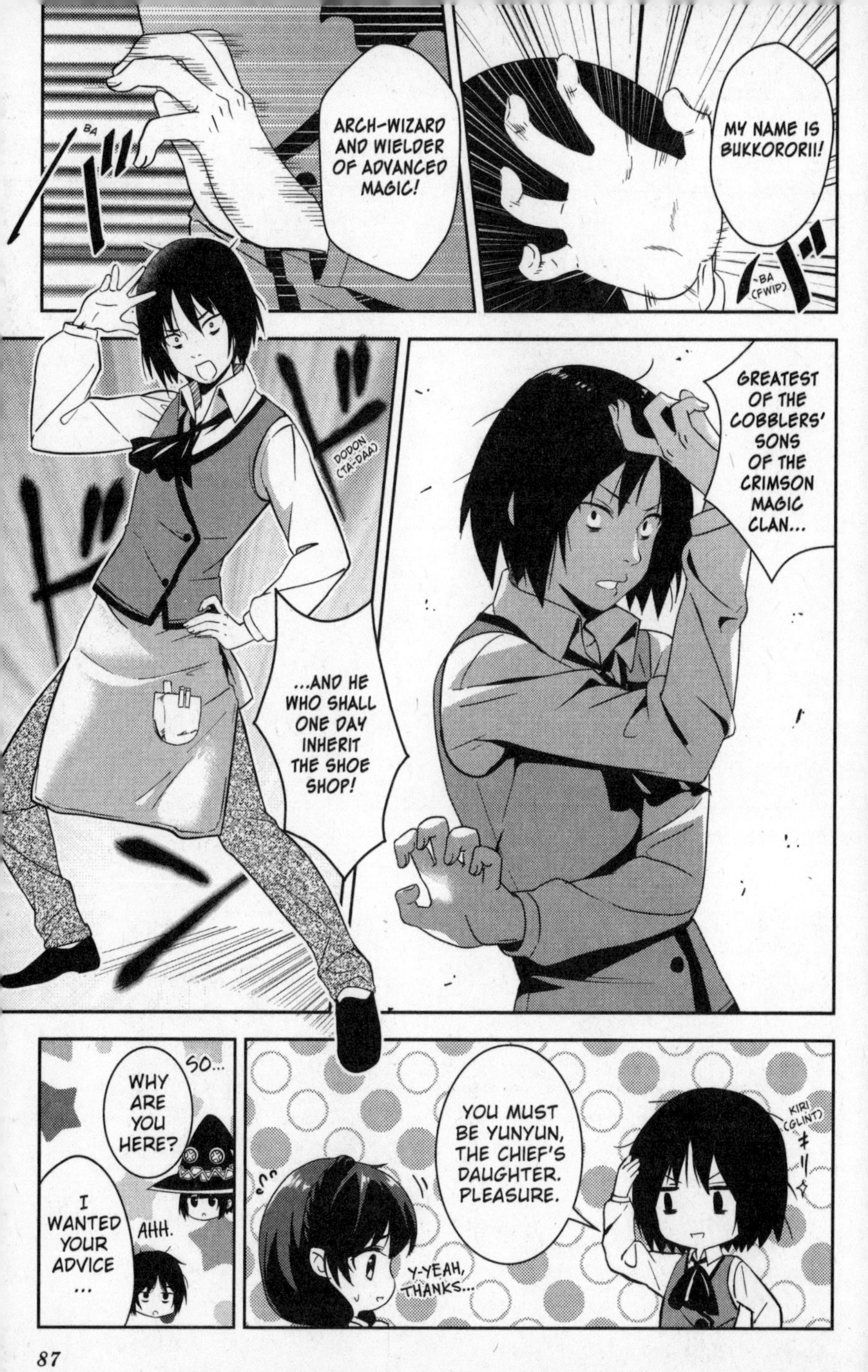
MY NAME IS BUKKORORII!
BA (FWIP)
ARCH-WIZARD AND WIELDER OF ADVANCED MAGIC!
BA
GREATEST OF THE COBBLERS' SONS OF THE CRIMSON MAGIC CLAN...
...AND HE WHO SHALL ONE DAY INHERIT THE SHOE SHOP!
DODON (TA-DAA)
KIRI (GLINT)
YOU MUST BE YUNYUN, THE CHIEF'S DAUGHTER. PLEASURE.
Y-YEAH, THANKS...
SO...
WHY ARE YOU HERE?
I WANTED YOUR ADVICE ...
AHH.

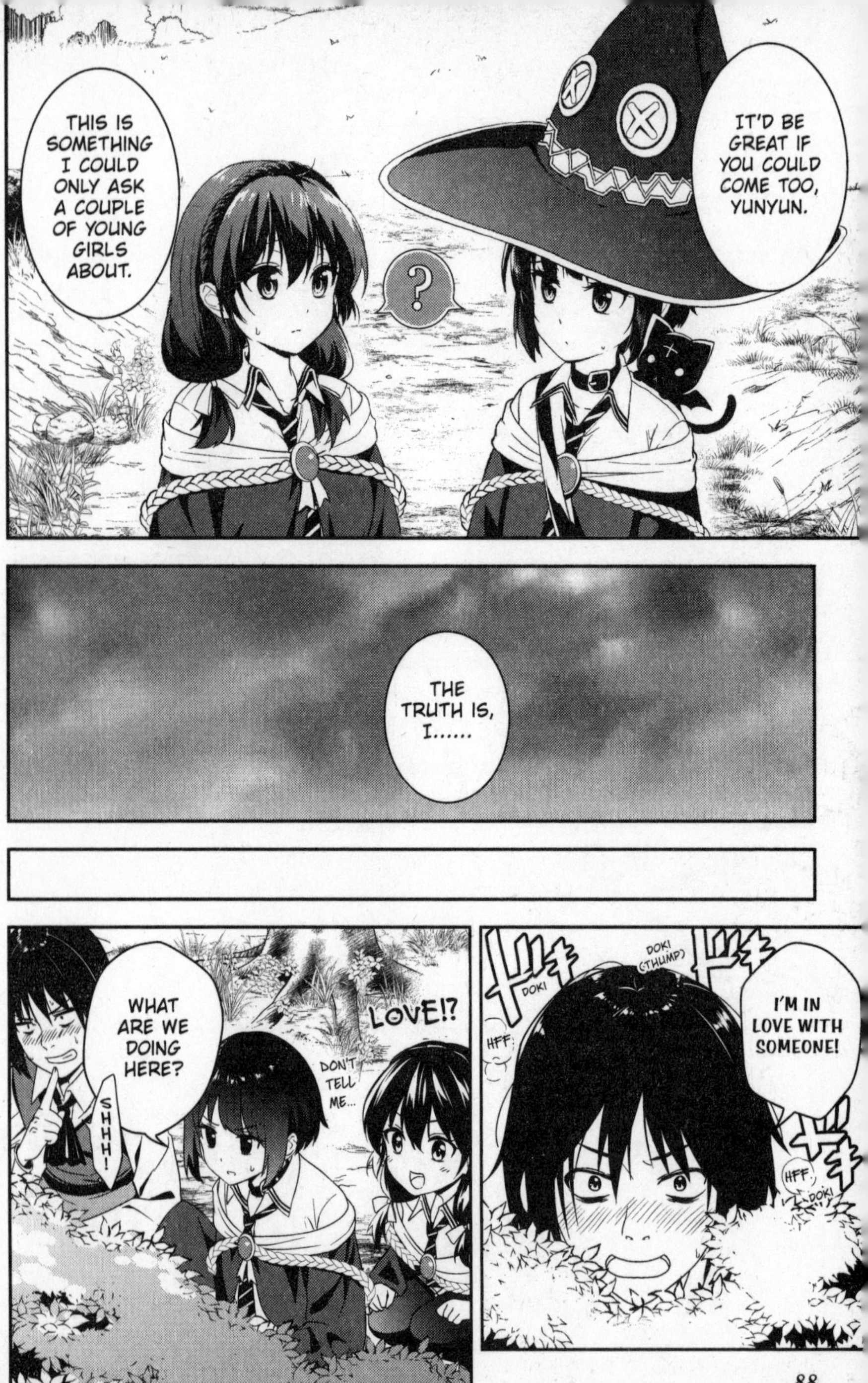
IT'D BE GREAT IF YOU COULD COME TOO, YUNYUN.
?
THIS IS SOMETHING I COULD ONLY ASK A COUPLE OF YOUNG GIRLS ABOUT.
THE TRUTH IS, I......
DOKI (THUMP)
DOKI
HFF
I'M IN LOVE WITH SOMEONE!
HFF
DOKI
LOVE!?
DON'T TELL ME...
WHAT ARE WE DOING HERE?
SHHH!

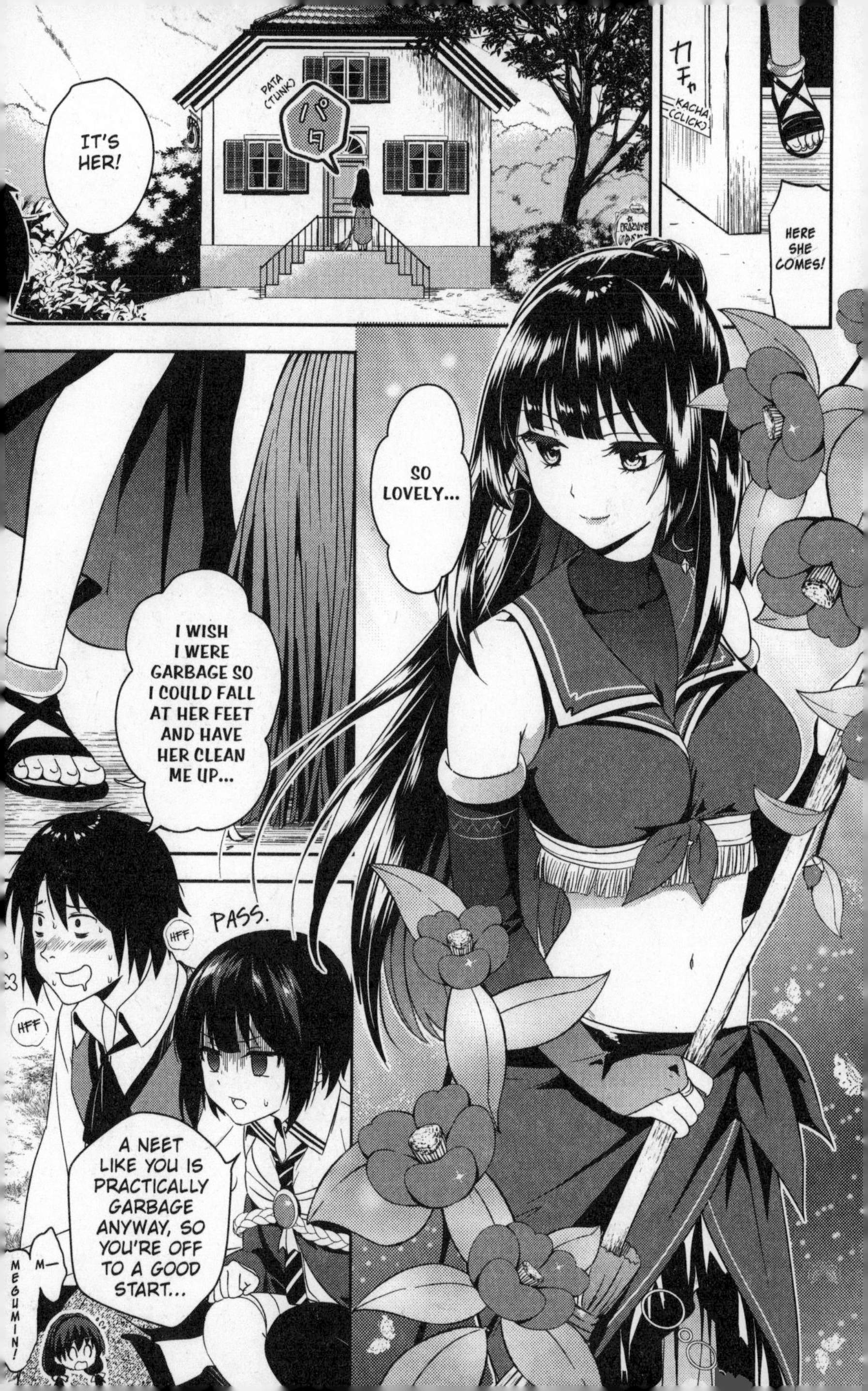
カチャ
KACHA (CLICK)
HERE SHE COMES!
パタ
PATA (TUNK)
IT'S HER!
SO LOVELY...
I WISH I WERE GARBAGE SO I COULD FALL AT HER FEET AND HAVE HER CLEAN ME UP...
PASS.
HFF
HFF
A NEET LIKE YOU IS PRACTICALLY GARBAGE ANYWAY, SO YOU'RE OFF TO A GOOD START...
M—
MEGUMIN!

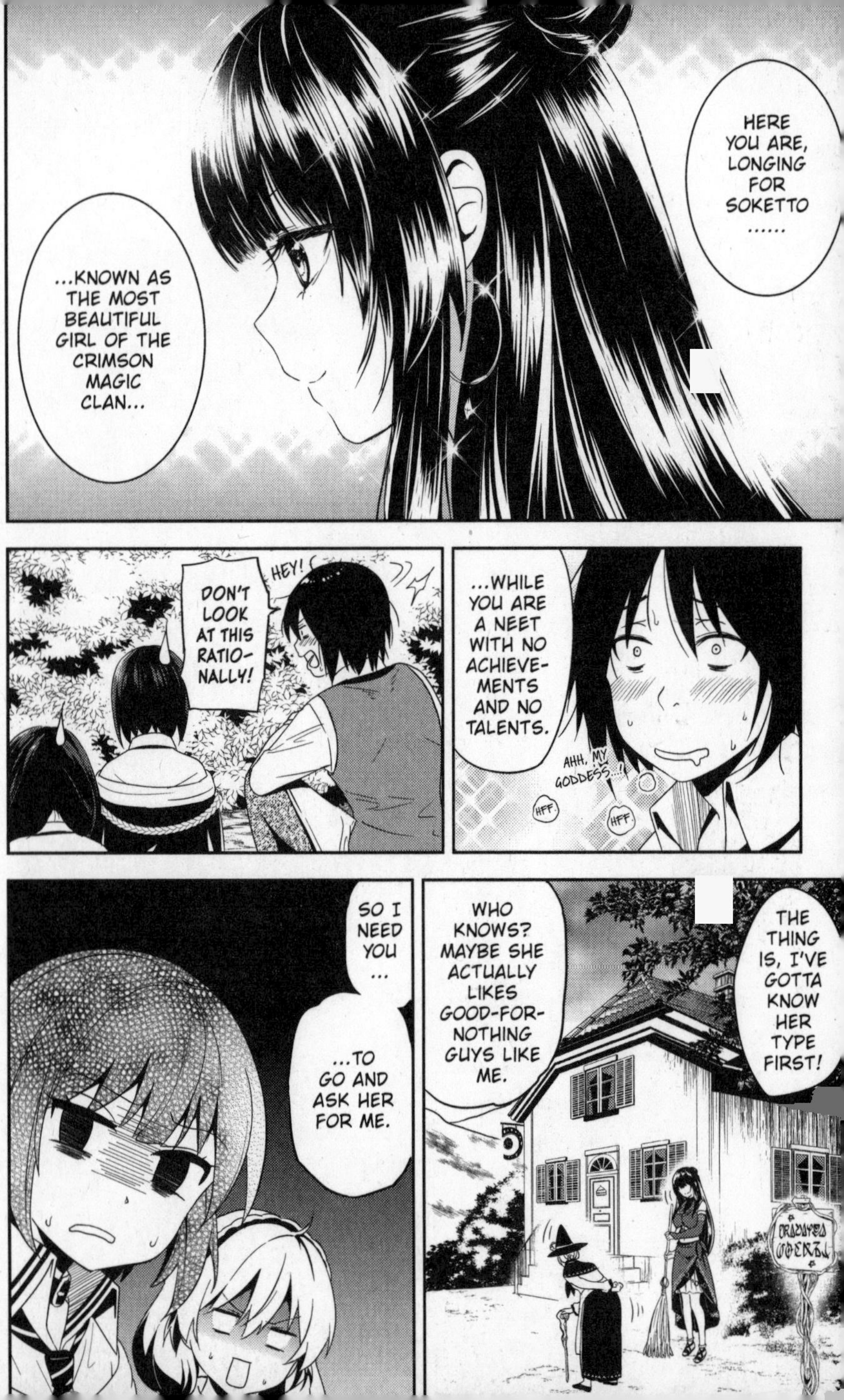
HERE YOU ARE, LONGING FOR SOKETTO......
...KNOWN AS THE MOST BEAUTIFUL GIRL OF THE CRIMSON MAGIC CLAN...
...WHILE YOU ARE A NEET WITH NO ACHIEVEMENTS AND NO TALENTS.
AHH, MY GODDESS...!
HFF
HFF
HEY!
DON'T LOOK AT THIS RATIONALLY!
THE THING IS, I'VE GOTTA KNOW HER TYPE FIRST!
WHO KNOWS? MAYBE SHE ACTUALLY LIKES GOOD-FOR-NOTHING GUYS LIKE ME.
SO I NEED YOU...
...TO GO AND ASK HER FOR ME.

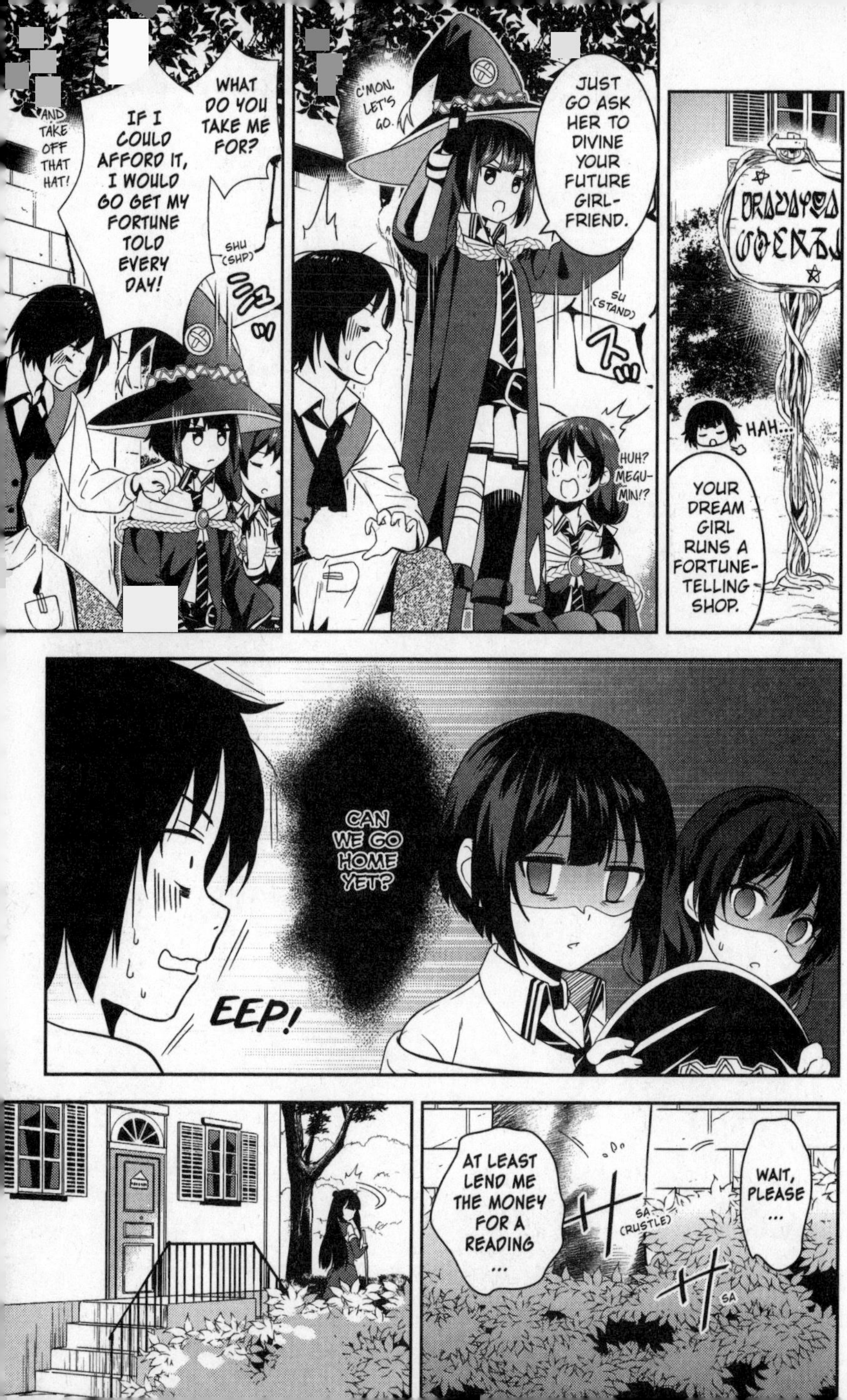
HAH...
YOUR DREAM GIRL RUNS A FORTUNE-TELLING SHOP.
JUST GO ASK HER TO DIVINE YOUR FUTURE GIRL-FRIEND.
C'MON, LET'S GO.
SU (STAND)
HUH? MEGU-MIN!?
WHAT DO YOU TAKE ME FOR?
IF I COULD AFFORD IT, I WOULD GO GET MY FORTUNE TOLD EVERY DAY!
SHU (SHP)
AND TAKE OFF THAT HAT!
CAN WE GO HOME YET?
EEP!
WAIT, PLEASE ...
SA (RUSTLE)
SA
AT LEAST LEND ME THE MONEY FOR A READING ...

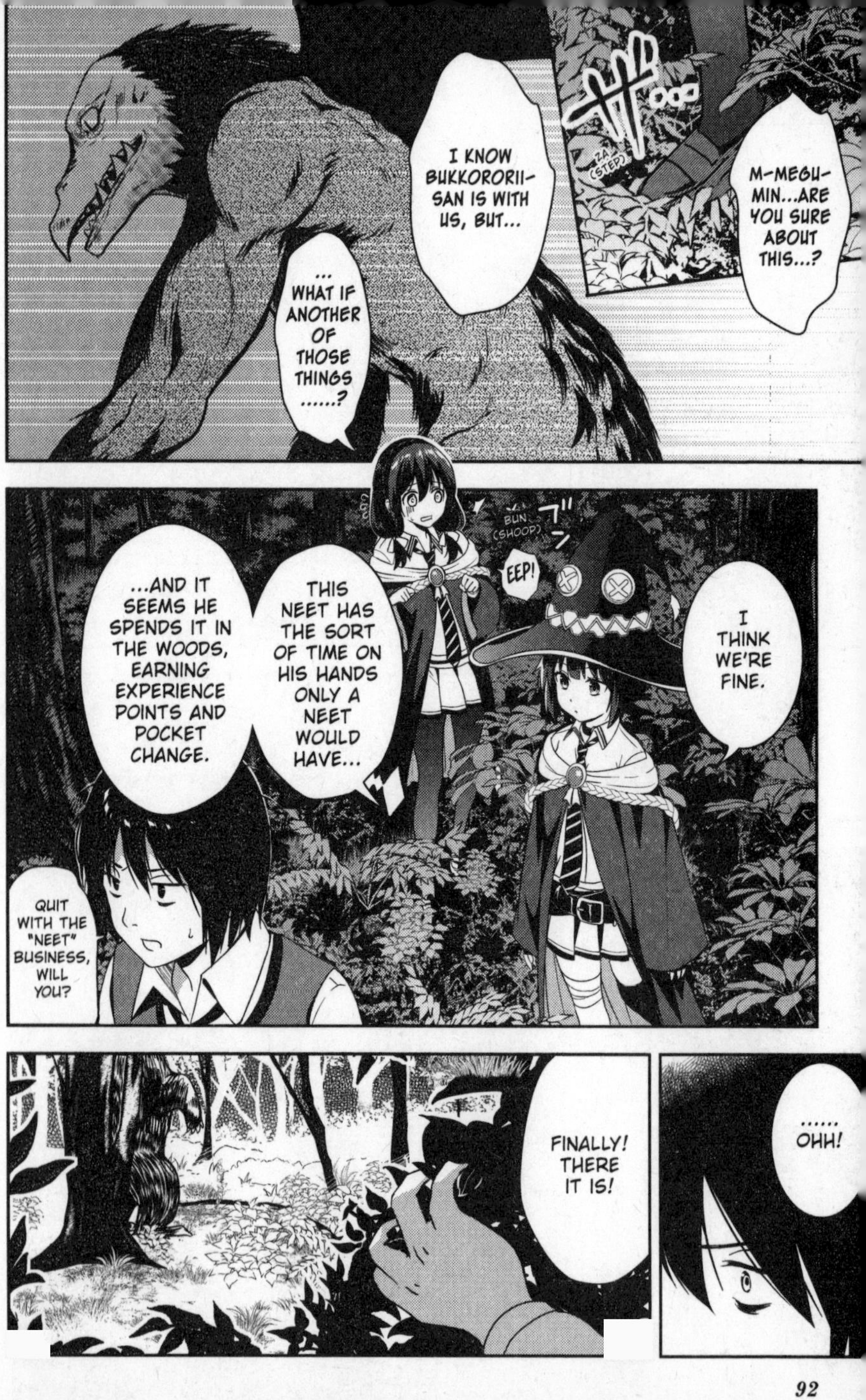
ZA (STEP)
M-MEGUMIN...ARE YOU SURE ABOUT THIS...?
I KNOW BUKKORORII-SAN IS WITH US, BUT...
...WHAT IF ANOTHER OF THOSE THINGS ......?
BUN (SHOOP)
EEP!
I THINK WE'RE FINE.
THIS NEET HAS THE SORT OF TIME ON HIS HANDS ONLY A NEET WOULD HAVE...
...AND IT SEEMS HE SPENDS IT IN THE WOODS, EARNING EXPERIENCE POINTS AND POCKET CHANGE.
QUIT WITH THE "NEET" BUSINESS, WILL YOU?
......OHH!
FINALLY! THERE IT IS!

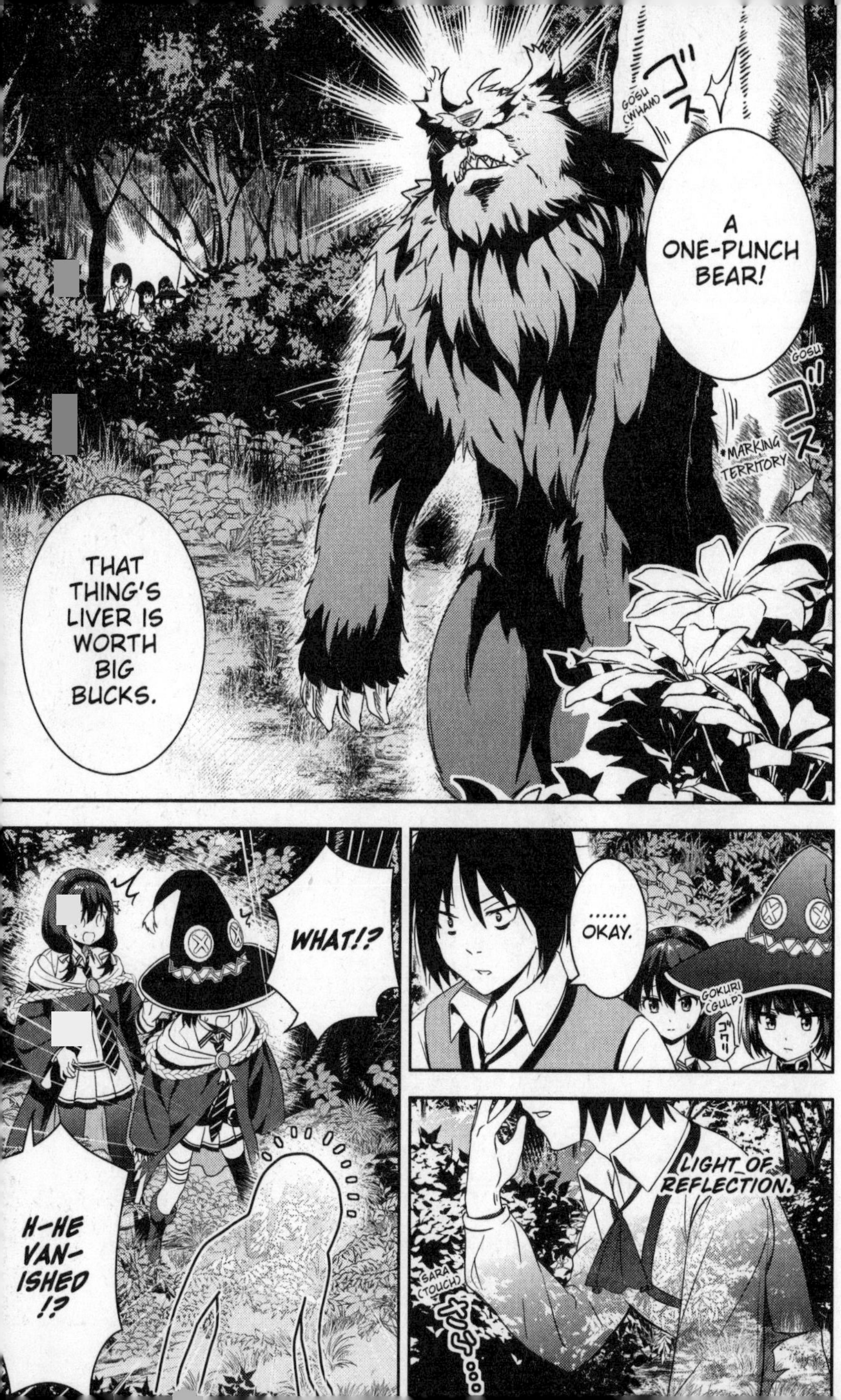

GOSU (WHAM)
ゴス
A ONE-PUNCH BEAR!
GOSU
ゴス
*MARKING TERRITORY
THAT THING'S LIVER IS WORTH BIG BUCKS.
...... OKAY.
GOKURI (GULP)
ゴクリ
LIGHT OF REFLECTION.
SARA (TOUCH)
サラ...
WHAT!?
H-HE VAN-ISHED!?

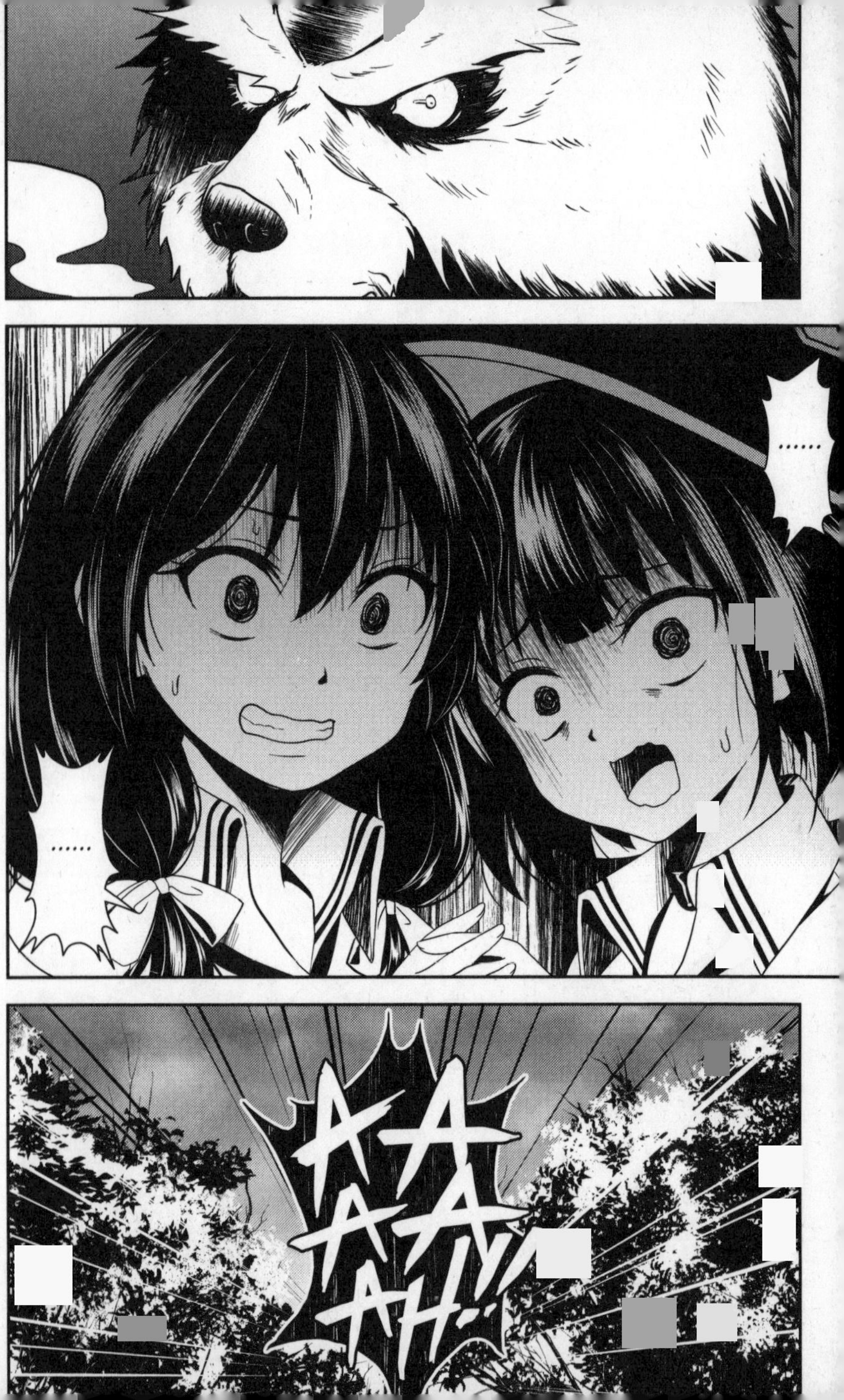
......
......
AAAAAH!!

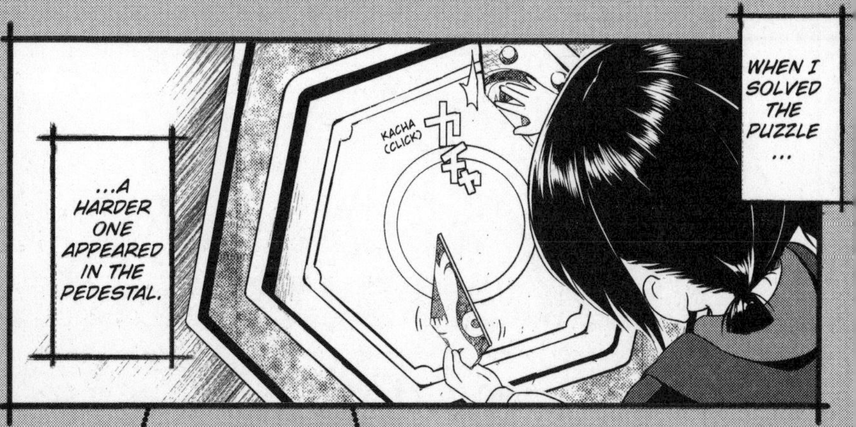
WHEN I SOLVED THE PUZZLE ...
KACHA (CLICK)
カチャ
...A HARDER ONE APPEARED IN THE PEDESTAL.

KOMEKKO'S STORY 2 INTERLUDE THEATRE

KOMEKKO-SAN AND HOST-SAMA

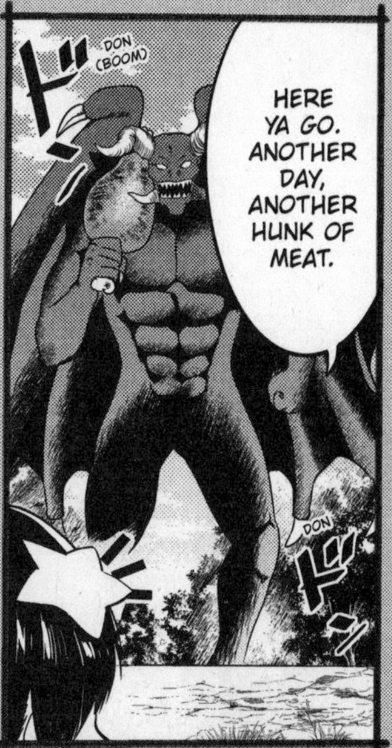
DON (BOOM)
ド
HERE YA GO. ANOTHER DAY, ANOTHER HUNK OF MEAT.
DON
ドンッ

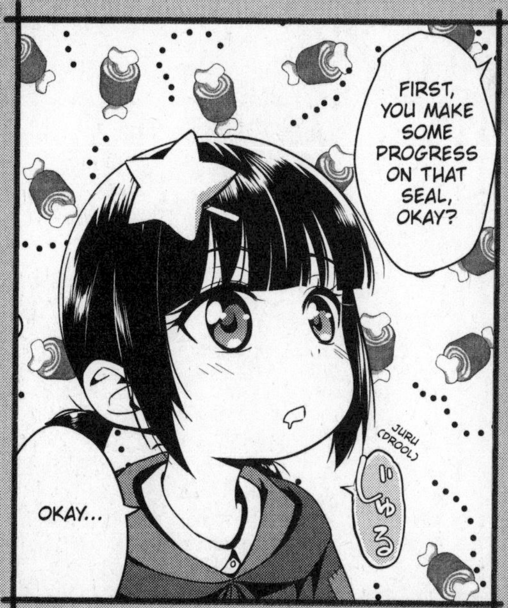
FIRST, YOU MAKE SOME PROGRESS ON THAT SEAL, OKAY?
JURU (DROOL)
じゅる
OKAY...

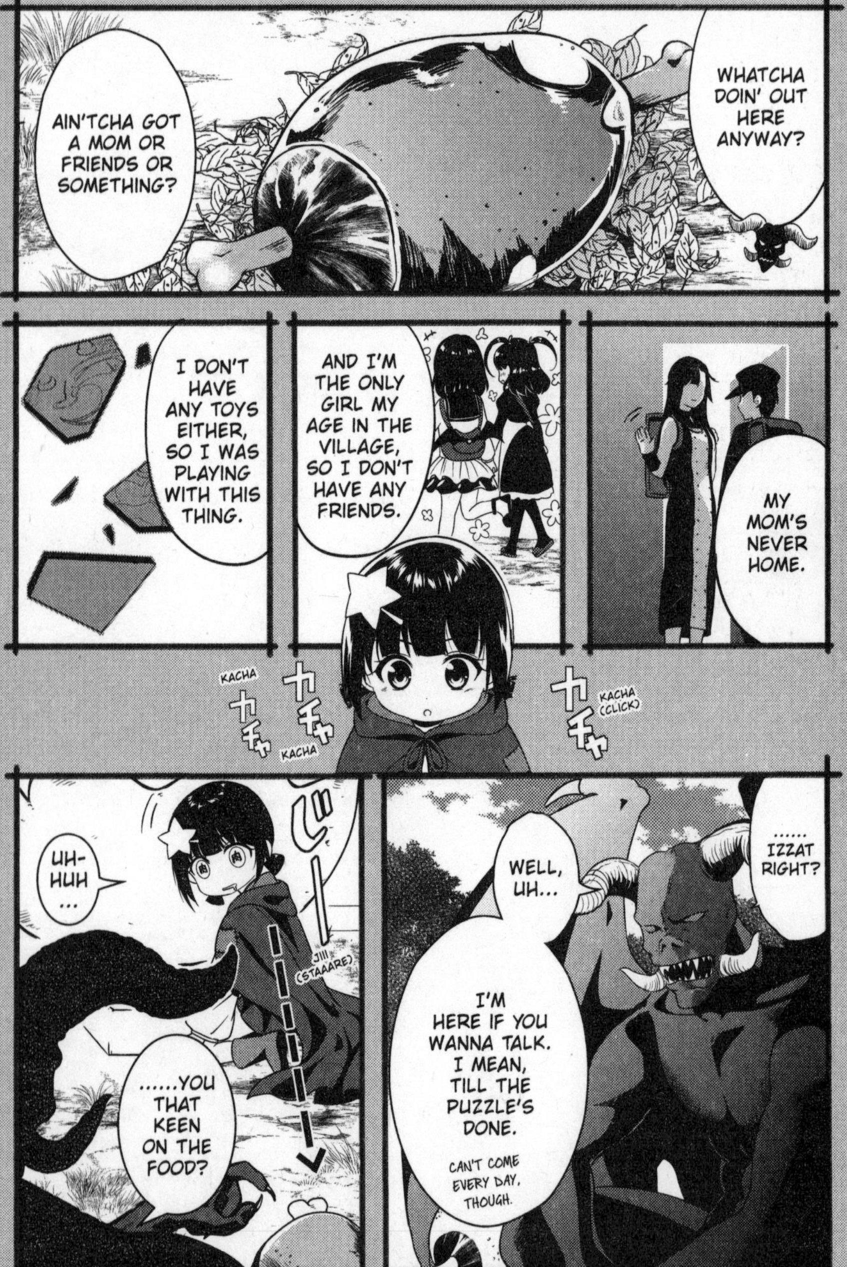
WHATCHA DOIN' OUT HERE ANYWAY?
AIN'TCHA GOT A MOM OR FRIENDS OR SOMETHING?
MY MOM'S NEVER HOME.
AND I'M THE ONLY GIRL MY AGE IN THE VILLAGE, SO I DON'T HAVE ANY FRIENDS.
I DON'T HAVE ANY TOYS EITHER, SO I WAS PLAYING WITH THIS THING.
カチャ KACHA (CLICK)
カチャ KACHA
カチャ KACHA
...... IZZAT RIGHT?
WELL, UH...
I'M HERE IF YOU WANNA TALK. I MEAN, TILL THE PUZZLE'S DONE.
CAN'T COME EVERY DAY, THOUGH.
UH-HUH...
じーー JIII (STAAARE)
......YOU THAT KEEN ON THE FOOD?

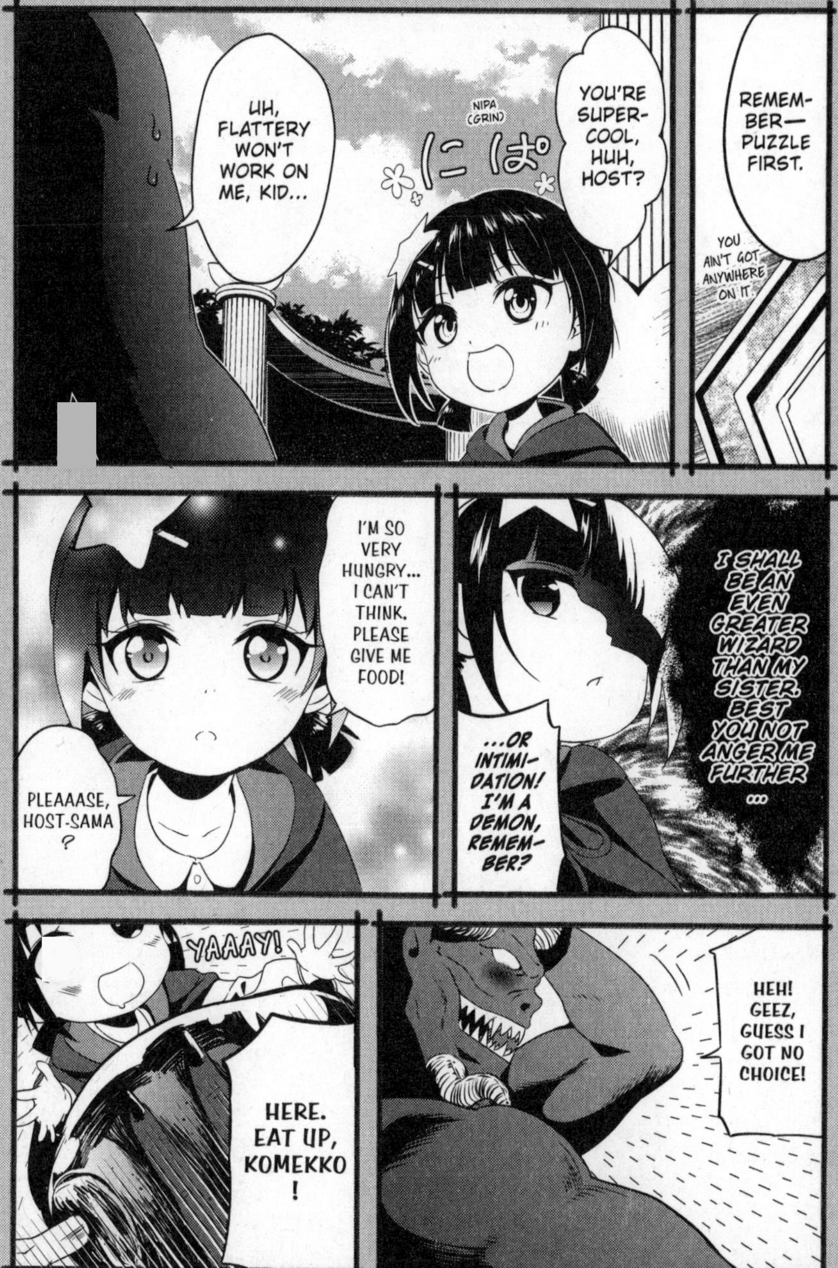
REMEMBER—PUZZLE FIRST.
YOU AIN'T GOT ANYWHERE ON IT.
YOU'RE SUPER-COOL, HUH, HOST?
NIPA (GRIN)
にぱ
UH, FLATTERY WON'T WORK ON ME, KID...
I SHALL BE AN EVEN GREATER WIZARD THAN MY SISTER. BEST YOU NOT ANGER ME FURTHER...
...OR INTIMIDATION! I'M A DEMON, REMEMBER?
I'M SO VERY HUNGRY... I CAN'T THINK. PLEASE GIVE ME FOOD!
PLEAAASE, HOST-SAMA?
HEH! GEEZ, GUESS I GOT NO CHOICE!
YAAAY!
HERE. EAT UP, KOMEKKO!

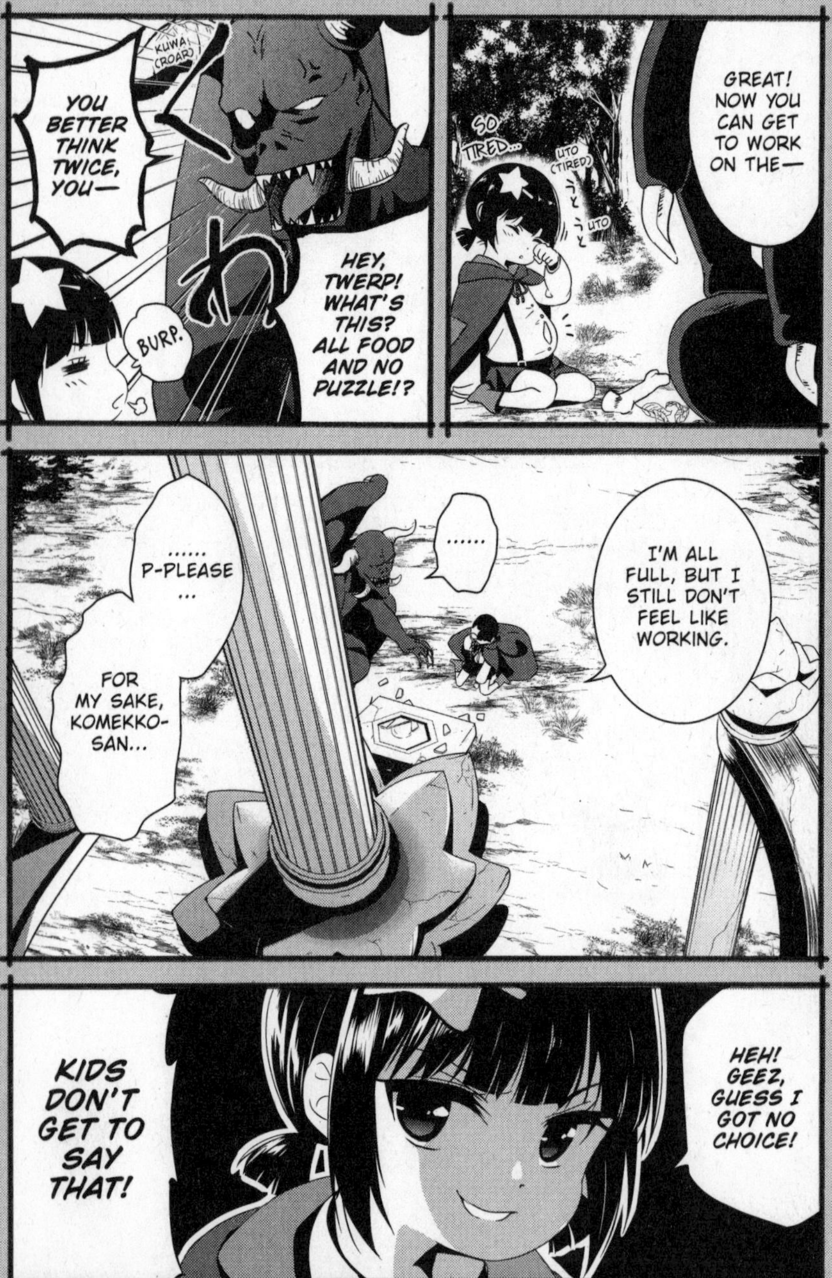
GREAT! NOW YOU CAN GET TO WORK ON THE—
SO TIRED...
UTO (TIRED)
UTO
KUWA (ROAR)
HEY, TWERP! WHAT'S THIS? ALL FOOD AND NO PUZZLE!?
YOU BETTER THINK TWICE, YOU—
BURP.
I'M ALL FULL, BUT I STILL DON'T FEEL LIKE WORKING.
......
...... P-PLEASE ...
FOR MY SAKE, KOMEKKO-SAN...
HEH! GEEZ, GUESS I GOT NO CHOICE!
KIDS DON'T GET TO SAY THAT!

KONOSUBA: AN EXPLOSION ON THIS WONDERFUL WORLD!

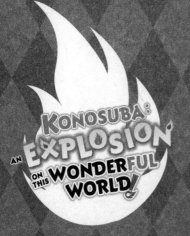

KONOSUBA: AN EXPLOSION ON THIS WONDERFUL WORLD!

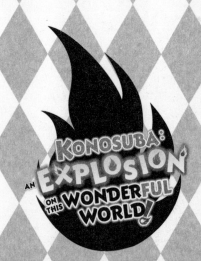

CHAPTER 4

MAY WE CONSULT THIS GENIUS OF THE CRIMSON MAGIC CLAN!

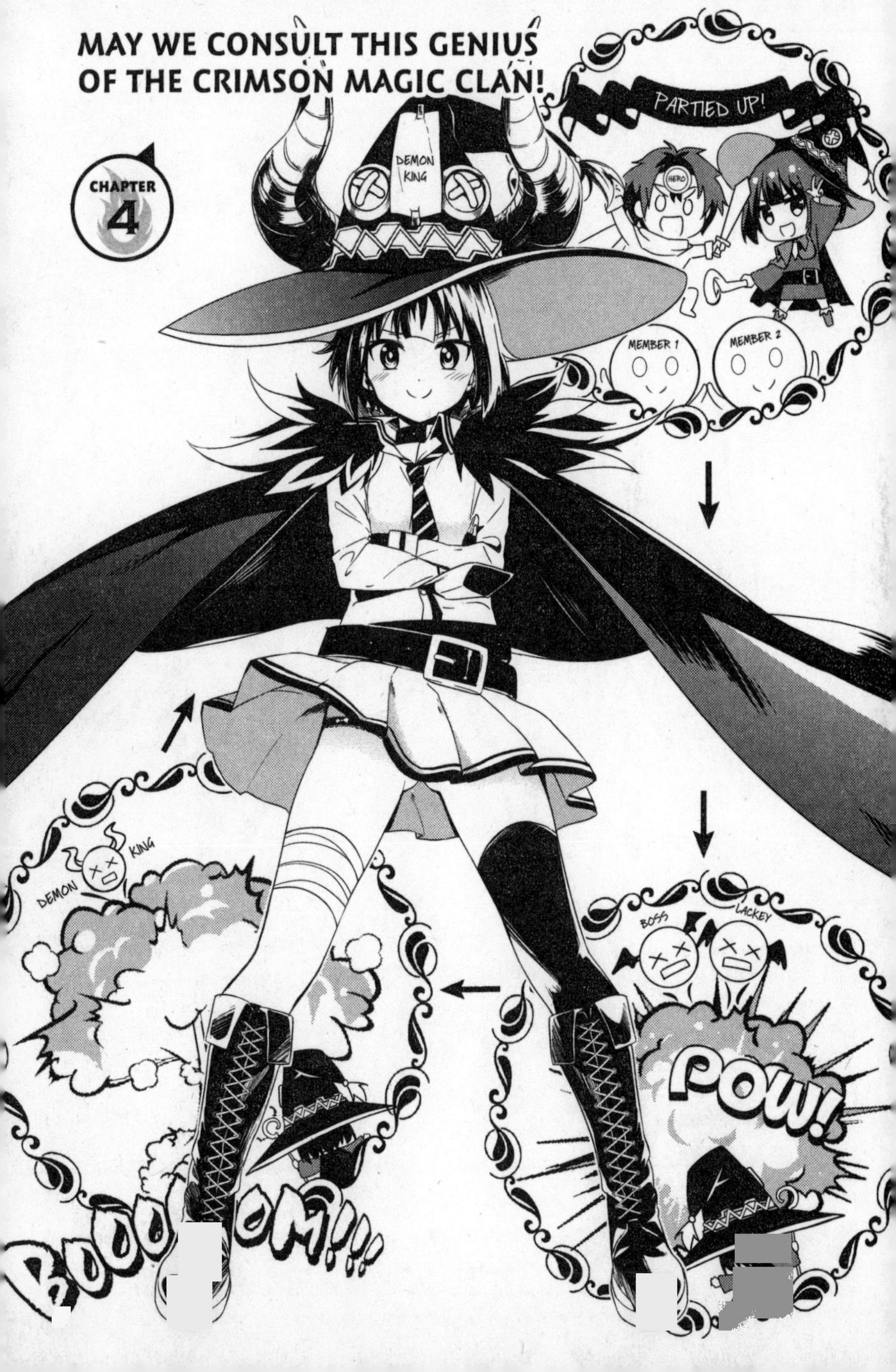
PARTIED UP!
DEMON KING
HERO
MEMBER 1
MEMBER 2
BOSS
LACKEY
POW!
DEMON KING
BOOO OM!!!

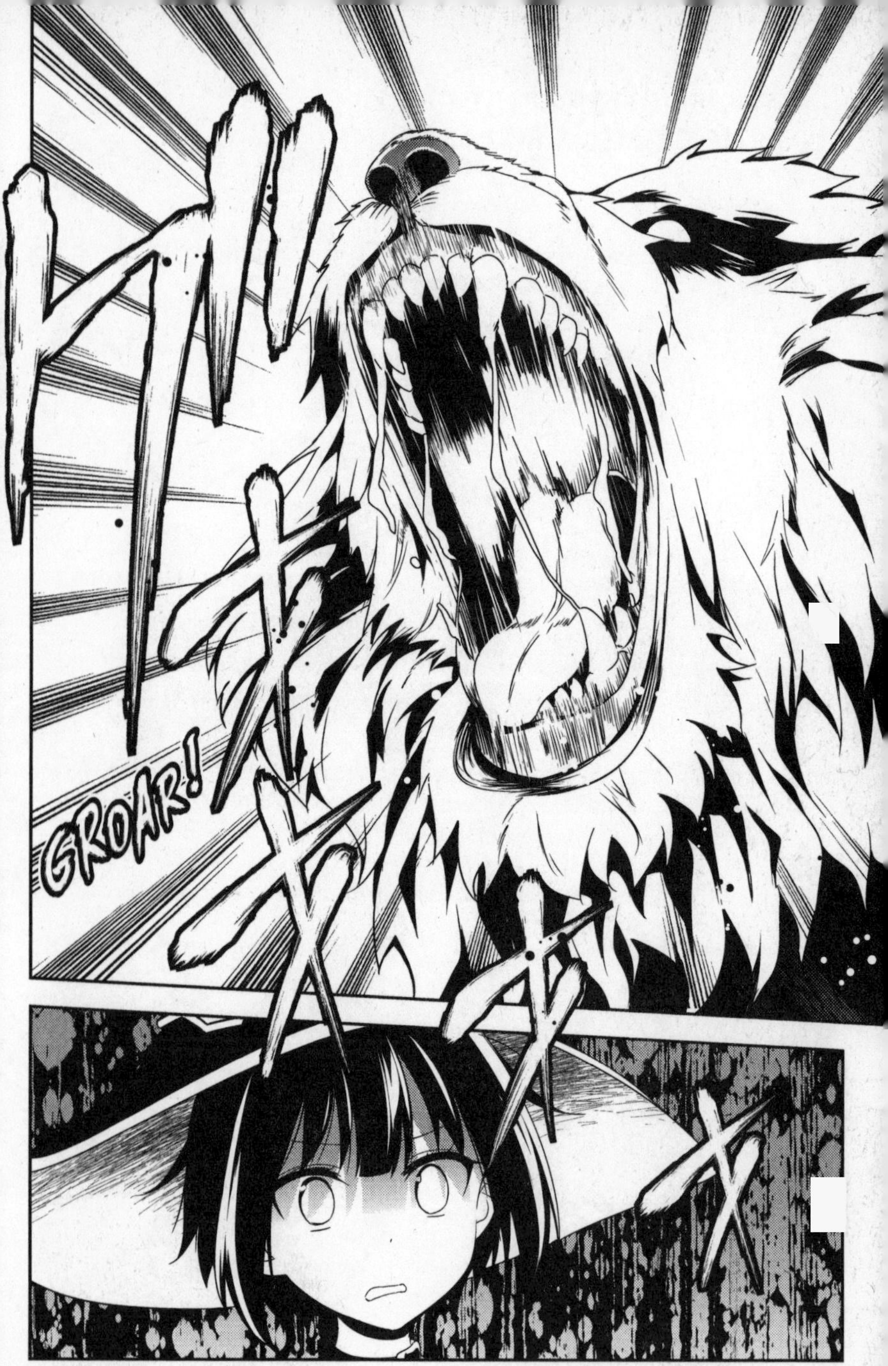
GROAR!

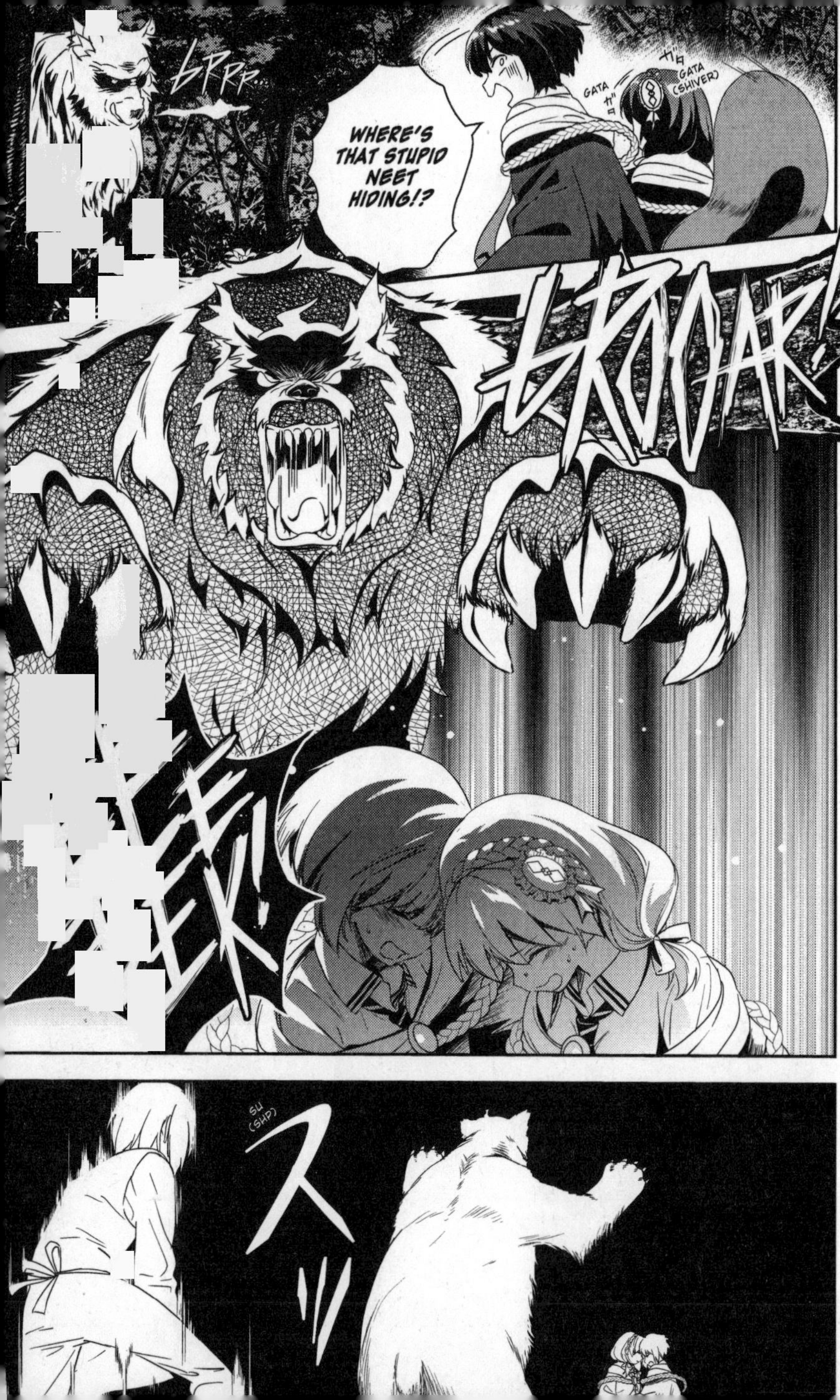
GATA
ガタ
GATA (SHIVER)
ガタ
WHERE'S THAT STUPID NEET HIDING!?
GRRR...
GROOAR!
EEK!
SU (SHP)
スッ

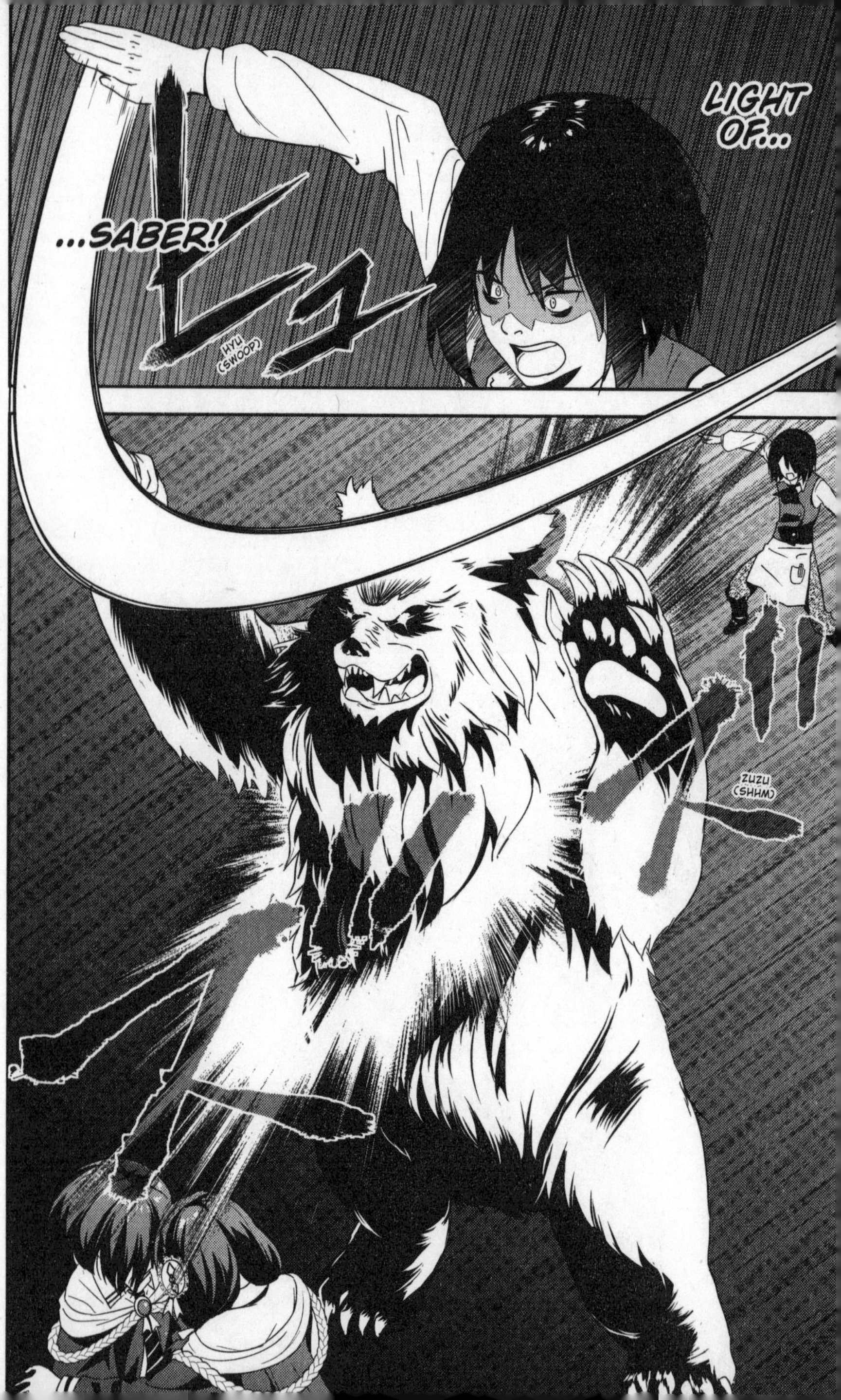
LIGHT OF...
...SABER!
HYU (SWOOP)
ZUZU (SHHM)

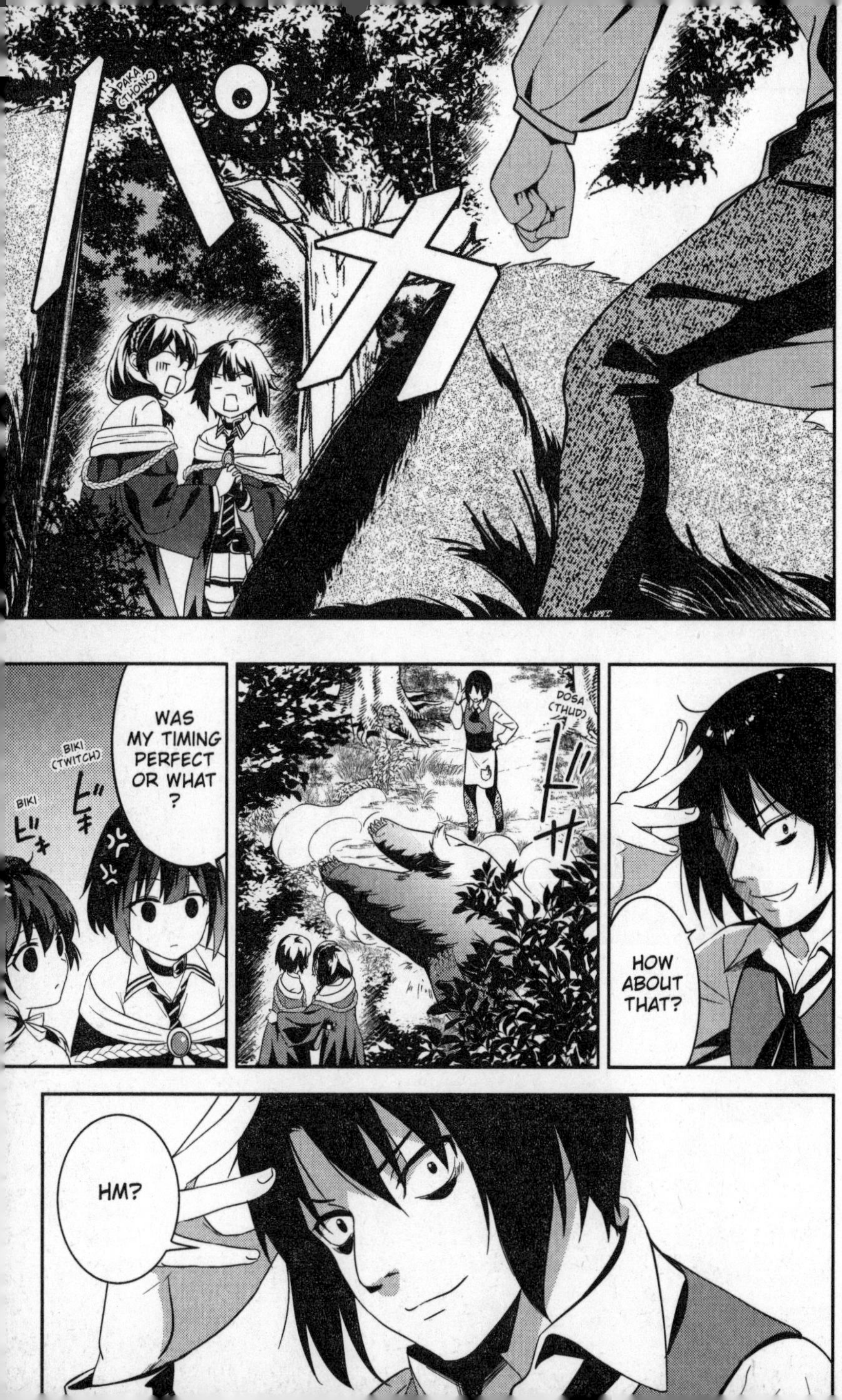
PAKA (THONK)
HOW ABOUT THAT?
DOSA (THUD)
WAS MY TIMING PERFECT OR WHAT?
BIKI (TWITCH)
BIKI
HM?

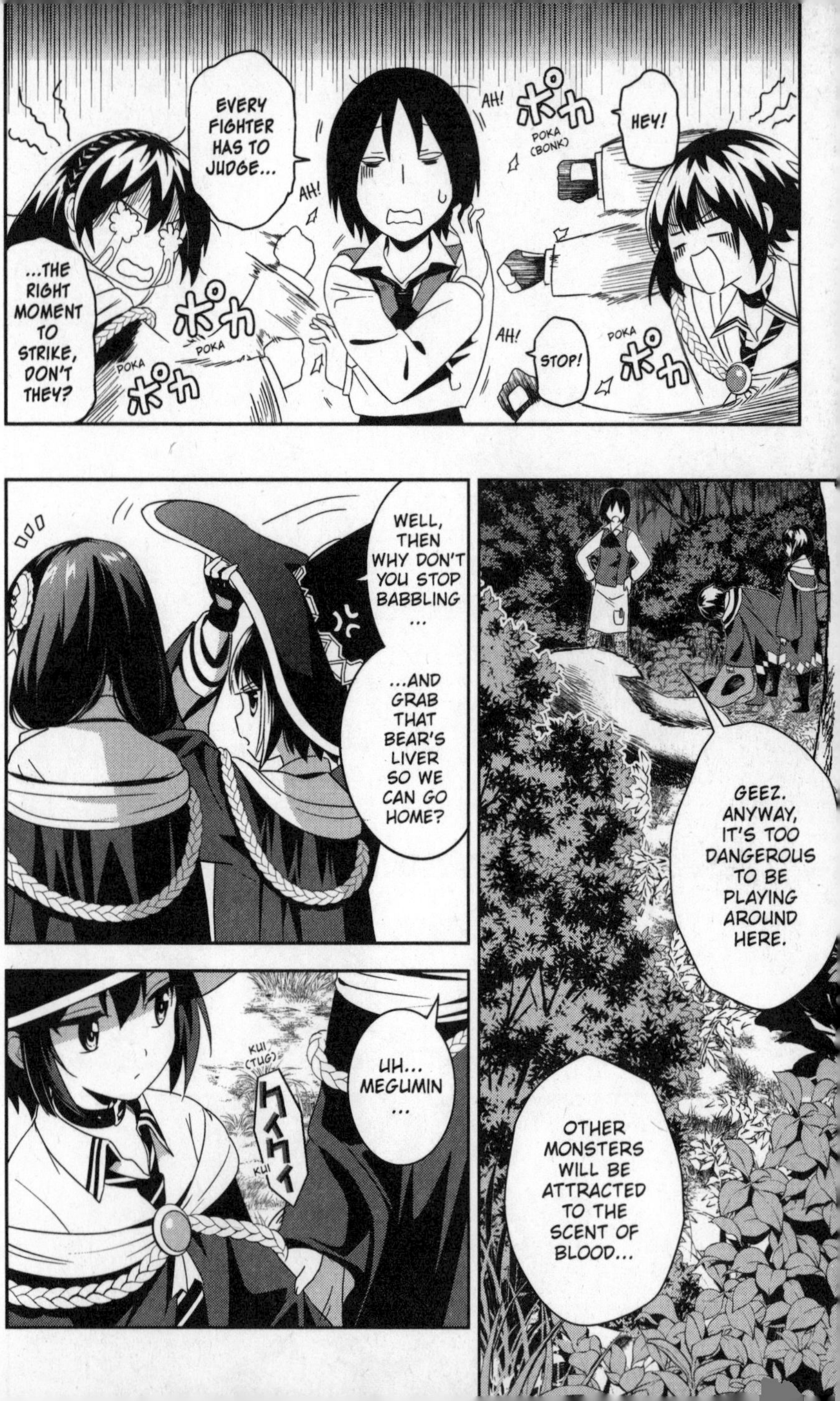
HEY!
ポカ
POKA (BONK)
AH!
AH!
STOP!
ポカ
POKA
EVERY FIGHTER HAS TO JUDGE...
AH!
...THE RIGHT MOMENT TO STRIKE, DON'T THEY?
ポカ
POKA
POKA
ポカ
GEEZ. ANYWAY, IT'S TOO DANGEROUS TO BE PLAYING AROUND HERE.
OTHER MONSTERS WILL BE ATTRACTED TO THE SCENT OF BLOOD...
WELL, THEN WHY DON'T YOU STOP BABBLING ...
...AND GRAB THAT BEAR'S LIVER SO WE CAN GO HOME?
UH... MEGUMIN ...
KUI (TUG)
クイクイ
KUI

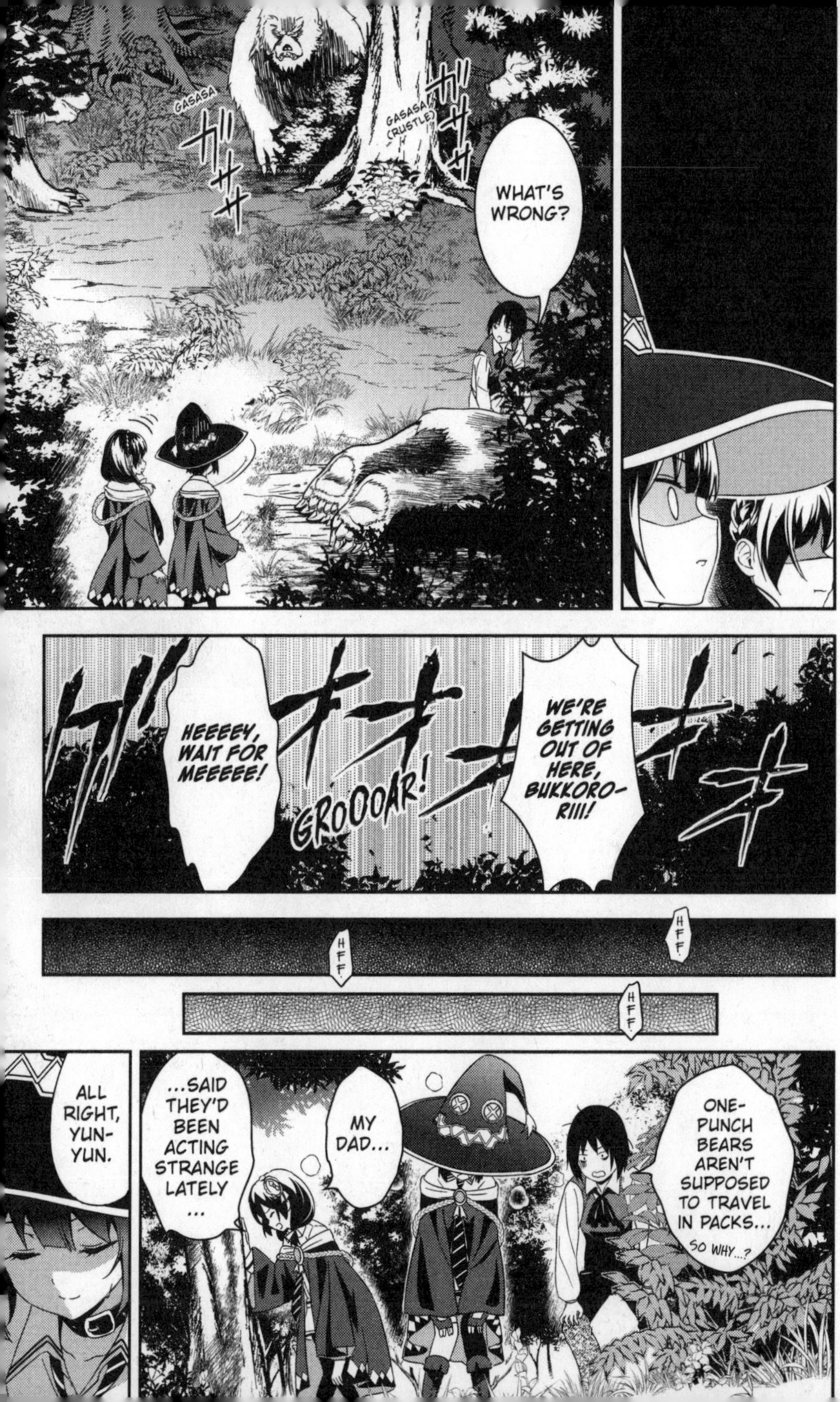
WHAT'S WRONG?
GASASA (RUSTLE)
GASASA
WE'RE GETTING OUT OF HERE, BUKKORO-RIII!
GROOOAR!
HEEEEY, WAIT FOR MEEEEE!
HFF
HFF
HFF
ONE-PUNCH BEARS AREN'T SUPPOSED TO TRAVEL IN PACKS...
SO WHY...?
MY DAD...
...SAID THEY'D BEEN ACTING STRANGE LATELY...
ALL RIGHT, YUN-YUN.

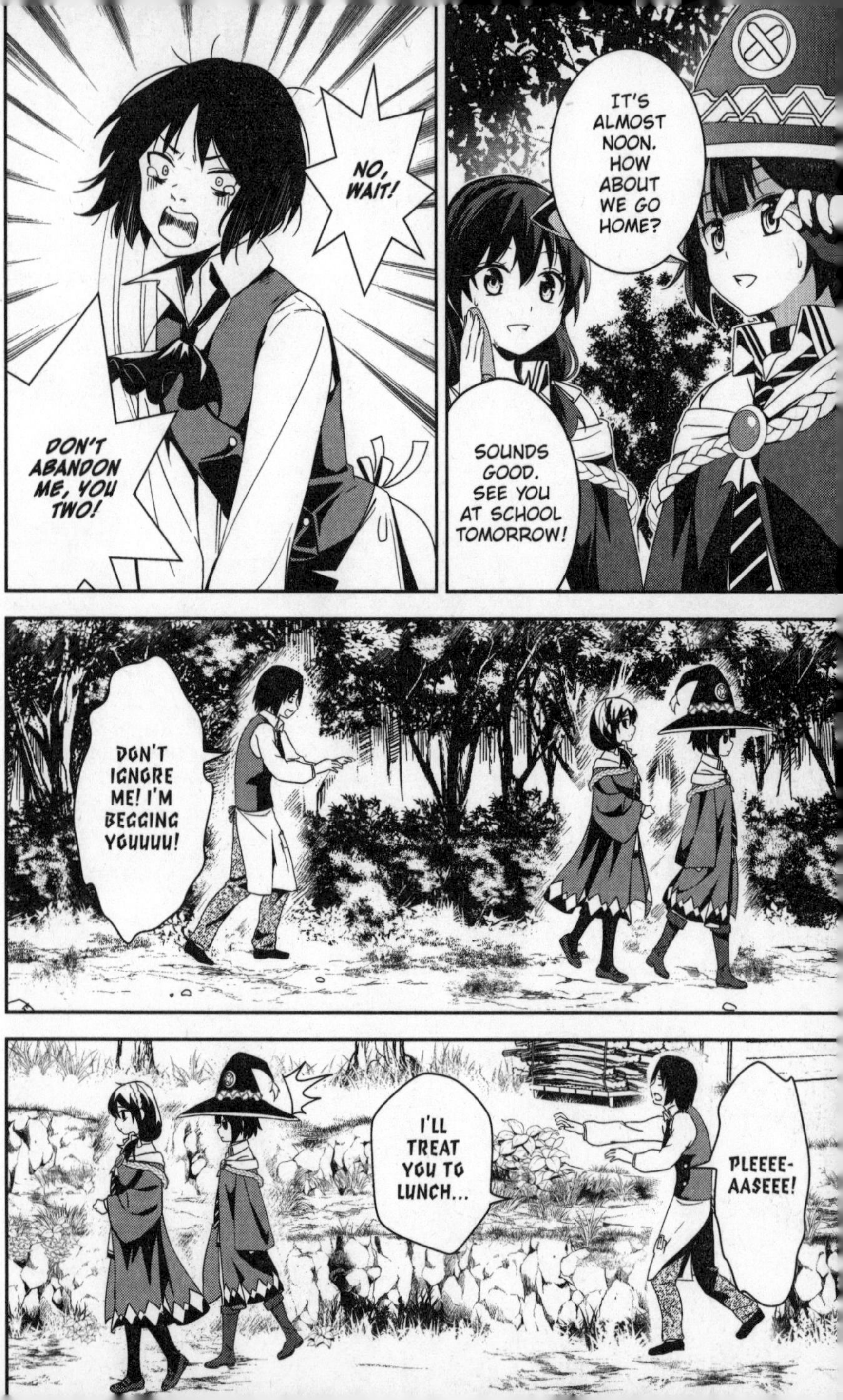
IT'S ALMOST NOON. HOW ABOUT WE GO HOME?
SOUNDS GOOD. SEE YOU AT SCHOOL TOMORROW!
NO, WAIT!
DON'T ABANDON ME, YOU TWO!
DON'T IGNORE ME! I'M BEGGING YOUUUU!
PLEEEE-AASEEE!
I'LL TREAT YOU TO LUNCH...

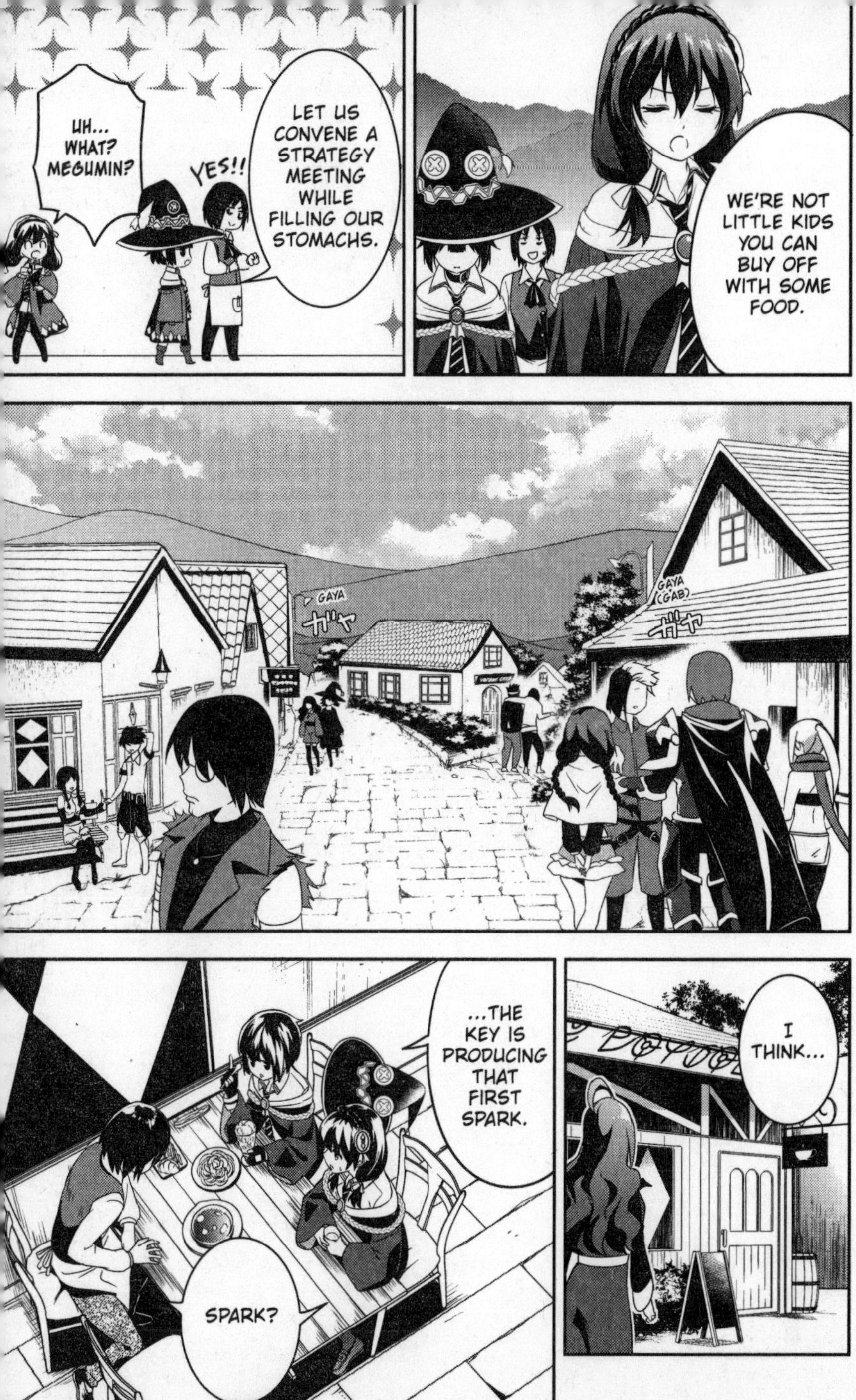
WE'RE NOT LITTLE KIDS YOU CAN BUY OFF WITH SOME FOOD.
LET US CONVENE A STRATEGY MEETING WHILE FILLING OUR STOMACHS.
YES!!
UH... WHAT? MEGUMIN?
GAYA (GAB)
ガヤ
GAYA
ガヤ
I THINK...
...THE KEY IS PRODUCING THAT FIRST SPARK.
SPARK?

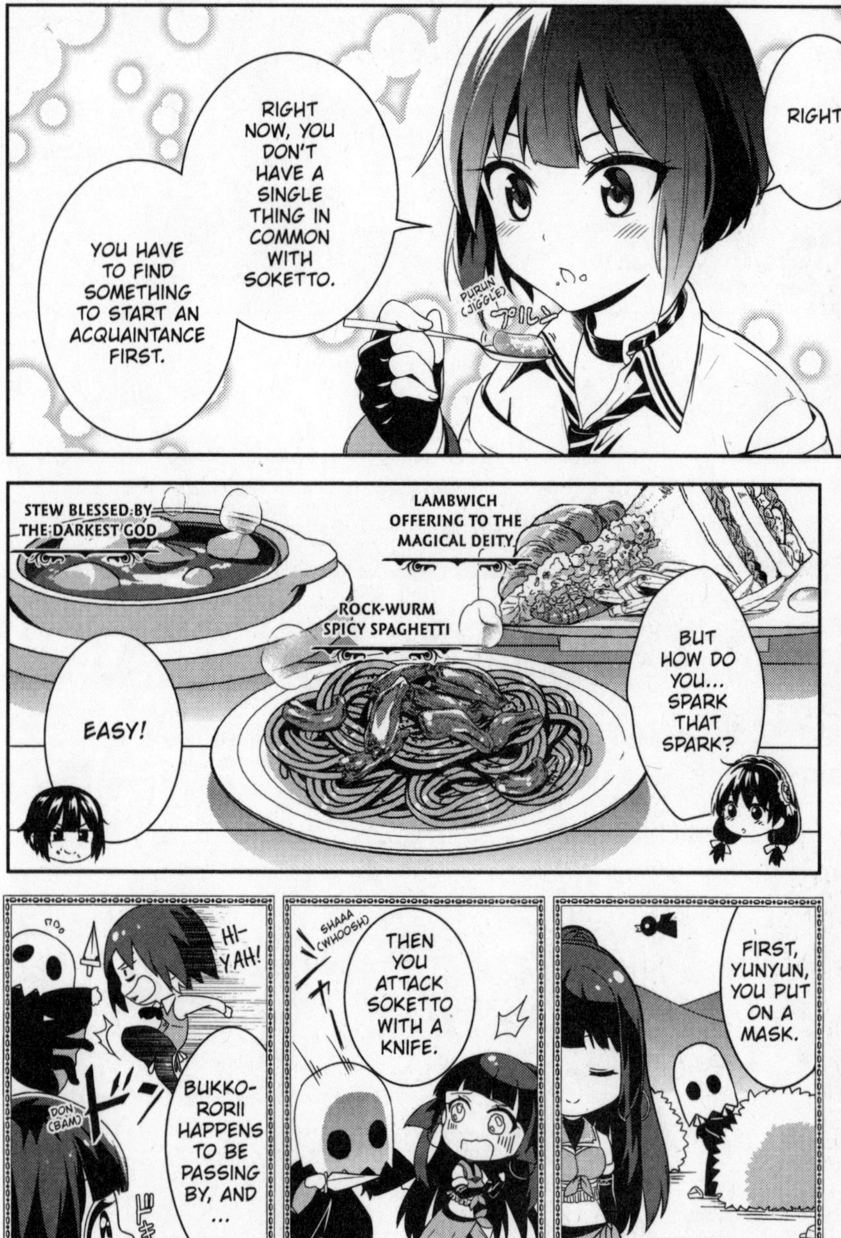
RIGHT.
RIGHT NOW, YOU DON'T HAVE A SINGLE THING IN COMMON WITH SOKETTO.
YOU HAVE TO FIND SOMETHING TO START AN ACQUAINTANCE FIRST.
PURUN (JIGGLE)
LAMBWICH OFFERING TO THE MAGICAL DEITY
STEW BLESSED BY THE DARKEST GOD
ROCK-WURM SPICY SPAGHETTI
BUT HOW DO YOU... SPARK THAT SPARK?
EASY!
FIRST, YUNYUN, YOU PUT ON A MASK.
SHAAA (WHOOSH)
THEN YOU ATTACK SOKETTO WITH A KNIFE.
HI-YAH!
BUKKO-RORII HAPPENS TO BE PASSING BY, AND ...
DON (BAM)
DOKI (THUMP)

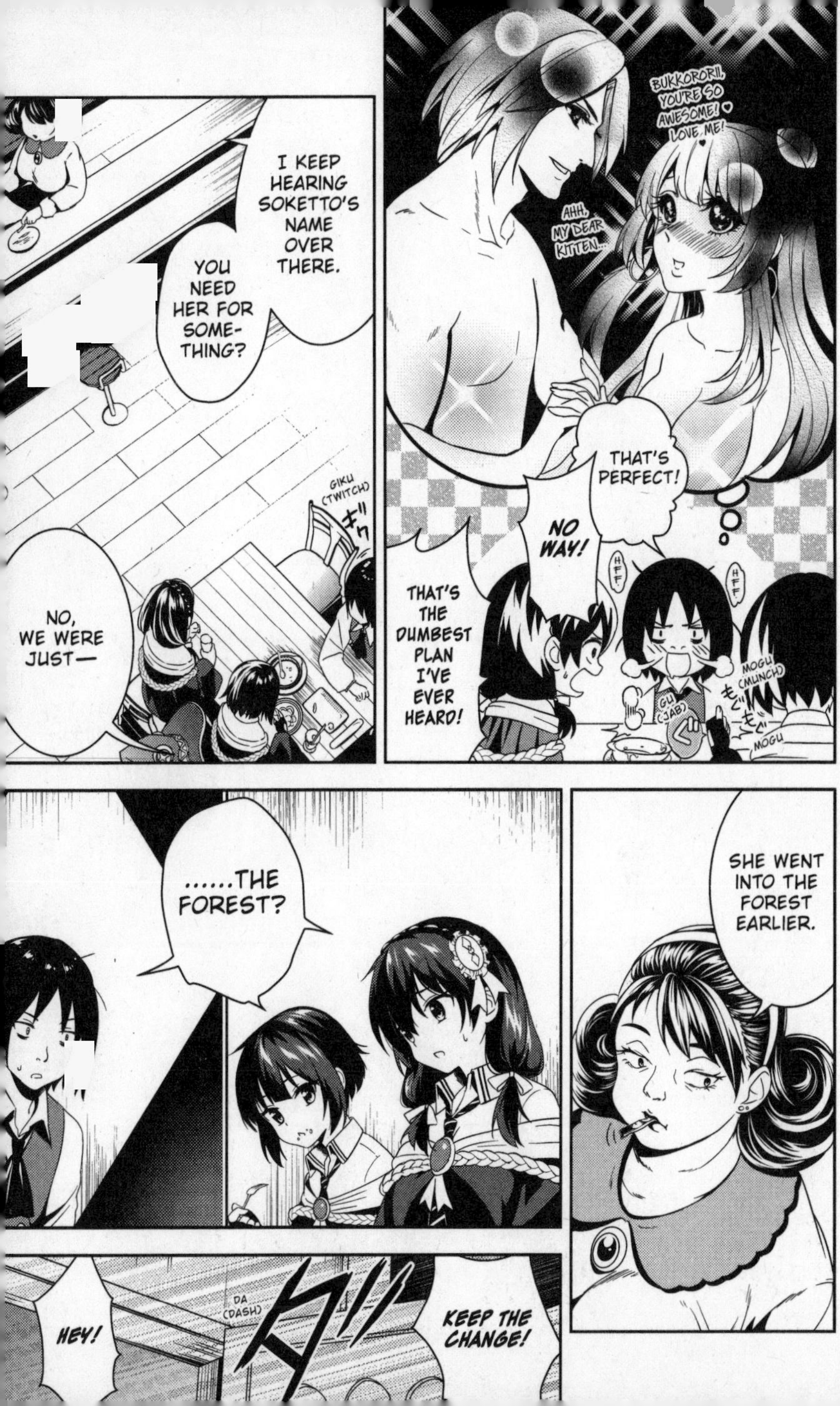
BUKKORORI, YOU'RE SO AWESOME! ♥ LOVE ME! ♥
AHH, MY DEAR KITTEN...
THAT'S PERFECT!
NO WAY!
HFF
HFF
THAT'S THE DUMBEST PLAN I'VE EVER HEARD!
GU (JAB)
MOGU (MUNCH)
MOGU
I KEEP HEARING SOKETTO'S NAME OVER THERE.
YOU NEED HER FOR SOMETHING?
GIKU (TWITCH)
NO, WE WERE JUST—
SHE WENT INTO THE FOREST EARLIER.
......THE FOREST?
KEEP THE CHANGE!
DA (DASH)
HEY!

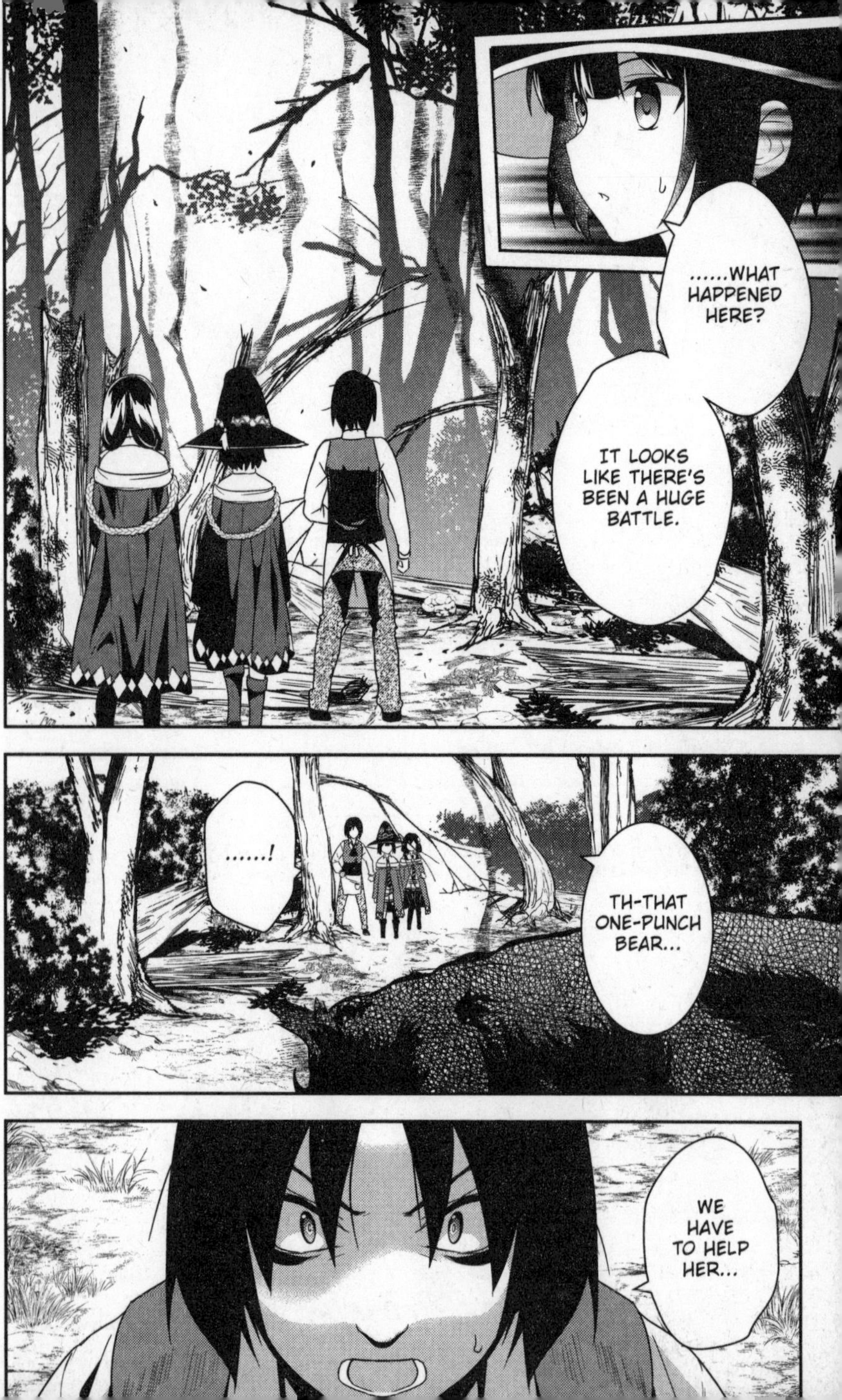
......WHAT HAPPENED HERE?
IT LOOKS LIKE THERE'S BEEN A HUGE BATTLE.
TH-THAT ONE-PUNCH BEAR...
......!
WE HAVE TO HELP HER...

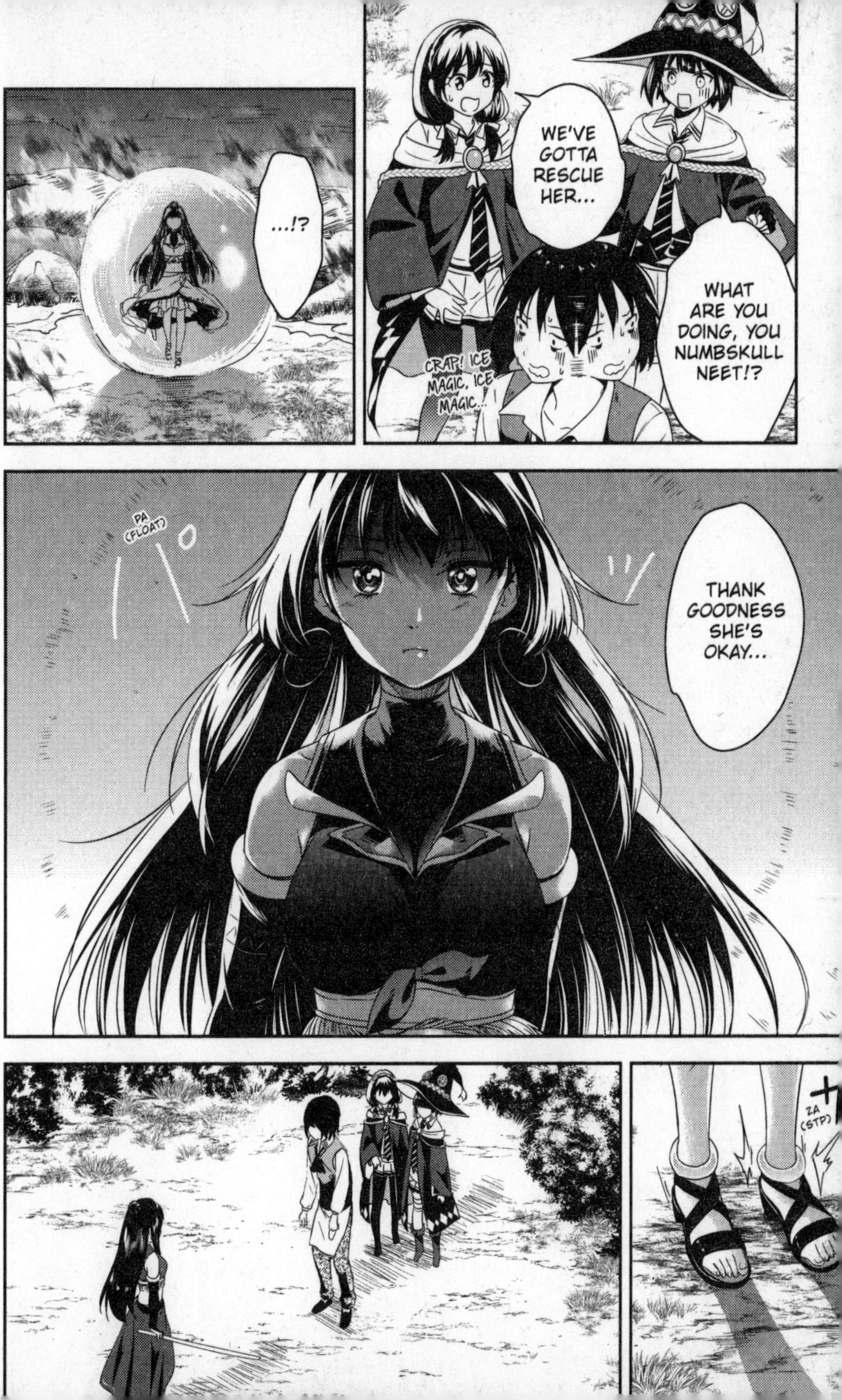
WE'VE GOTTA RESCUE HER...
WHAT ARE YOU DOING, YOU NUMBSKULL NEET!?
CRAP! ICE MAGIC, ICE MAGIC...
...!?
THANK GOODNESS SHE'S OKAY...
PA (FLOAT)
ZA (STP)

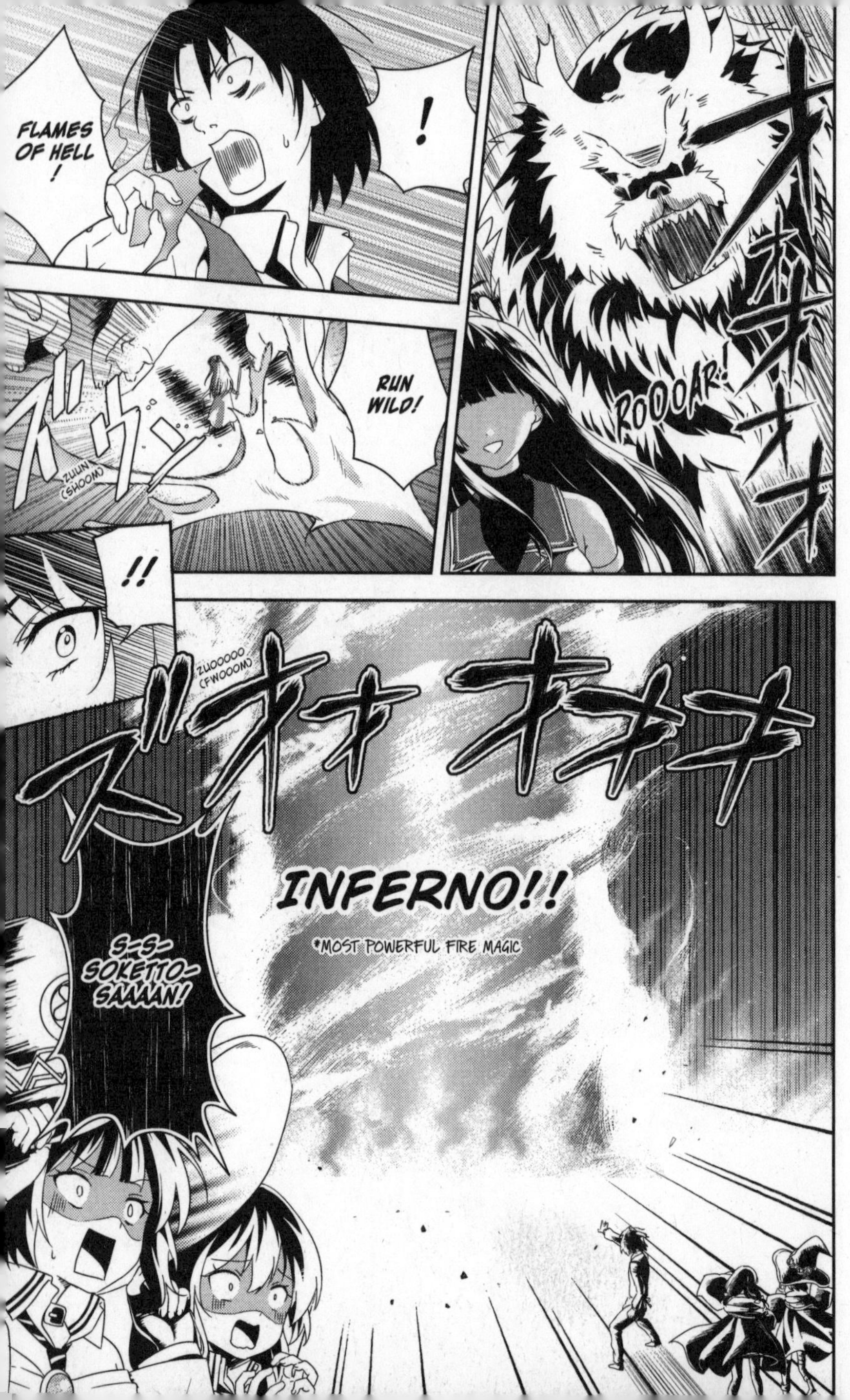
ROOOAR!
FLAMES OF HELL !
!
RUN WILD!
ZUUN (SHOOM)
!!
ZUOOOOO (FWOOOM)
INFERNO!!
*MOST POWERFUL FIRE MAGIC
S-S-SOKETTO-SAAAAN!

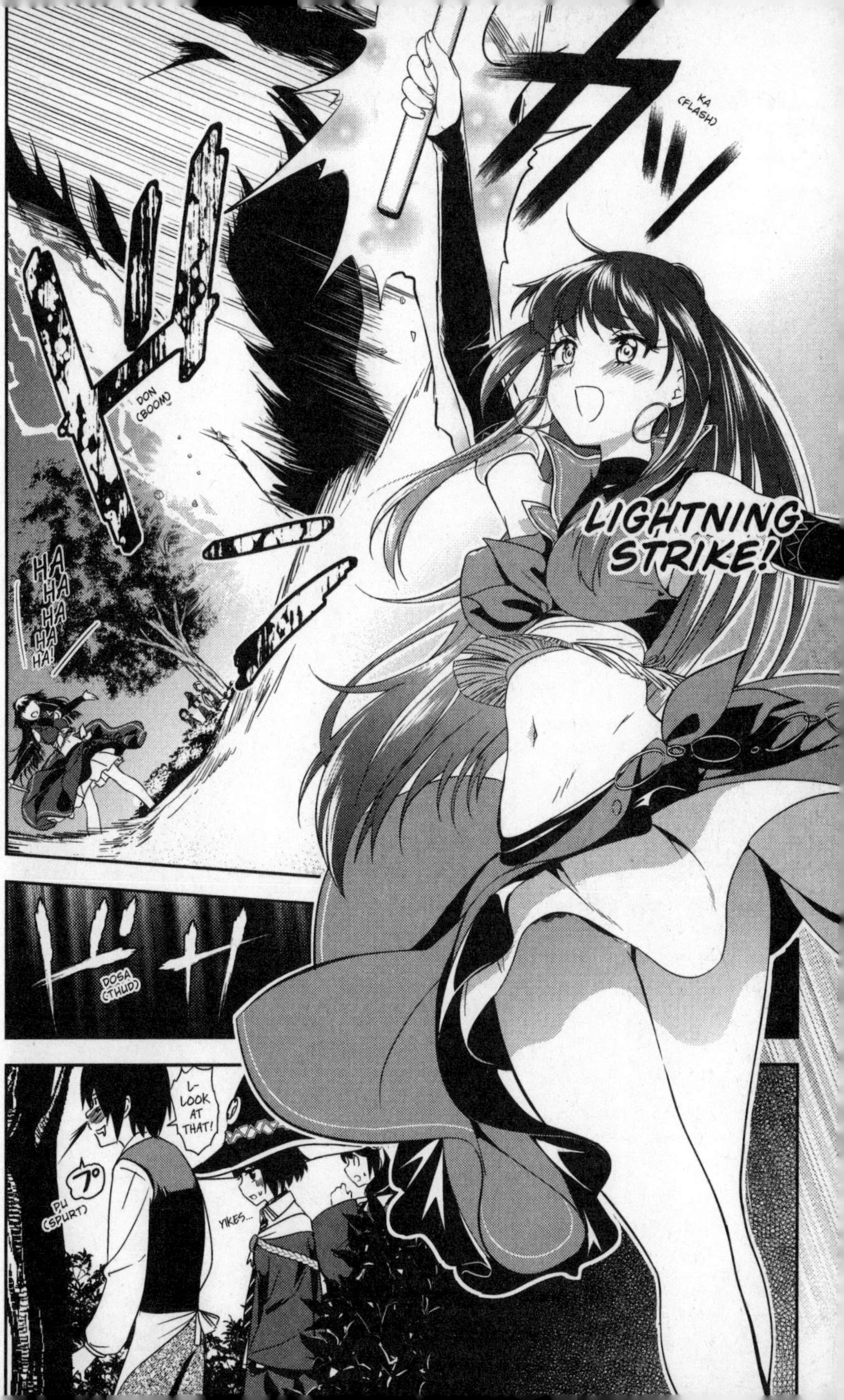
KA (FLASH)
LIGHTNING STRIKE!
DON (BOOM)
HA HA HA HA HA!
DOSA (THUD)
YIKES...
L-LOOK AT THAT!
PU (SPURT)

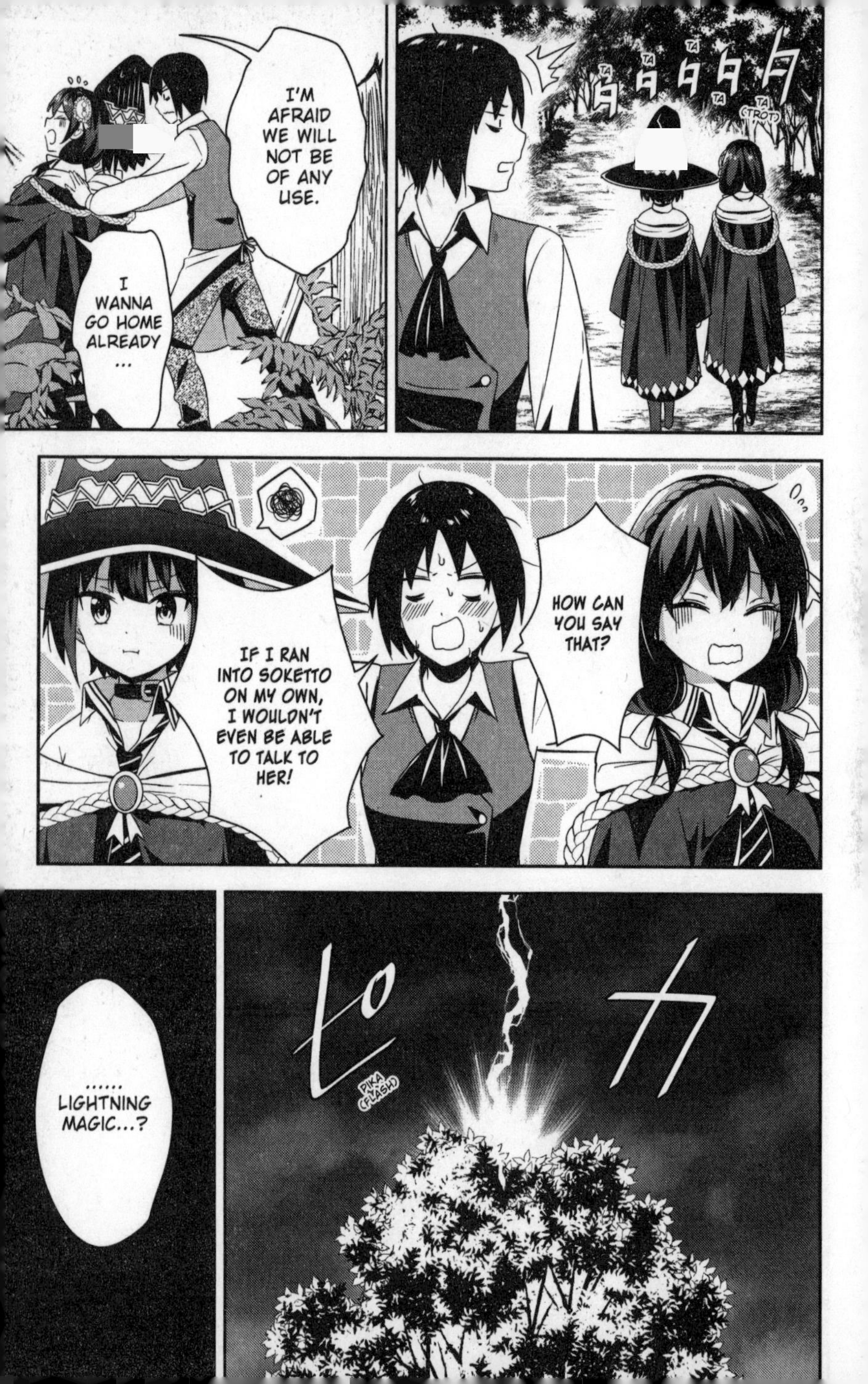
TA TA TA TA TA
(TROT)
I'M AFRAID WE WILL NOT BE OF ANY USE.
I WANNA GO HOME ALREADY ...
HOW CAN YOU SAY THAT?
IF I RAN INTO SOKETTO ON MY OWN, I WOULDN'T EVEN BE ABLE TO TALK TO HER!
ピカ
PIKA (FLASH)
...... LIGHTNING MAGIC...?

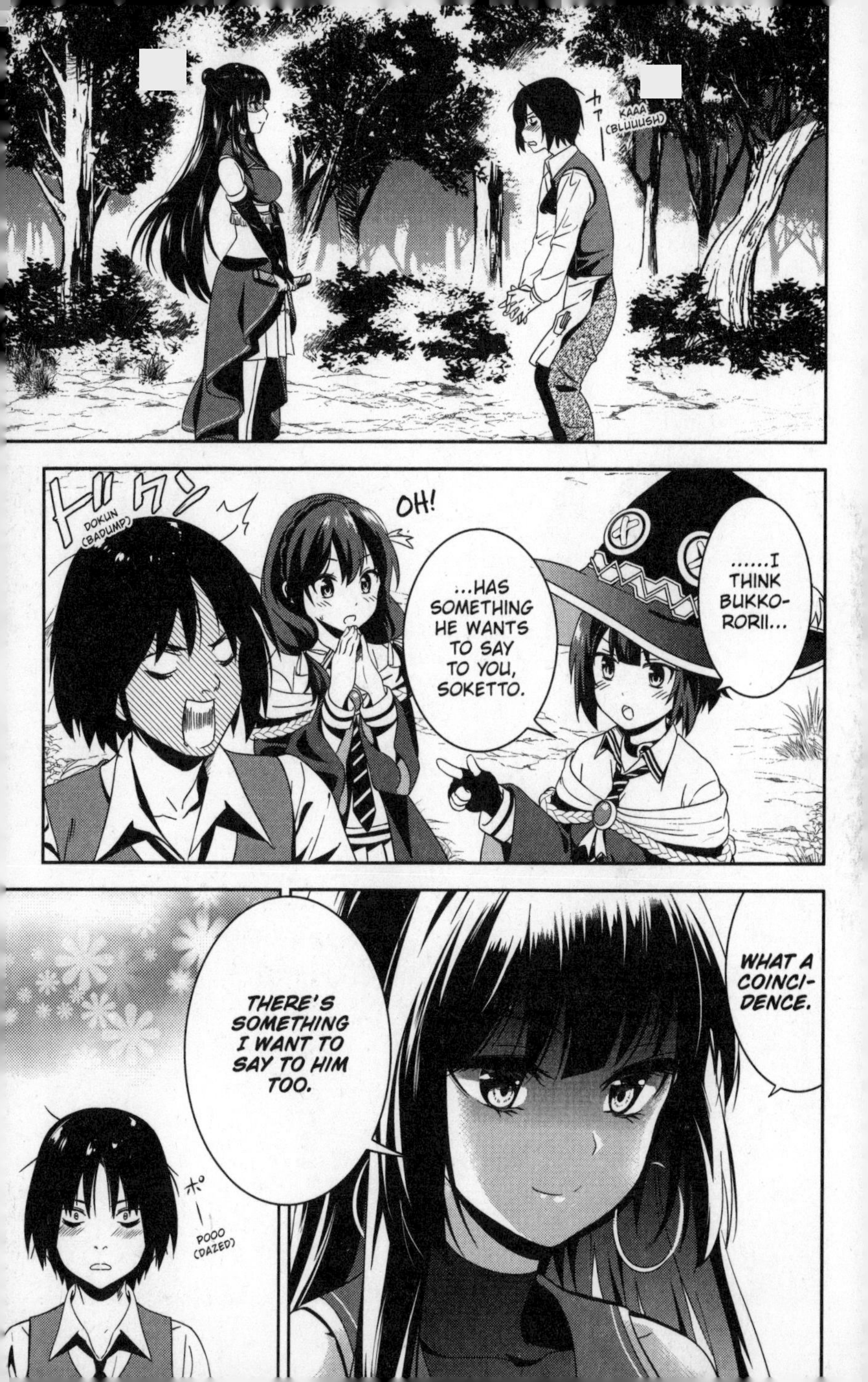
KAAA (BLUUUSH)
......I THINK BUKKO-RORII...
...HAS SOMETHING HE WANTS TO SAY TO YOU, SOKETTO.
OH!
DOKUN (BADUMP)
WHAT A COINCI-DENCE.
THERE'S SOMETHING I WANT TO SAY TO HIM TOO.
POOO (DAZED)

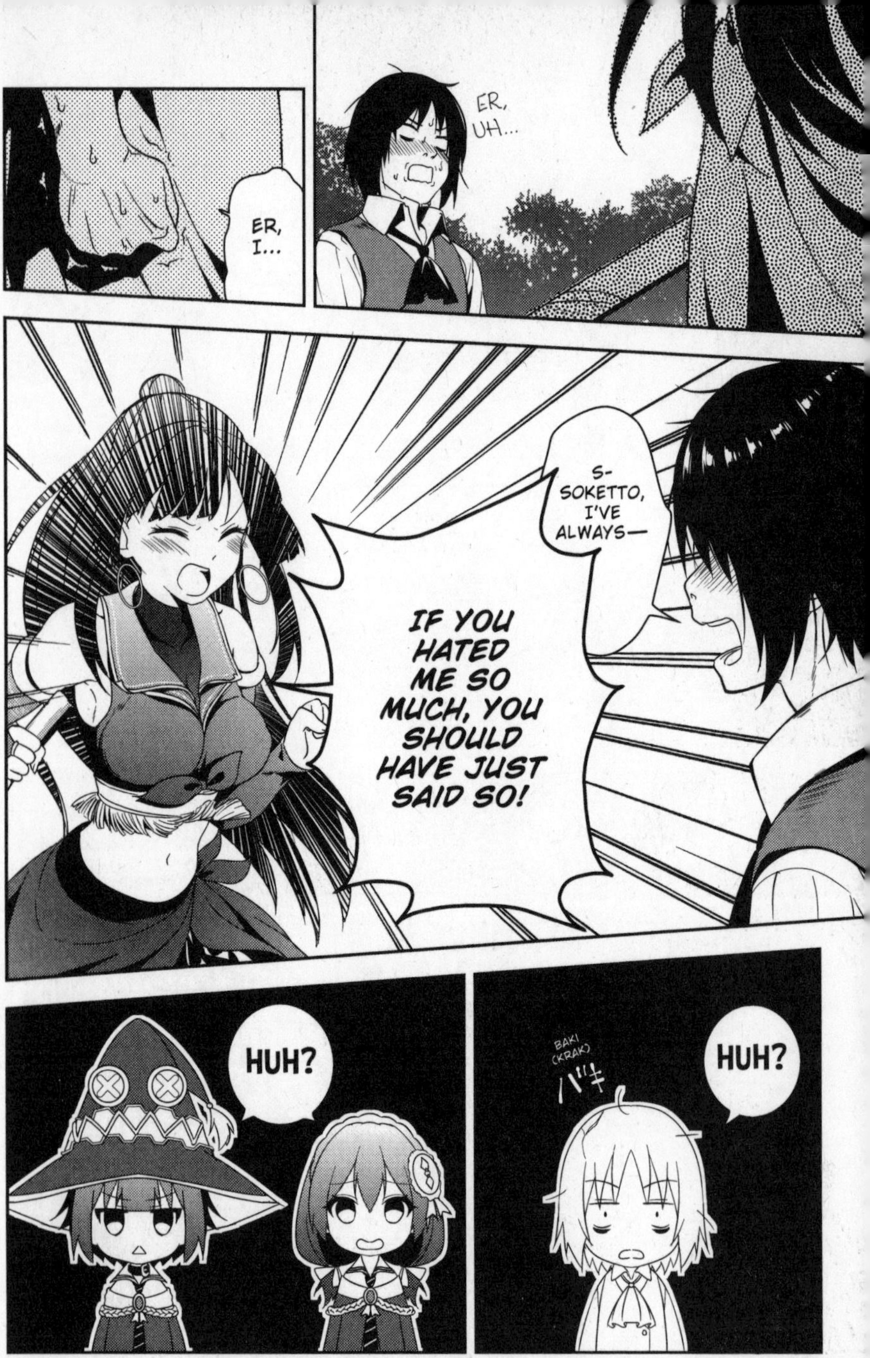
ER, UH...
ER, I...
S-SOKETTO, I'VE ALWAYS—
IF YOU HATED ME SO MUCH, YOU SHOULD HAVE JUST SAID SO!
BAKI (KRAK)
バキ
HUH?
HUH?

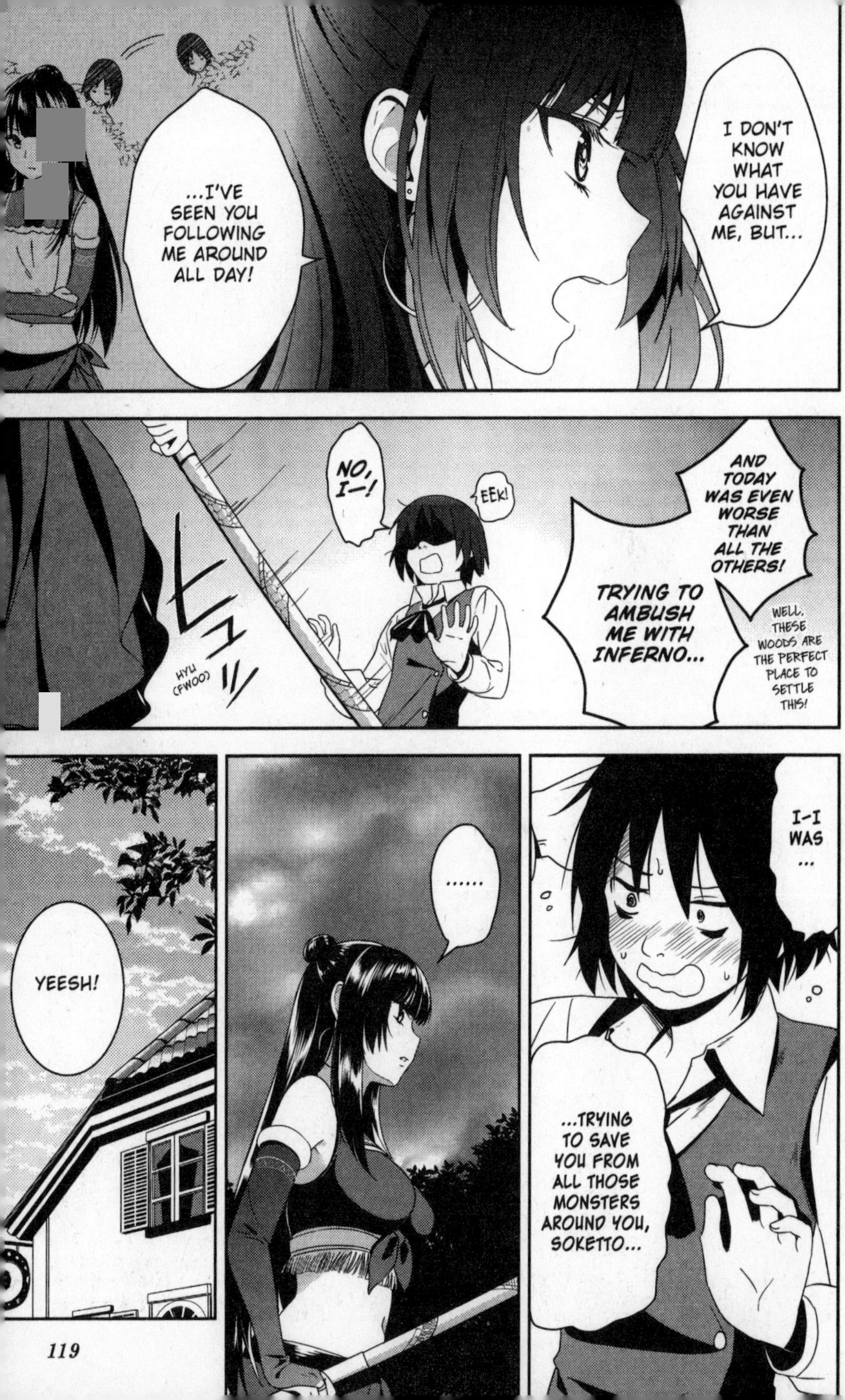
I DON'T KNOW WHAT YOU HAVE AGAINST ME, BUT...
...I'VE SEEN YOU FOLLOWING ME AROUND ALL DAY!
AND TODAY WAS EVEN WORSE THAN ALL THE OTHERS!
TRYING TO AMBUSH ME WITH INFERNO...
WELL, THESE WOODS ARE THE PERFECT PLACE TO SETTLE THIS!
NO, I—!
EEK!
HYU (FWOO)
I-I WAS...
...TRYING TO SAVE YOU FROM ALL THOSE MONSTERS AROUND YOU, SOKETTO...
......
YEESH!

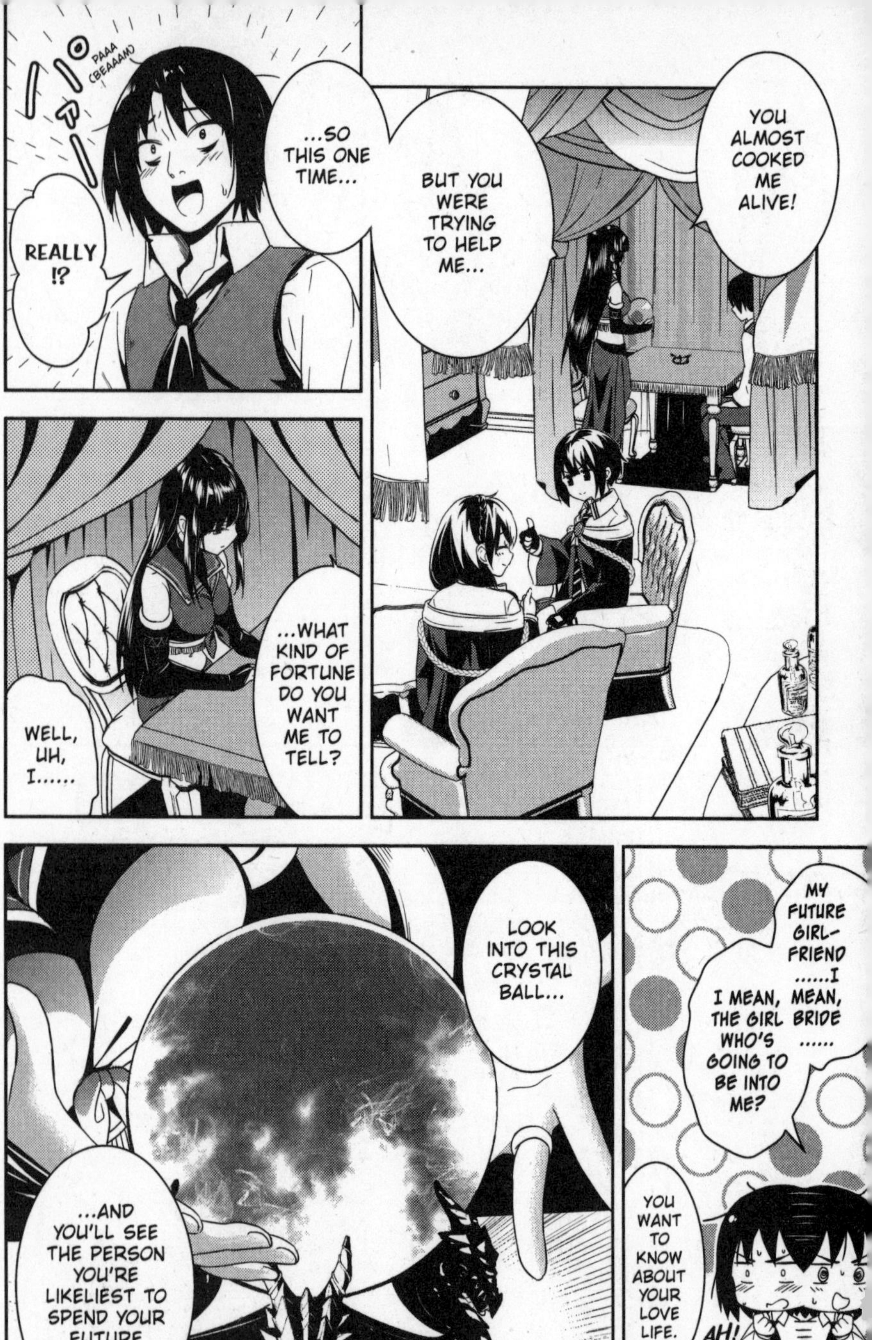
YOU ALMOST COOKED ME ALIVE!
BUT YOU WERE TRYING TO HELP ME...
...SO THIS ONE TIME...
PAAA (BEAAAM)
REALLY !?
...WHAT KIND OF FORTUNE DO YOU WANT ME TO TELL?
WELL, UH, I......
MY FUTURE GIRL-FRIEND ......I MEAN, BRIDE ......
I MEAN, THE GIRL WHO'S GOING TO BE INTO ME?
YOU WANT TO KNOW ABOUT YOUR LOVE LIFE.
AH!
LOOK INTO THIS CRYSTAL BALL...
...AND YOU'LL SEE THE PERSON YOU'RE LIKELIEST TO SPEND YOUR FUTURE WITH.

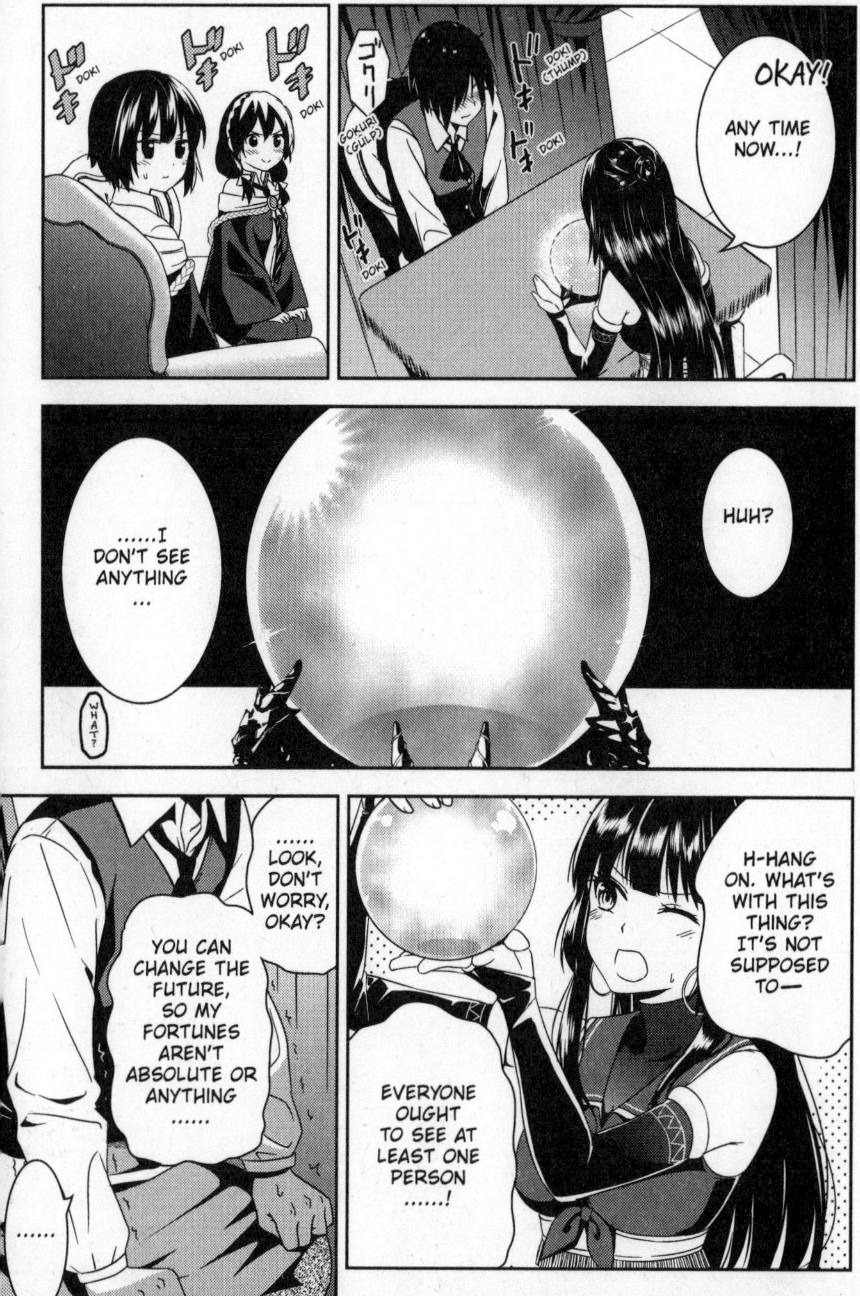
OKAY!!
ANY TIME NOW...!
DOKI (THUMP)
DOKI
ゴクリ
GOKURI (GULP)
DOKI
DOKI
DOKI
DOKI
HUH?
......I DON'T SEE ANYTHING ...
WHAT?
H-HANG ON. WHAT'S WITH THIS THING? IT'S NOT SUPPOSED TO—
EVERYONE OUGHT TO SEE AT LEAST ONE PERSON ......!
...... LOOK, DON'T WORRY, OKAY?
YOU CAN CHANGE THE FUTURE, SO MY FORTUNES AREN'T ABSOLUTE OR ANYTHING ......
......

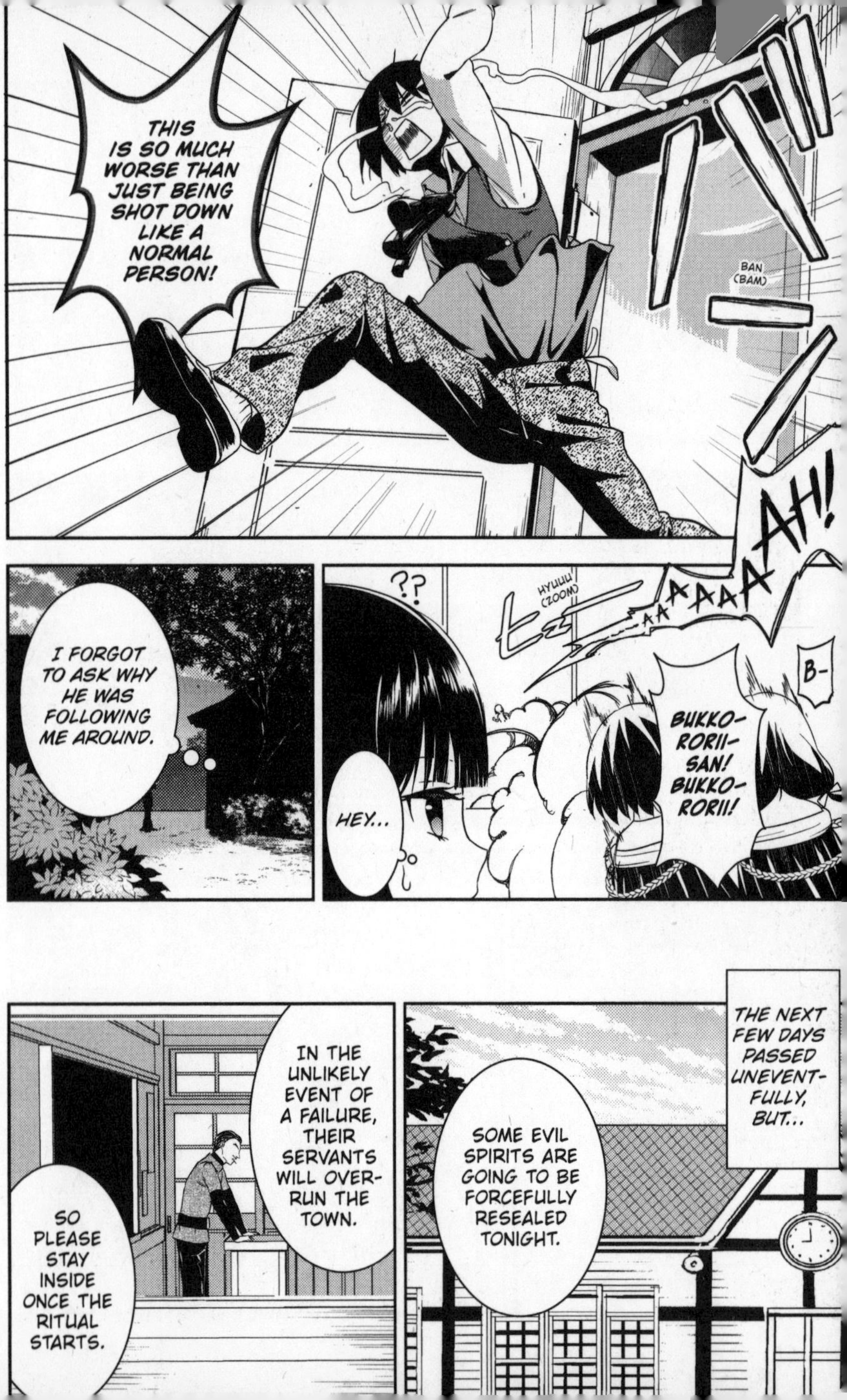
THIS IS SO MUCH WORSE THAN JUST BEING SHOT DOWN LIKE A NORMAL PERSON!
BAN (BAM)
AAAAAAAAH!
HYUUU (ZOOM)
B-
BUKKORORII-SAN! BUKKORORII!
??
HEY...
I FORGOT TO ASK WHY HE WAS FOLLOWING ME AROUND.
THE NEXT FEW DAYS PASSED UNEVENTFULLY, BUT...
SOME EVIL SPIRITS ARE GOING TO BE FORCEFULLY RESEALED TONIGHT.
IN THE UNLIKELY EVENT OF A FAILURE, THEIR SERVANTS WILL OVERRUN THE TOWN.
SO PLEASE STAY INSIDE ONCE THE RITUAL STARTS.

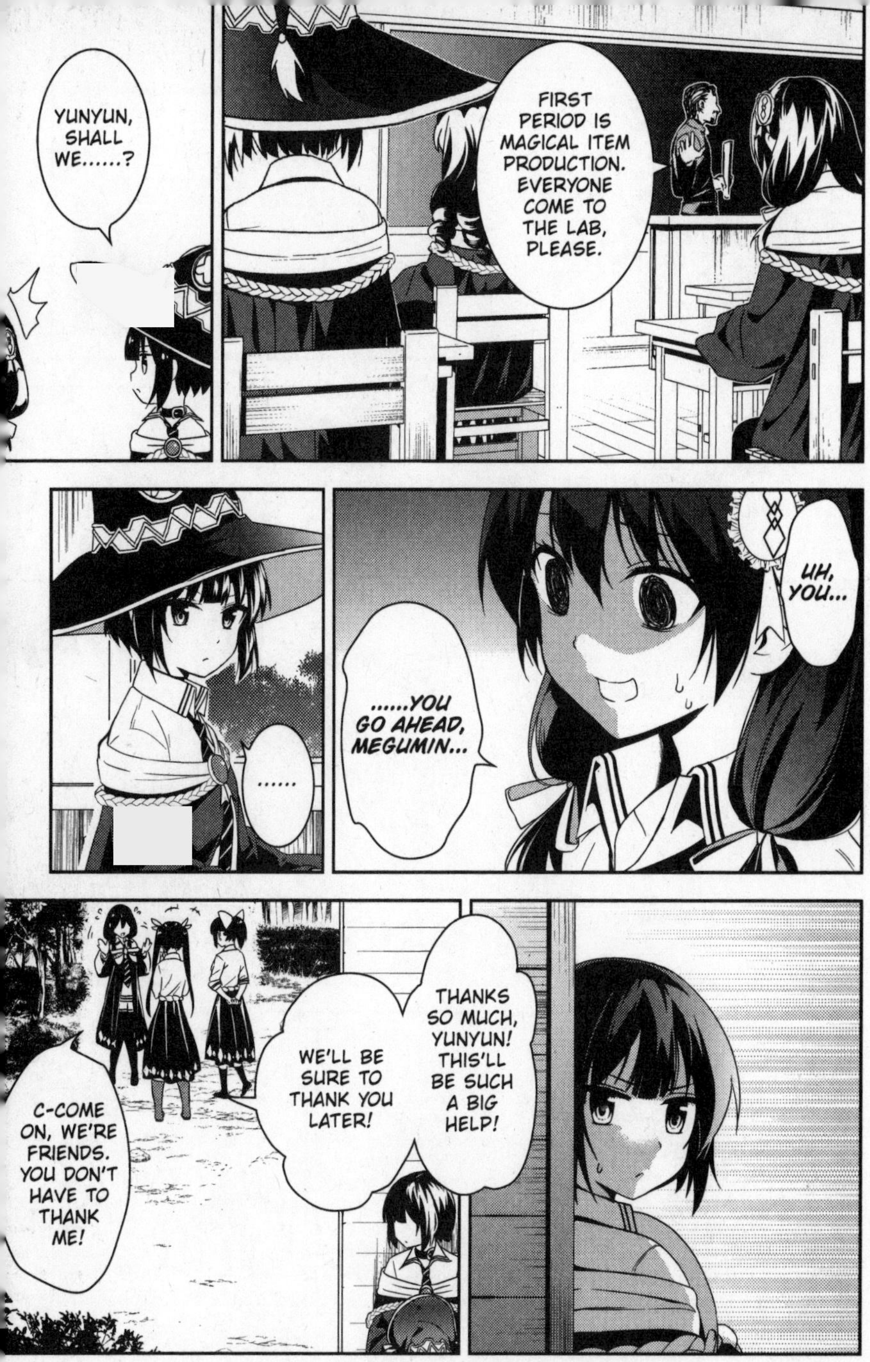
FIRST PERIOD IS MAGICAL ITEM PRODUCTION. EVERYONE COME TO THE LAB, PLEASE.
YUNYUN, SHALL WE......?
UH, YOU...
......YOU GO AHEAD, MEGUMIN...
......
THANKS SO MUCH, YUNYUN! THIS'LL BE SUCH A BIG HELP!
WE'LL BE SURE TO THANK YOU LATER!
C-COME ON, WE'RE FRIENDS. YOU DON'T HAVE TO THANK ME!

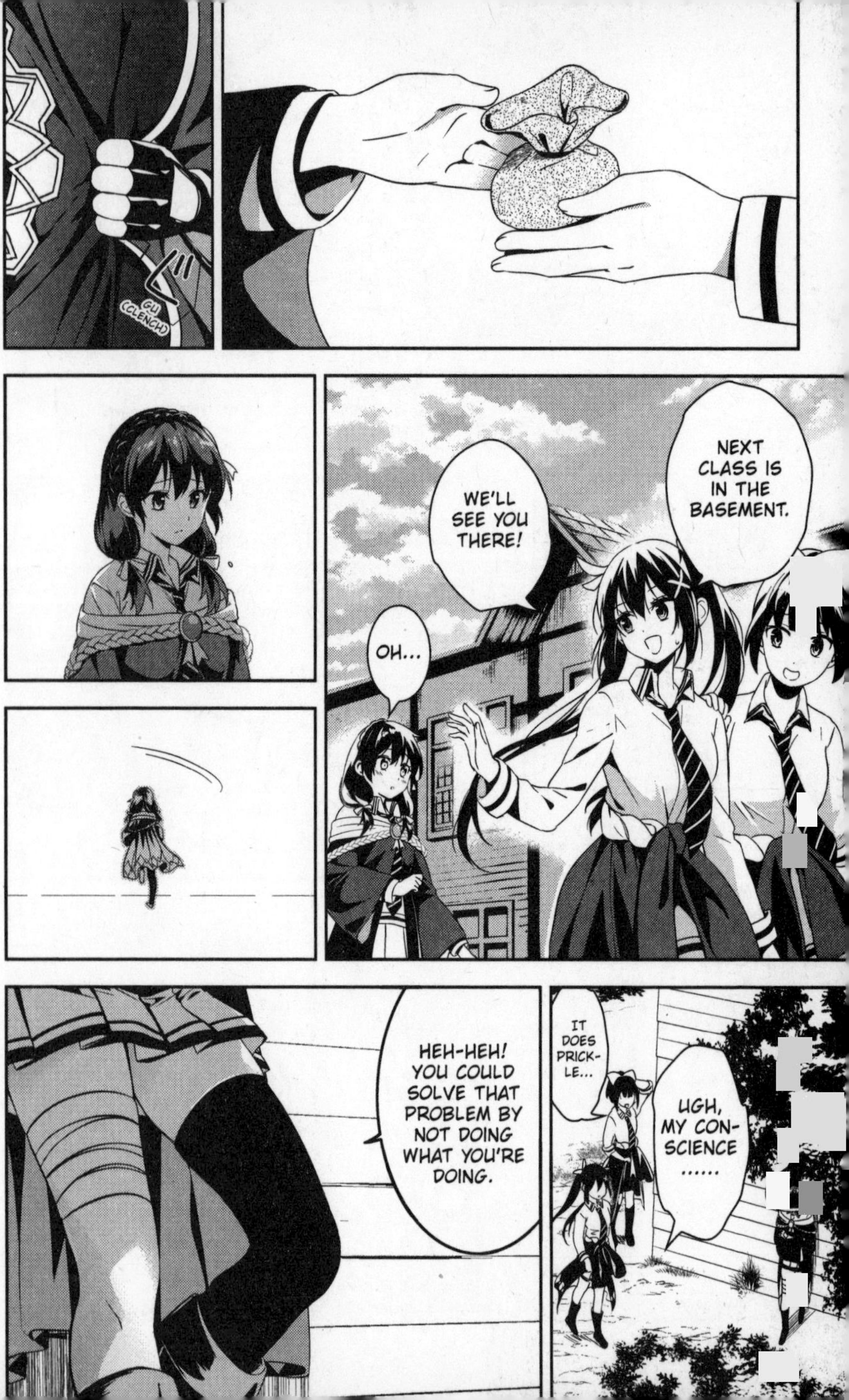
GU
(CLENCH)
NEXT CLASS IS IN THE BASEMENT.
WE'LL SEE YOU THERE!
OH...
UGH, MY CON-SCIENCE ......
IT DOES PRICK-LE...
HEH-HEH! YOU COULD SOLVE THAT PROBLEM BY NOT DOING WHAT YOU'RE DOING.

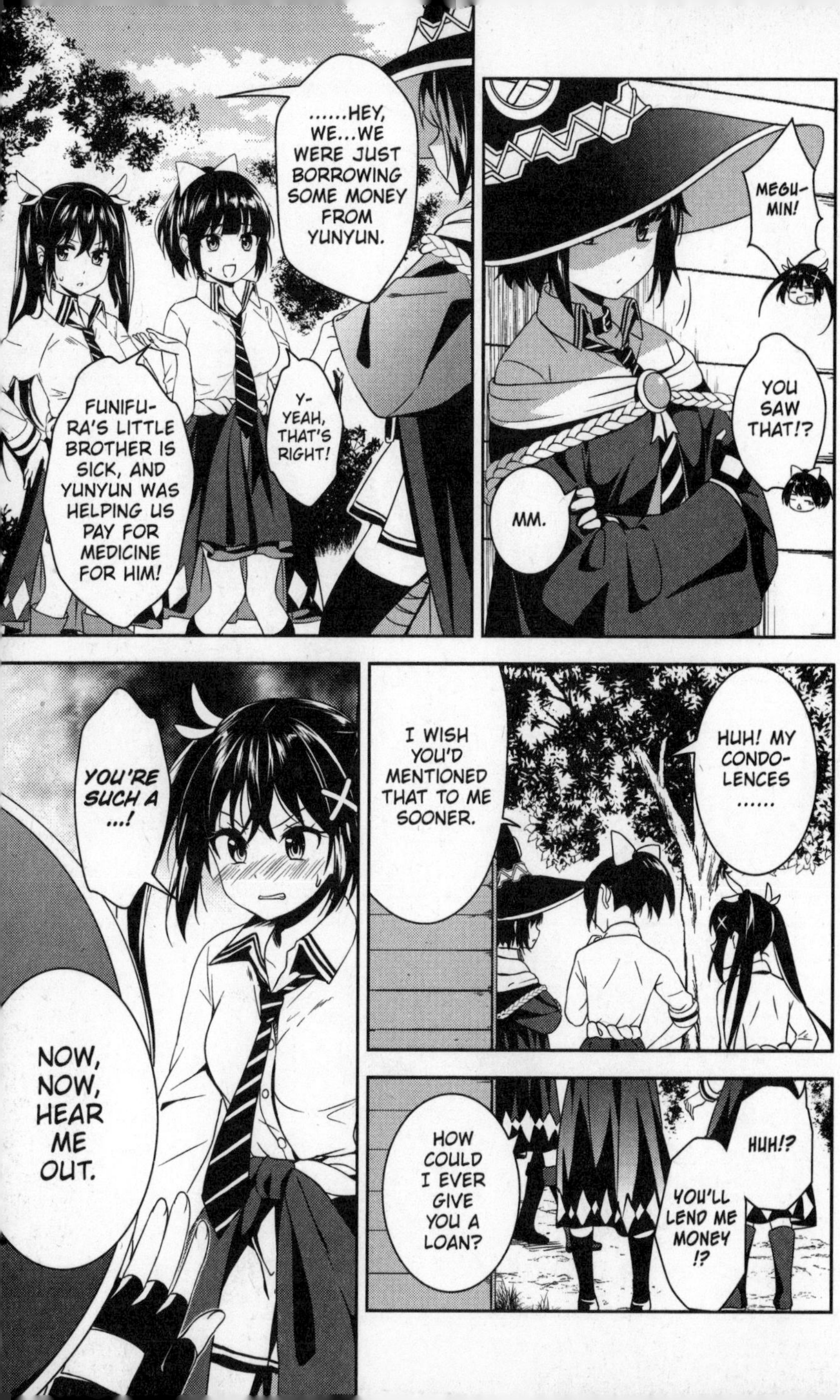
MEGU-MIN!
YOU SAW THAT!?
MM.
......HEY, WE...WE WERE JUST BORROWING SOME MONEY FROM YUNYUN.
Y-YEAH, THAT'S RIGHT!
FUNIFU-RA'S LITTLE BROTHER IS SICK, AND YUNYUN WAS HELPING US PAY FOR MEDICINE FOR HIM!
HUH! MY CONDO-LENCES ......
I WISH YOU'D MENTIONED THAT TO ME SOONER.
HUH!?
YOU'LL LEND ME MONEY !?
HOW COULD I EVER GIVE YOU A LOAN?
YOU'RE SUCH A ...!
NOW, NOW, HEAR ME OUT.

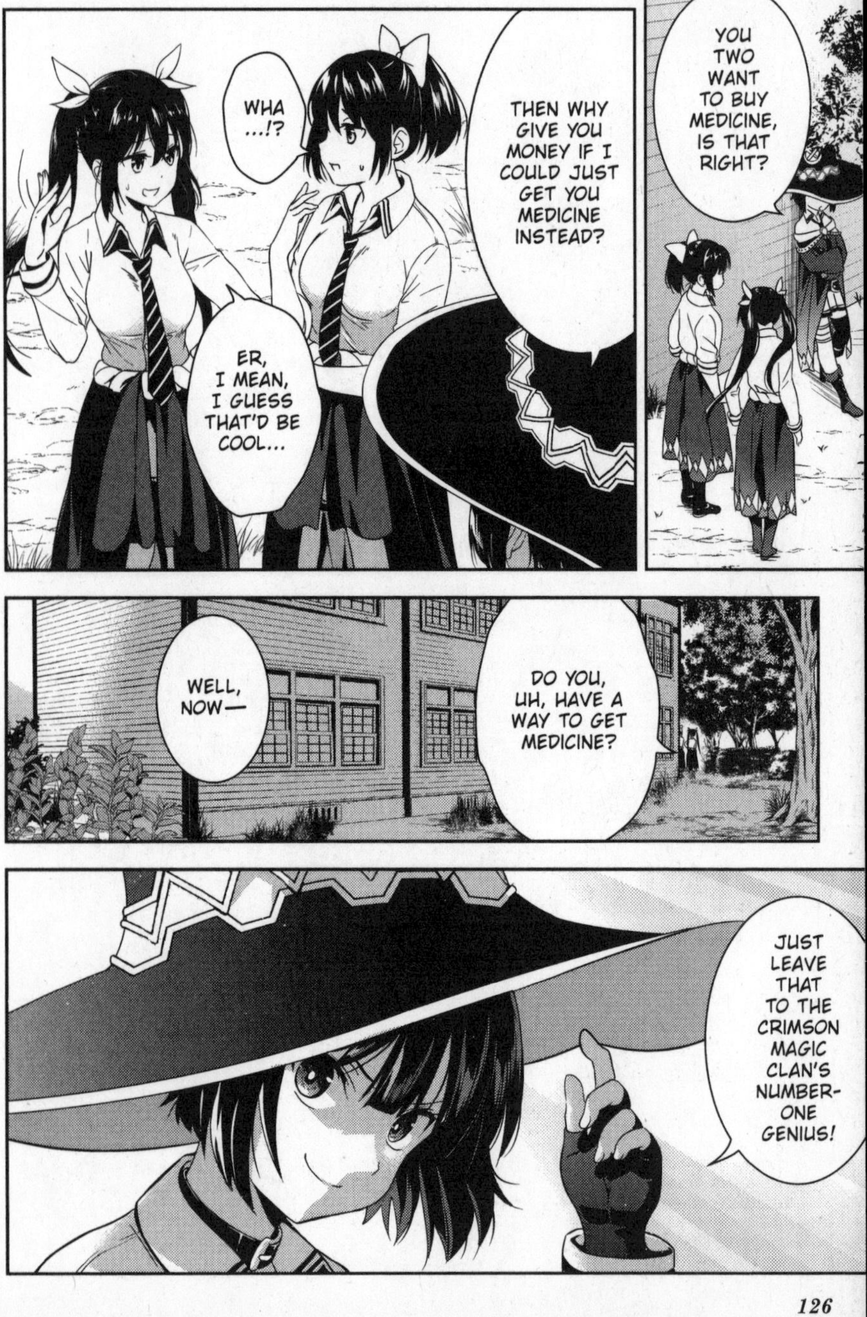
YOU TWO WANT TO BUY MEDICINE, IS THAT RIGHT?
THEN WHY GIVE YOU MONEY IF I COULD JUST GET YOU MEDICINE INSTEAD?
WHA ...!?
ER, I MEAN, I GUESS THAT'D BE COOL...
DO YOU, UH, HAVE A WAY TO GET MEDICINE?
WELL, NOW—
JUST LEAVE THAT TO THE CRIMSON MAGIC CLAN'S NUMBER-ONE GENIUS!

THE SECOND PUZZLE IS SOLVED...

...AND KOMEKKO FACES A NEW TEST.

I GIVE UP!

OOOH...

ガクガク (GAKU) (SLUMP)

......HEY, YOU'RE REALLY COMING ALONG!

HEH HEH!

ATTAGIRL!

バタ (BATAN) (BAMP)

HRM?

WHAT'S WRONG?

 KOMEKKO'S STORY 3 INTERLUDE THEATRE

THE MOST DEVILISH LITTLE SISTER AMONG THE CRIMSON MAGIC CLAN

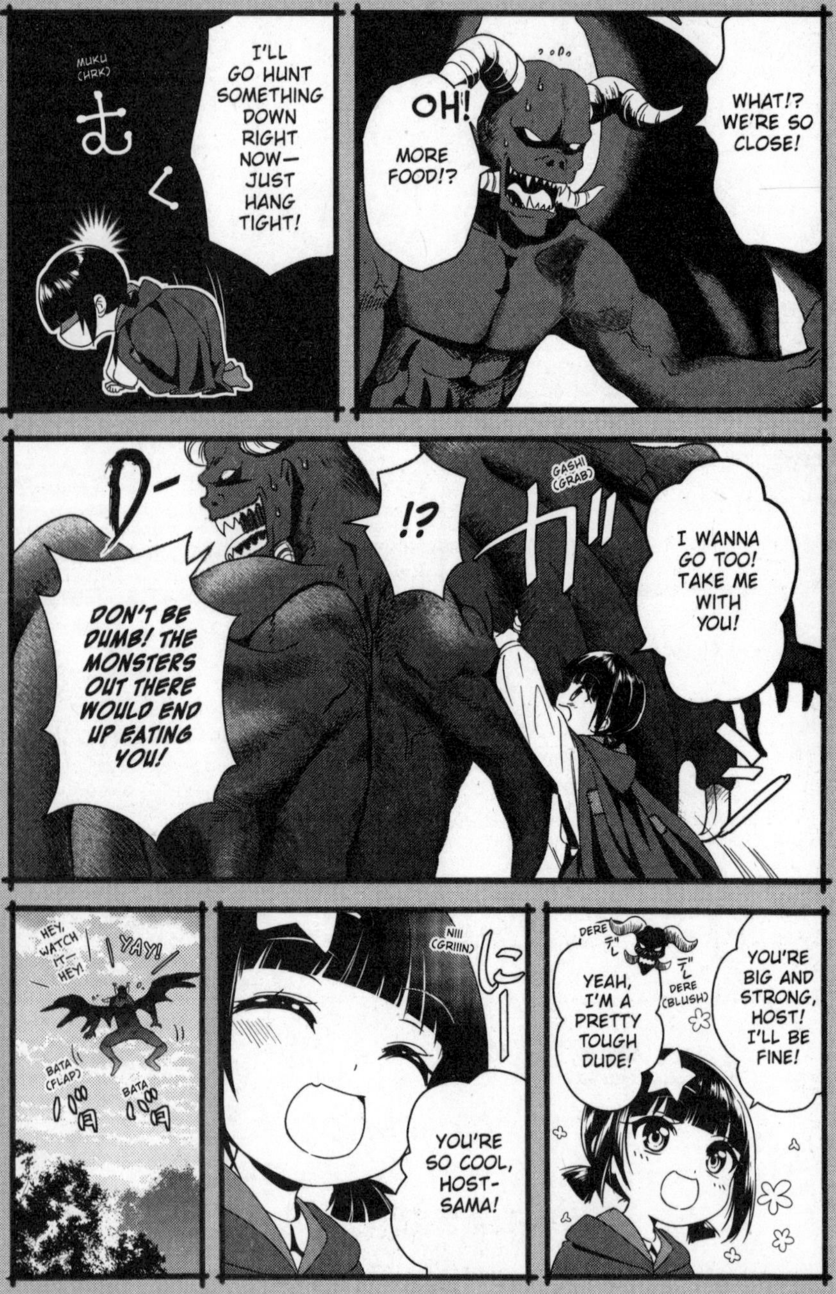
WHAT!? WE'RE SO CLOSE!
OH!
MORE FOOD!?
I'LL GO HUNT SOMETHING DOWN RIGHT NOW—JUST HANG TIGHT!
MUKU (HRK)
I WANNA GO TOO! TAKE ME WITH YOU!
GASHI (GRAB)
!?
D-
DON'T BE DUMB! THE MONSTERS OUT THERE WOULD END UP EATING YOU!
YOU'RE BIG AND STRONG, HOST! I'LL BE FINE!
DERE DERE (BLUSH)
YEAH, I'M A PRETTY TOUGH DUDE!
NIII (GRIIIN)
YOU'RE SO COOL, HOST-SAMA!
YAY!
HEY, WATCH IT— HEY!
BATA (FLAP)
BATA

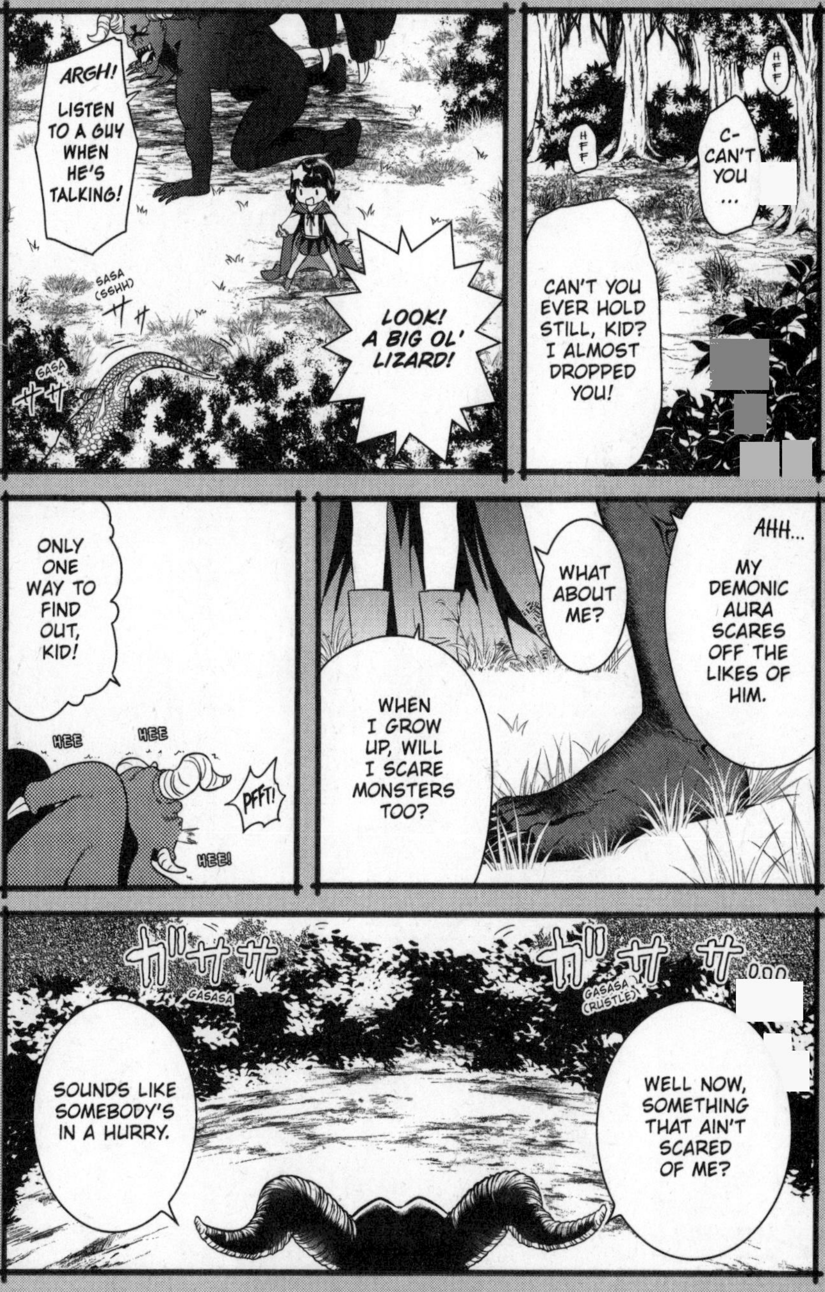
HFF
C-CAN'T YOU ...
HFF
CAN'T YOU EVER HOLD STILL, KID? I ALMOST DROPPED YOU!
ARGH!
LISTEN TO A GUY WHEN HE'S TALKING!
LOOK! A BIG OL' LIZARD!
SASA (SSHH)
SASA
AHH...
MY DEMONIC AURA SCARES OFF THE LIKES OF HIM.
WHAT ABOUT ME?
WHEN I GROW UP, WILL I SCARE MONSTERS TOO?
ONLY ONE WAY TO FIND OUT, KID!
HEE
HEE
PFFT!
HEE!
GASASA (RUSTLE)
WELL NOW, SOMETHING THAT AIN'T SCARED OF ME?
GASASA
SOUNDS LIKE SOMEBODY'S IN A HURRY.

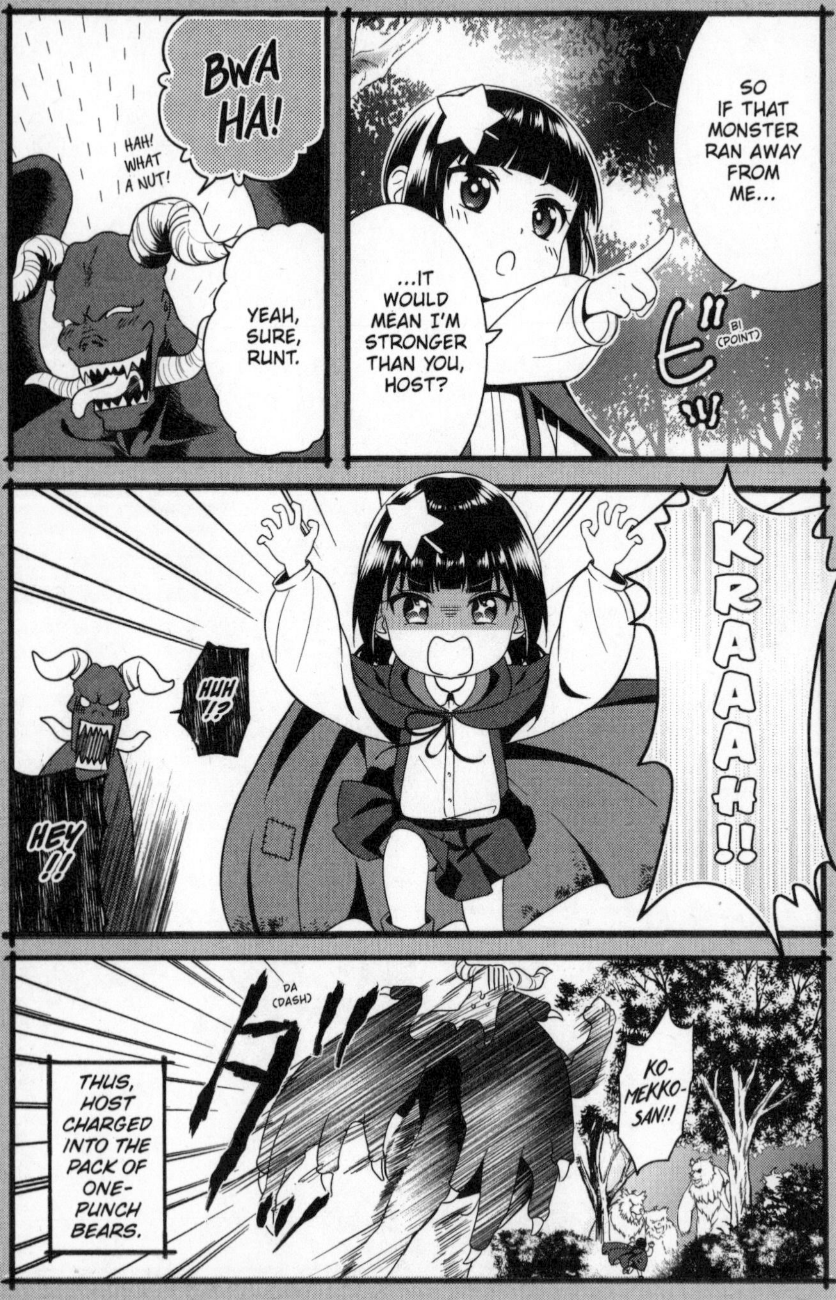
SO IF THAT MONSTER RAN AWAY FROM ME...
BI (POINT)
...IT WOULD MEAN I'M STRONGER THAN YOU, HOST?
BWA HA!
HAH! WHAT A NUT!
YEAH, SURE, RUNT.
KRAAAAH!!
HUH!?
HEY!!
DA (DASH)
KO-MEKKO-SAN!!
THUS, HOST CHARGED INTO THE PACK OF ONE-PUNCH BEARS.

—TO BE CONTINUED...

KONOSUBA: AN EXPLOSION ON THIS WONDERFUL WORLD!

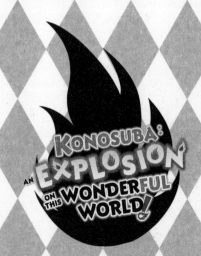

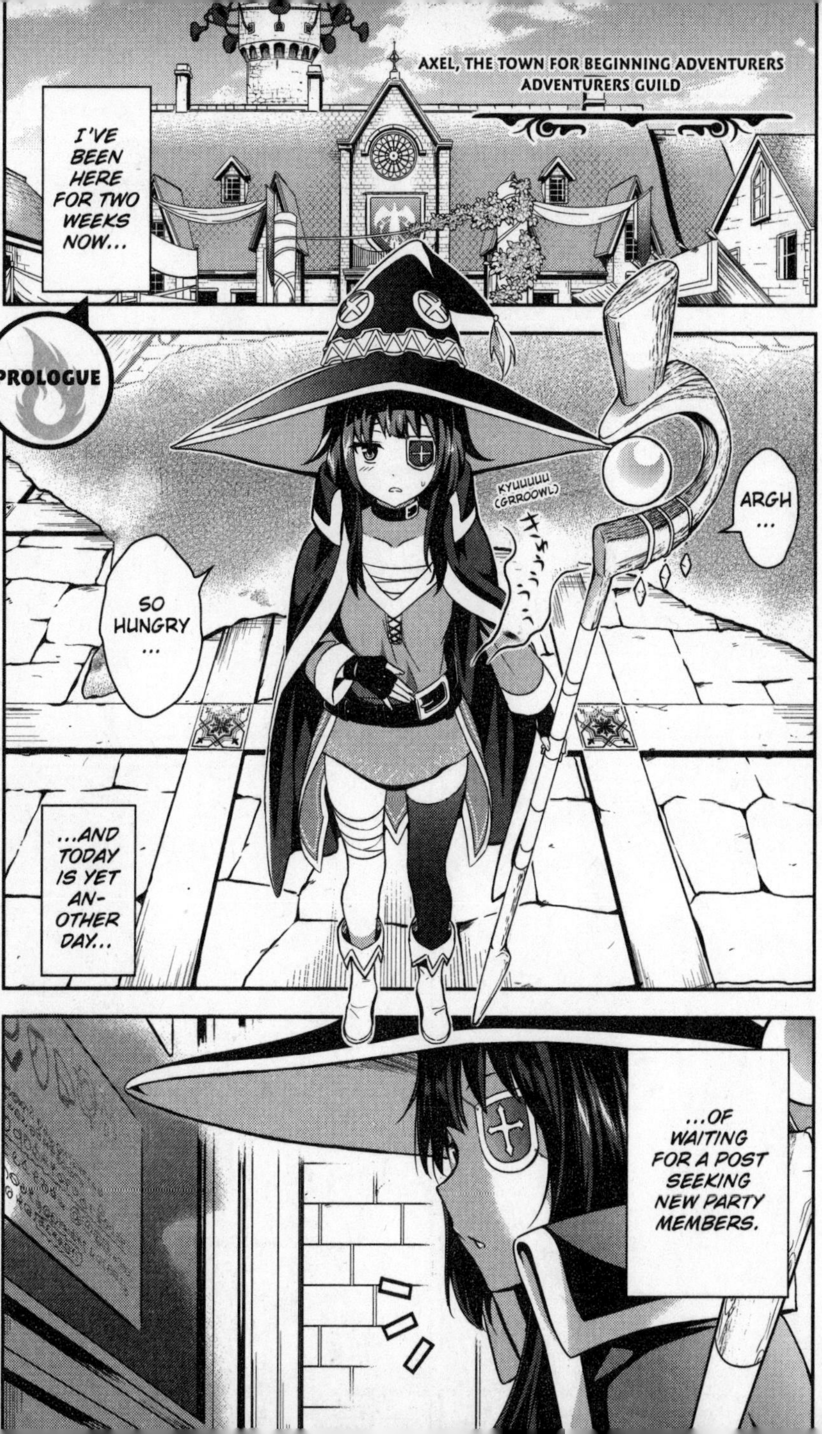
AXEL, THE TOWN FOR BEGINNING ADVENTURERS
ADVENTURERS GUILD
I'VE BEEN HERE FOR TWO WEEKS NOW...
PROLOGUE
ARGH ...
KYUUUUU (GRROOWL)
SO HUNGRY ...
...AND TODAY IS YET AN-OTHER DAY...
...OF WAITING FOR A POST SEEKING NEW PARTY MEMBERS.

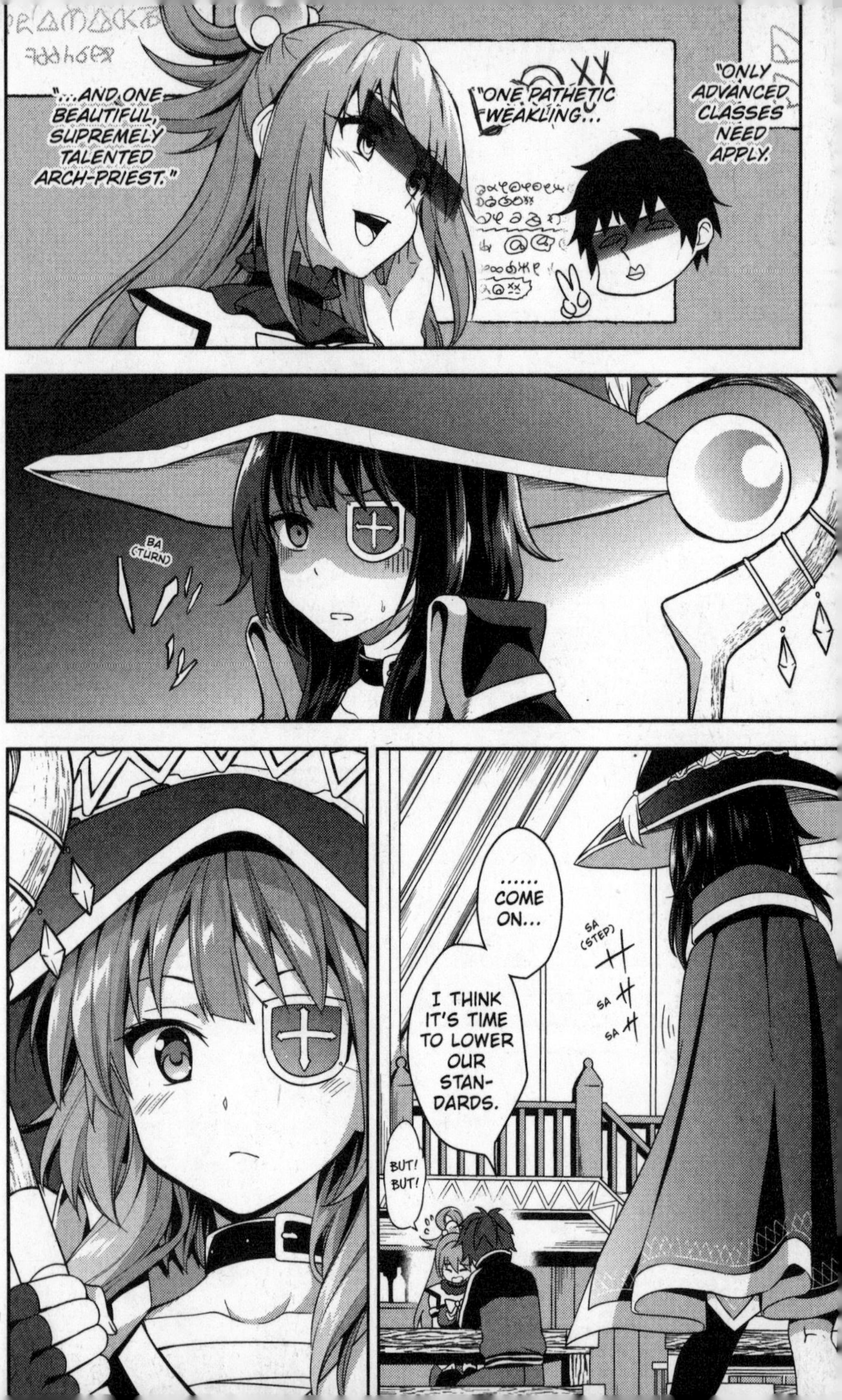
"ONLY ADVANCED CLASSES NEED APPLY.
"ONE PATHETIC WEAKLING...
"...AND ONE BEAUTIFUL, SUPREMELY TALENTED ARCH-PRIEST."
BA (TURN)
...... COME ON...
I THINK IT'S TIME TO LOWER OUR STAN-DARDS.
SA (STEP)
SA
SA
BUT! BUT!

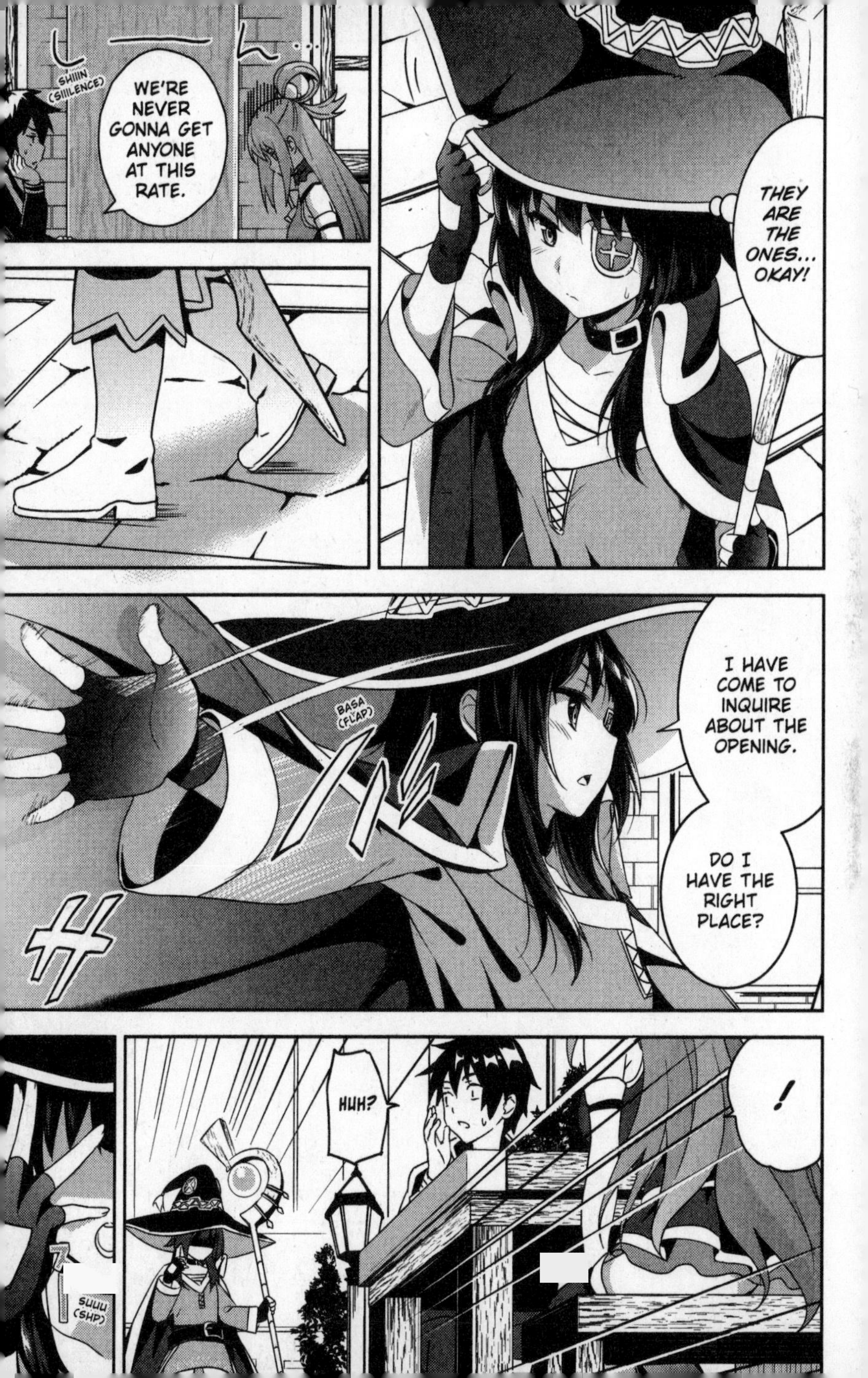
THEY ARE THE ONES... OKAY!
SHIIIN (SIIILENCE)
WE'RE NEVER GONNA GET ANYONE AT THIS RATE.
BASA (FLAP)
I HAVE COME TO INQUIRE ABOUT THE OPENING.
DO I HAVE THE RIGHT PLACE?
!
HUH?
SUUU (SHP)

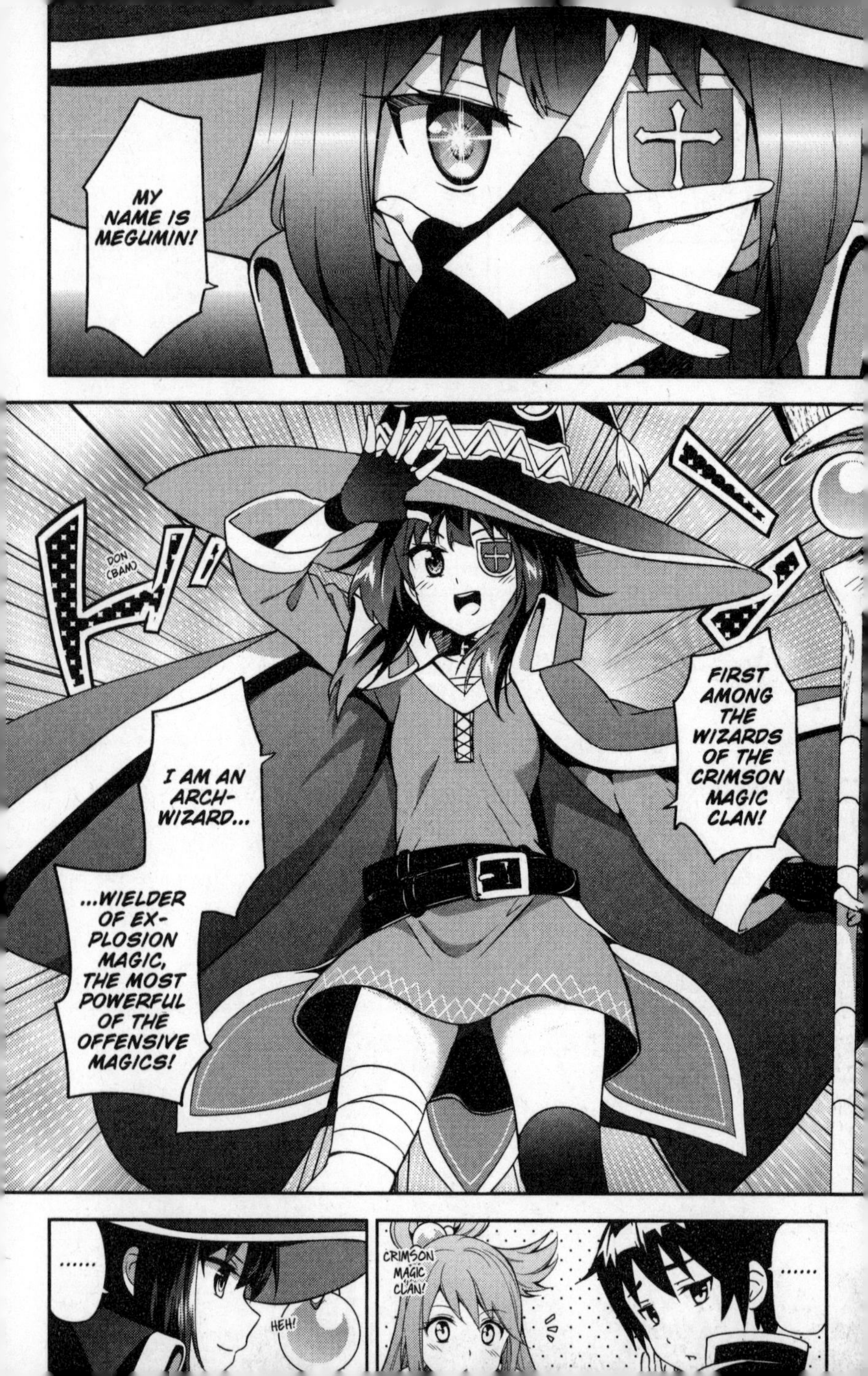
MY NAME IS MEGUMIN!
FIRST AMONG THE WIZARDS OF THE CRIMSON MAGIC CLAN!
DON (BAM)
I AM AN ARCH-WIZARD...
...WIELDER OF EX-PLOSION MAGIC, THE MOST POWERFUL OF THE OFFENSIVE MAGICS!
......
CRIMSON MAGIC CLAN!
......
HEH!

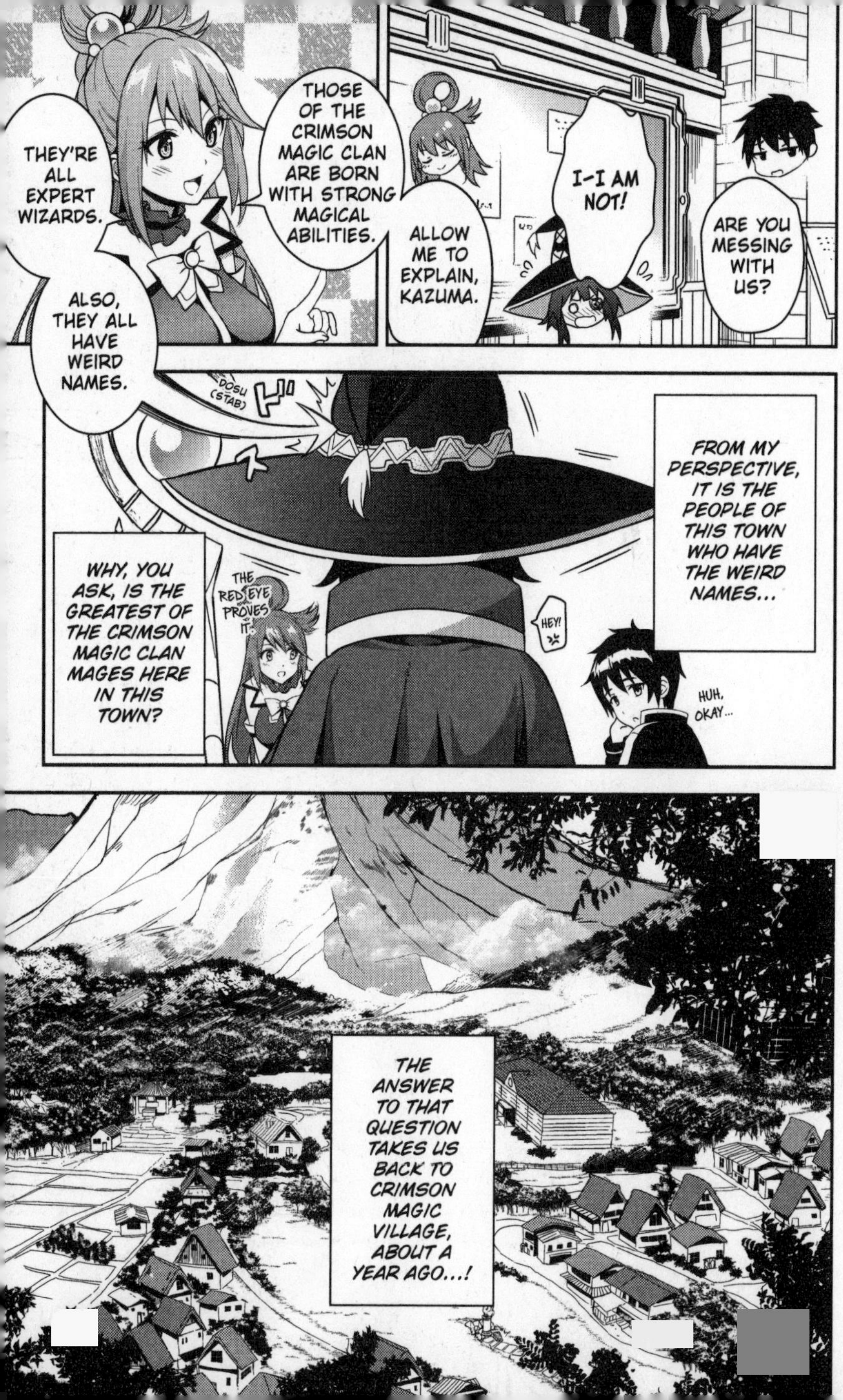
ARE YOU MESSING WITH US?
I-I AM NOT!
ALLOW ME TO EXPLAIN, KAZUMA.
THOSE OF THE CRIMSON MAGIC CLAN ARE BORN WITH STRONG MAGICAL ABILITIES.
THEY'RE ALL EXPERT WIZARDS.
ALSO, THEY ALL HAVE WEIRD NAMES.
FROM MY PERSPECTIVE, IT IS THE PEOPLE OF THIS TOWN WHO HAVE THE WEIRD NAMES...
DOSU (STAB)
HEY!
HUH, OKAY...
THE RED EYE PROVES IT.
WHY, YOU ASK, IS THE GREATEST OF THE CRIMSON MAGIC CLAN MAGES HERE IN THIS TOWN?
THE ANSWER TO THAT QUESTION TAKES US BACK TO CRIMSON MAGIC VILLAGE, ABOUT A YEAR AGO...!

KONOSUBA: AN EXPLOSION ON THIS WONDERFUL WORLD!

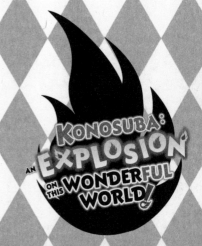

You're reading the wrong way!
Flip to the back to read
a bonus short story by
Konosuba original creator
Natsume Akatsuki!

When she intoned this spell, I found I couldn't move.

"What is this—? What do you mean to do, immobilizing me? I'll tell the village grown-ups! When I get home, I'll tell my mom and dad a golden-eyed lady with big boobs was mean to me. Stop that... St-stooop!"

"I'm just having a look at your Adventurer's Card! Come on, all that shouting is going to get a girl in trouble!"

I tried to resist but couldn't move a muscle, and my hidden card was quickly taken from me.

After she'd had her look, the woman removed the spell on me and muttered, "There, see? Explosion magic is right here on the skill li— Huh? All these other spells I showed you are here, too?! Slow learner, my butt! You remembered every single thing I showed you after seeing them just one time!"

I pointedly turned my back to her, whereupon the woman, looking upset, said, "Come on, sweetheart. I've got places to go, things to do. I taught you explosion magic. Can I go now?"

"Uh-uh. If you go, I won't be able to see explosions anymore."

The woman smiled bitterly, then crouched down so her gaze was level with mine. "But you're set on learning Explosion yourself, aren't you? If you really do manage it, you'll be able to see all the explosions you want."

And then, she smiled.

"Well, I guess this is good-bye. It starts getting dangerous the farther you go from the village, so you don't have to see me any farther. Frankly, I feel like I've done something kind of awful, but it's your life, young lady. I won't stop you—do whatever you want." The woman looked out at the road stretching away from the village.

I had really enjoyed training with her every day, even for just this short time. She'd given me food, shown me where to hunt powerful monsters, and demonstrated all sorts of magic.

And...

"All right, I'm off. If you ever really do learn Explosion, I want you to show it to me."

"Very well. Remember me until that day comes, then."

"H-how could I ever forget? I mean your name, or the way you behave, or the way you live. Just watching you ticks me off... Have you ever thought about living a quieter life?"

And then, there was the magic I'd fallen instantly in love with, which she'd shown me so many times.

"My plans for the future include toppling the Demon King, so I cannot promise a quiet life. I can and do, however, promise to come show you my Explosion. Thus..."

I could tell from the woman's smile that she already knew what I was going to ask.

"Could you possibly show me your Explosion just one more time?"

Because, one day, you'll definitely see mine.

know why it's got its back to us, terrified, but now's our chance—let's catch it and make bear stew!"

We were chasing after a One-Punch Bear that was fleeing from us for some inexplicable reason. Maybe my level had gone up from those crawdads we beat up for dinner the other day.

"Aww, hold on. The whole reason I brought you here was so you could see how useful advanced magic is against the worst monsters around! Nobody said you should go hand to hand with a One-Punch Bear!"

"It's okay. Right now, I somehow feel as if I could win even bare-handed. The power of the deity of destruction sleeping within me must be trying to awaken."

"This is the problem with the Crimson Magic Clan! Do all of you act like this from such a young age?!" the woman screamed and then started incanting some magic. "Freeze Gust!"

A white mist emerged from her palm and wrapped itself around the One-Punch Bear—

"Ooh. If I could take that thing back to the village, I think it would make a fine tourist attraction."

"No one's taking anything back! I told you, this is a lesson about the usefulness of other magic!"

There was a One-Punch Bear, completely frozen from the neck down. It could only howl helplessly. The woman looked at it and smiled with just a touch of personal satisfaction.

"What you just saw was Freeze Gust, a bit of intermediate magic. Like that? If the user has enough magical power, even intermediate magic can be a potent weapon. And it takes so much less MP than explosion magic. If you were thoughtful about how you used advanced and intermediate magic, I'm sure you'd become one of the world's most— Hey, what do you think you're doing?!"

She frantically tried to stop me as I approached the bear with a wooden club in my hand.

"I finally have a One-Punch Bear, a huge catch, immobilized in front of me. I want to finish it off and gain the experience points. It's a standard leveling-up technique among the grown-ups in my village—freeze a monster in ice and then have someone else deal the final blow. We call it farming."

"What?! Hey, don't Crimson Magic Clan members have consciences?!"

And so, we spent many delightful days together. Eventually, the woman seemed to grow listless.

"Sweetheart, can I ask you something?"

"What is it? If it's about where the crayfish hide, I won't tell you, you know."

"Don't worry—I won't ask about that. Listen, Crimson Magic Clan members have an Adventurer's Card made for them when they're born, right? Could you show me yours?"

I quickly hid the card hanging around my neck.

The woman noticed and let out a soft breath. "I thought not. So explosion magic is already on your list of available skills, isn't it?"

"It is not," I replied immediately. "I'm a slow learner, so I think it'll take some time yet."

The woman leveled her palm at me. "Paralyze."

then put a hand to her cheek in dismay.

At last, she intoned the chant—with my personal touches.

"Explosion!"

A fresh hole was added to the growing collection of craters that had been accumulating in this field over the past days.

"I don't understand it… How can it have gotten more powerful?!" the woman exclaimed, astonished by the spell she herself had cast.

"Of course a spell is more powerful with a cool chant."

"But magic isn't that simple! …I get that you're a genius, sweetheart, but don't go modifying spells anymore, okay?"

"Absolutely not okay," I answered promptly. The woman looked like she was going to cry.

She was older than me, very cool, and also beautiful, but I couldn't help thinking she cried a lot for a grown-up.

"Okay. There's something I want you to see before we start today's training. I know you're a child, though. And it's something very scary and very dangerous, so I won't force you if you don't want to. What do you say?"

"My mom is scary and dangerous. I think I'll be fine."

The woman giggled at that. "What we're about to see is a lot worse than your mother—I promise you that."

"Really?! Once, when my dad took out a loan to make these weird magical items, my mom froze him in ice from the neck down and then left him crying in the woods. Is it scarier than that?"

"…True. I forgot your mother would be a member of the Crimson Magic Clan. But I think we're dealing with something just about on par with her."

Something almost as scary as my mom…

"Are we going to go see the Demon King or an evil spirit?"

"Just how scary do you think your mother is?! …Hey, I see how your eyes are sparkling. Do you want to see the Demon King or an evil spirit?"

I nodded impishly at the woman. "I am considering calling myself the new Demon King the day I defeat the old one."

"Well, you can't! The Demon King is literally the king of all demons. It's not just a nickname you pick up off the street!" Then, looking unusually sanguine, she said, "…But when it comes to evil spirits, who knows? You may have already met one without realizing it."

She sounded kind of teasing and had a weird smile on her face.

"That simply isn't possible. If any evil spirit invaded this village, the people would immediately catch it and seal it away, and it would become our newest tourist attraction."

"I really think you Crimson Magic people should learn that the gods and spirits aren't your toys!"

In the vast woods beside the village…

Normally, we weren't allowed to enter because of all the dangerous monsters said to live in the area. But the woman had led me here…

"Come on, kid—let's go home! Please? It was my bad bringing you here!"

"The stomachs and livers of One-Punch Bears sell for a high price! I don't

And that was it. That was the beginning of my days training with this woman whose name I didn't even know...

"Okay, look, I really think you need to stop throwing in these little original touches of yours when you're chanting. They're cool, for sure. But they're not the spell we're working on."

"As a member of the Crimson Magic Clan, I want to include the word 'crimson.'"

Each time I tried to improvise, she would warn me not to.

"Sweetheart, the pose is not necessary! If you throw your arm out like that, who knows where the spell will go?!"

"The cobbler's son says that a Crimson Magic Clan member without a pose is hardly a member of the clan at all."

"The cobbler's son has a screw loose, so I wouldn't listen to him. In fact, I'd be careful not to follow his example."

Each time I posed, she would correct me.

"Here, look. This is the advanced spell Inferno! A big, mean piece of magic that burns everything before you to cinders. How about it? Aren't you even a little interested?"

"Not even a little. Now, come on, use explosion magic. Show me today's blast!"

"Explosion magic isn't a fireworks display, okay, sweetheart? If you do learn it, you can't go shooting it off just anywhere, all right?"

"Not all right."

My stubbornness brought the woman to tears as she tried to bring me in line.

"Let me give you some advice: Teleport paired with advanced magic can defeat almost any opponent. Did you know that?"

"Explosion!"

"And the Light of Saber spell can cut through anything at all if the caster has enough power."

"Explosion!"

"I've got an idea—instead of explosion magic, how about blasting or detonation magic? They're both very strong spells..."

"Explosion!"

"Take my advice—I'm begging you!"

Practicing cool ways of intoning the spell also brought the woman to tears.

Finally...

"I am not interested in learning anything except explosion magic. No matter how long it takes, even if I'm an old granny when I finally learn it, I will master this spell."

"Come on—what is it about explosion magic that has you so obsessed?"

I held a sheet of paper out to the woman, who was shuddering for some reason.

"Do Explosion with this, please."

"...Have you messed with the chant again? A spell's chant isn't just about imbuing it with power, you know. It also governs the actual control of the magic. So when you go making random changes to— Hm?" She looked at the paper,

Beneath her hood, the voluptuous older woman frowned as deeply as I had ever seen anyone frown.

"Erm, what did you just say?"

I dutifully repeated myself. "I said, 'Teach me that spell you just cast.'"

The woman looked at me, more apologetic than when I'd asked to take over the world. More than when I had requested huge boobs. Even more than when I'd said I wanted to be the Demon King.

"I can't— Look, you heard me, right? I really don't recommend this magic."

......

"Fine. Then just help me catch some crayfish for dinner."

"No, don't look at me like I'm a useless lump! Please! I can teach you the spell I used. I'm just saying it has some serious disadvantages…!"

Staring steadily at the frantic woman, I asked, "What kind of magic was that?"

"The spell I just used? It's the strongest magic of all—they call it explosion magic."

The strongest!

"But since it's the strongest, it takes a ton of skill points to learn. If you don't have enough inborn magical power, you might not even be able to use it, and even if a human did manage to cast the spell, it would take every ounce of their MP and leave them unable to m— H-hey, are you listening to me?"

"I am not. Teach it to me. I want to use this explosion magic." I took hold of her robe and gave it a stern shake.

"What in the world…? I was just trying to show some gratitude, but I'm going to end up turning this girl's life upside down…," the woman murmured, and then she heaved a deep sigh.

The next day…

The woman told me she couldn't cast explosion magic again yesterday, so my training was to start today. But…

"Listen, sweetheart—are you sure you won't reconsider?"

We met up in front of the tombstone, and the woman took me to a deserted wasteland some distance from the village.

My response was immediate. "Very sure. I can't imagine learning anything but explosion magic."

The woman sighed again, quieter this time.

"W-well, I guess it's just showing you a little spell. I assume it'll be a few decades before you can actually learn explosion magic. Plenty of time to give it up."

The woman seemed a bit concerned, but biting her lip, she began to chant. "Okay, now that was the incantation used for explosion magic. The first step will be to memorize—"

Before she had finished speaking, I flung my cape back dramatically and exclaimed, "I, Megumin, the True Crimson Goddess of Destruction, command you! By the Ancient True Name, unleash the primal power!"

"That's not how it goes! We've hardly even started, and you've already got it all messed up! I didn't say anything about a goddess of destruction, an ancient true name, or any of that stuff!"

SPECIAL SHORT STORY

Konosuba: God's Blessing on This Wonderful World! Spin-off

AN EXPLOSION ON THIS WONDERFUL WORLD!
EVERY EXPLOSION BEGINS WITH A SINGLE STEP

BY NATSUME AKATSUKI

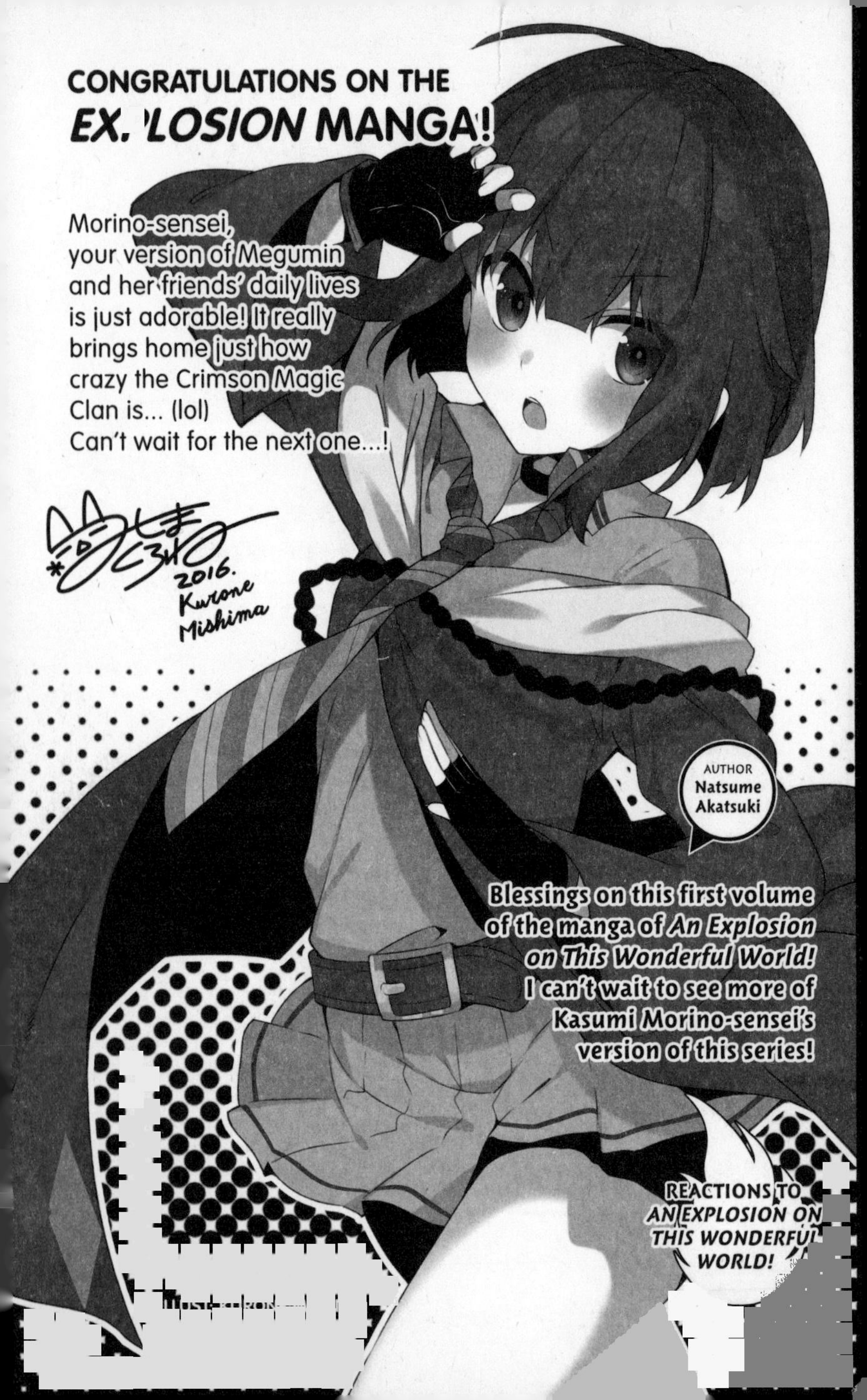
CONGRATULATIONS ON THE
EX. 'LOSION MANGA!
Morino-sensei, your version of Megumin and her friends' daily lives is just adorable! It really brings home just how crazy the Crimson Magic Clan is... (lol) Can't wait for the next one...!
2016. Kurone Mishima
AUTHOR Natsume Akatsuki
Blessings on this first volume of the manga of An Explosion on This Wonderful World! I can't wait to see more of Kasumi Morino-sensei's version of this series!
REACTIONS TO AN EXPLOSION ON THIS WONDERFUL WORLD!

CONTENTS

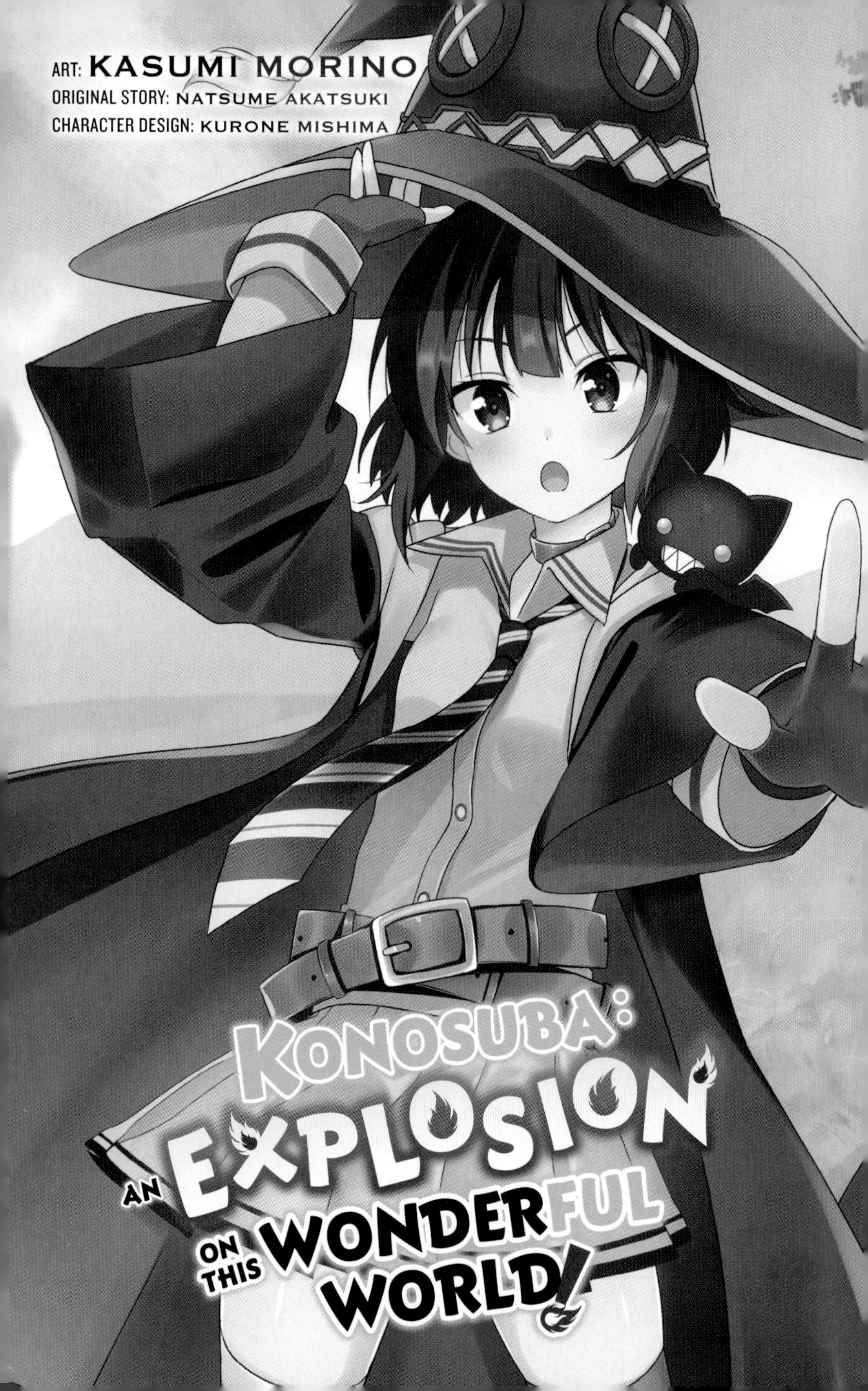
ART: KASUMI MORINO
ORIGINAL STORY: NATSUME AKATSUKI
CHARACTER DESIGN: KURONE MISHIMA
KONOSUBA:
AN EXPLOSION
ON THIS WONDERFUL
WORLD!